In a Glass Darkly
Seeking Vision for Public Life

In a Glass Darkly

Seeking Vision for Public Life

Christopher Sunderland

paternoster
press

First published in 2001 by Paternoster Press

07 06 05 04 03 02 01   7 6 5 4 3 2 1

Paternoster Press is an imprint of Paternoster Publishing,
P.O. Box 300, Carlisle, Cumbria, CA3 0QS, UK
and
P.O. Box 1047, Waynesboro, GA 30830-2047, USA

Website: www.paternoster-publishing.com

British Library Cataloguing in Publication Data
A catalogue record for this book is available from the British Library

ISBN 1-84227-093-1

Cover Design by Four Nine Zero
Typeset by WestKey Ltd, Falmouth, Cornwall
Printed in Great Britain by Omnia Books Ltd, Glasgow

*I went down a path less travelled
to see if I could get a better view*

Contents

Preface

This book has been an ambitious project. Some would call it foolhardy. The subjects covered embrace a huge range of disciplines, more than any traditional academic approach would normally allow. Yet I have written it because I believe this sort of broad approach is the only way to address the issues faced by humanity as the millennium turns. A little of my own story might help explain why I think this way.

In the mid-seventies I graduated in biochemistry and set out on a path of research in biochemistry and immunology that kept me occupied for close to ten years. My post-doctoral study was focused on the syncytiotrophoblast plasma membrane of the human placenta. Strange words perhaps, describing an esoteric field, relevant in one sense, and totally irrelevant in another. There were fifty or so scientists studying the syncytiotrophoblast membrane. We would meet at conferences. The work had a potential payoff in that it bore on knowledge about transplant rejection. This particular membrane is the outermost layer of fetal material in direct contact with the maternal bloodstream. It was semi-foreign material. So why wasn't it rejected? That was the big question and one we duly emphasised on all grant application forms. But it was really a very narrow world.

Since that time I have been ordained a priest in the Church of England and latterly served nine years in an inner city tower block estate in Bristol. My time there made me angry. Angry with a church and church doctrines that seemed to have no real bearing on the problems the people were facing and angry with a society that also did not seem to understand. I set myself to study again, but with a new purpose. I wanted to ask the big questions, to break out of the confines of the 'experts' and dare to reach across disciplines in the hope of actually being relevant. I grappled with the Enlightenment and the scientific rationalism that has given rise to our modern institutions. I saw how theology, and indeed the humanities as a whole, had become relegated to a second division of knowledge, and struggled with how they might become properly valued again. Gradually a pattern emerged out of the fog and I wrote it up for another research degree, this time nominally in theology. This book is a continuation of that process complete with its determination to think thoughts that count and apply to our lives. I know that there are questions in here that bear on philosophy, scientific method, history, theology, sociology, business, politics, and much else besides. I know that some will recoil at my attempt to take all these subjects in, but I sincerely believe that taking such a big view is the only way to address our modern problems.

Very little of what I have written is new in itself, though the synthesis may be. It is no coincidence that I have drawn heavily from others like Mary Midgley, Michael Polanyi, Frans de Waal, and Matt Ridley, all of whom are distinguished by having dared to cross disciplines and therefore by having said things that are directly and broadly relevant. It is easy to mine at the academic coal face, inventing your own language, affirming and publicising each other's work, but it is harder to take the view from the plain, to try to draw it all together and make sense of it.

In a sense I have tried to lay a new foundation for thinking about public life. Yet I do not mean by that that I have performed some absolutely rigorous logical analysis from which everyone might draw conclusions by means of chains of reason. That modernist view is a utopia, or a hell, but it is anyway not possible. At the same time I recognise that the verbose and destructively sceptical meanderings of the extreme postmodernists are also inadequate. The sort of foundation I have tried to lay is one in which human society is an open process, searching for all that is good and true and beautiful.

We need something to build on. We need to dare to try to make sense of the world we inhabit. We need a vision for life. If I am judged to have contributed anything to that end, I shall be satisfied.

Many people have contributed indirectly to the preparing of this manuscript. I am particularly grateful to the people of St Luke's Church in Barton Hill who taught me so much and gave me time to start these explorations. Also to those people at St Michael's Church in Bath and elsewhere who allowed me to interview them about their work and served as guinea pigs for some of these ideas. Several have commented helpfully on the manuscript, including Ian Donaldson and Ike Okonta. I have been supported by grants from Bristol Archdeaconry Charities, The Barrow Cadbury Trust and St Michael's Church House Trust, and also by my wife Bobbie who has brought in the lion's share of our income during this period. Thank you to you all.

Introduction

Life is happening to us. Blind, captives to fortune, free but not free, western humanity stumbles on. Ideology has fallen away in confusion. Pragmatism reigns. Without any compass to steer by, we are lost. And we are alone. The old places of meeting have gone. The clubs, the local communities, the traditional events that were the regular points where people met and talked and negotiated life and its purposes, these have gone. We are now alone with the TV, or with the paper. It is in these contexts that vast changes are taking place, but we have no means to assess them or criticise them, and even if we did no one would hear what we have to say. Who cares what we think? How can we express ourselves? Western humanity faces huge challenges and has no way of guiding itself through them. Individuals are caught in systems that are changing daily and yet have no effective comeback.

The workplace is coming under extraordinary pressure. David Prior works as a Christian minister in London's square mile. He reported a case of a young man of twenty-eight who had come to him complaining of stress. David discovered that this man had recently worked at his leading London law firm from 9.30a.m. on Sunday morning through to 4p.m. on Wednesday. David is familiar with the scene and asked whether the firm provided any sleeping arrangements. The young man replied, 'No, I just crash out at my desk.' Apparently law firms in London are increasingly worried that their young lawyers choose to leave the practice of law after two to three years. Who can blame them? Lawyers take a long time to train. Such a departure rate is very costly. One law firm has just hired its second psychotherapist.

There are massive pressures on people in public life and much confusion as to how to handle them. I have a friend who is a senior member of the medical profession. In the hospital where he works, he is known as a particularly compassionate man, one who is able to draw alongside patients and offer real comfort in times of distress. His integrity is such that his leadership in the academic environment was once half-jokingly criticised for being 'too honest'. Now sixty years of age this man is shortly to retire, seriously concerned for the future of medicine in this country. He carries with him an immense amount of experience, wisdom and discernment, but the performance indicators to which his department is subject mark him out as a substandard performer. The indicators do not measure experience, wisdom, compassion, honesty or integrity, but are concerned with numbers of papers published, operations performed, beds vacated and all sorts of easily measured goods. He now feels a burden on the system. So he is getting out.

Despite these pressures the workplace has actually become more important to us all. A psychiatrist once told me that one of his key opening questions is to ask people to complete the saying 'I am [John] and I am …' Whatever the person says next reveals the heart of their self-identity. Most people now answer this question by reference to their work. Negotiating this new public world can be a real struggle.

The purpose of this book is to help the reader make sense of public life and so find some vision and proper confidence that can withstand today's pressures and integrate them into truly wholesome and fruitful living. I am going to use the term *public life* for those situations where we need to deal with all sorts of people. Typically we might take up a role, with duties and responsibilities, and be required to interact with others with whom we may have little in common and who we would not necessarily choose as friends. Public life therefore includes the whole spectrum of people's work lives and the world of politics. As we have seen, it can be a confusing world to negotiate.

My hope is to help you in your attempt to make sense of some of this. 'Making sense' is, I believe, a reasonable goal. For the past few centuries we have tried to construct the rational society. Some bold sociologists have tried to figure out the whole of human life on rational grounds. We expected to be able to design society and to bring it into being in accordance with our wishes, but it was all fool's gold.

After a particularly brutal century, we need to take stock. We need a new humility about ourselves and our potential, including our potential to understand. As a young animal leaves its nest for the first time, it ventures very carefully. Any sign of threat and it bolts for home. Gradually it extends its range, gets to know the area, its threats and its refuges. Finally it feels reasonably confident outside on its territory. It has 'made sense' of its own patch. It is in this way that I hope we might seek to make sense of public life. Not to define all its detail; not to know everything about it; but simply to know enough that we can negotiate it with a proper confidence. To achieve this task I am going to suggest that we need to face two aspects of life that people in the west have generally come to shy away from. These are animal behaviour and religious faith.

Many people are still basically in denial about evolution. As Samuel Wilberforce initially reacted with shock and horror to the suggestion that we derived from primates, so many still today have not faced the fact that we are animals and that we may have something to learn from the study of their behaviour. Conversations about animals and humans typically try to pick out the one thing that separates us from 'them'. However spurious the handle we find for such a separation, it gives us some emotional distance, a height from which to look down. Yet sadly it also prevents us from learning from animals. The philosopher Mary Midgely describes how animals are typically our source of bad words.[1] We speak of them as 'wild', implying that they are chaotic, dangerous and unpredictable. Animal words, like beastly and brutal, are used to describe bad behaviour. Similarly in the intellectual establishment there has been a common assumption that we have transcended our animal heritage by means of our rationality. Philosophies like existentialism have offered us a view of ourselves as free agents who choose our own destiny, without any constraints from our inherited nature. Society has risen above all influence from our natural heritage. The past might be described as a 'state of nature', but now we are different. Cultural anthropology set out as a discipline this century with the blatant assumption that there was no 'nature' that constrained the human being.[2] All things were possible for human societies, so it was said, and the world was explored specifically to prove that thesis. They looked for non-aggressive people. They looked for perfect egalitarian societies. At first they 'discovered' what they predicted. Later things turned up that did not fit with what they had presupposed. It's a long story, but it has left everyone rather confused.

The religious angle has not helped either. Although the church came to terms with evolution relatively quickly and has contained many theistic evolutionists since, in recent years the most influential Christian apologists have been concerned with the inorganic world, with relativity and quantum theory. This has meant that there has been little response to an increasingly vociferous band of atheistic biologists who have triumphantly proclaimed that a belief in God and a belief in evolution are utterly inconsistent. But what if both are required to make sense of the world?

Religion has been boxed into a corner. The modern era has

[1] Midgely, *Beast and Man.*

[2] A review of this literature can be found in Matt Ridley, *The Origins of Virtue*, pp. 256ff.

sought to make sense of everything in the world solely on the grounds of scientific rationality, and has sidelined religion. Religion is seen as a matter of personal preference, but of no relevance to public policy. Of course the scientific approach to society has not been without its problems. From the London School of Economics through to communist Russia, much energy has been devoted to rethinking the grand enterprise of designing the rational society. This has been brought into focus more recently by the wholesale abandonment of the project by the postmodern school, who have powerfully refuted the false certainties of the past. Accurately exposing the false assumptions of pseudo-science as applied to human society, the postmodernists have nothing with which to replace it. Zygmunt Bauman has characterised postmodernism as like a soldier standing on a battleground indiscriminately shooting at anything that moves.[3] Such scepticism leaves us little ground for hope or vision. We are left only with ourselves, our own lives. There is no common good to be searched for; we have only personal preference to guide us. The isolated individual is left only with the struggle for self-fulfilment as we hire a new generation of counsellors to soothe us through our demise.

I believe that now is the time to try to find something positive amidst the wreckage. This book will try to demonstrate that religious faith, and in particular the Christian faith, can provide for a society that is always looking to hold on to what is good and yet reform itself around a fuller vision. It will claim that a faith understood in this way can provide purpose for us as humans, yet a purpose that does not cage us in, or deny our individuality, but rather opens us up to creatively seek new solutions to the age old problem of being a social animal.

In both these areas of religious faith and animal behaviour, there will be those who find the idea of looking into these things threatening. They will already be holding this book lightly, ready

---

[3] Bauman, *Intimations of Postmodernity*, from the introduction.

to put it down. My plea is to hang on in there. I believe the potential rewards of such an approach are truly great. If we are to find our way out of the confusions of the present, we are going to need to suspend some of our prejudices.

Part one

Setting the Scene

1

A new look at our roots

Animals we are, like it or not. The purpose of this chapter is to
try to show that the idea of ourselves as animals is not quite so
threatening to our humanity as we perhaps have feared. Indeed
an approach to culture through the constraints of human nature
can offer practical insights of real importance.

Basic conflicts and the development of the mind

According to evolutionary biology the life of every organism has
one most basic function, which is the passing on of its genes to
the next generation. Surviving species must be those that have
achieved this. Such gene propagation depends in turn on the fulfilment of certain key tasks. Typically they may need to feed,
keep safe, mate and rear their young. In the simplest organisms
such functions may be almost totally determined at the genetic
level. There may be relatively little learning or spontaneity. Yet
even so there can be problems. There are certain flies that eat
other flies, but they are not too discerning about who they eat.
This means that when the male approaches the female he has a
problem. How does he get near enough to mate without being
eaten? The answer that has evolved is to come up with a little
ritual. He kills a fly and presents it to the female. While she is

eating, he hops round the back and does the business.[1] It is a clever little ruse. Much better than the praying mantis family of insects where the front half of the male frequently gets eaten while the back half copulates!

So, clearly, conflicts can develop through the need to co-ordinate one aspect of life with another. As organisms grew in complexity the development of new ways through such conflicts was one of the principle reasons for the development of the brain. The brain allowed the translation of the fundamental needs of life into mental processes, into motivations. These could take a general form, such as hunger, lust or fear, but they could also involve very specific information hard-wired into the brain circuits. Genetically determined behavioural patterns remained as part of the system. Invariant behaviours, such as the dance of the honeybee, could still be found in abundance in higher and more complex animals. A young gull recognises the shape of the shadow of the predator circling above its head and can therefore take avoiding action.[2] An orphan squirrel still knows how to hide its nuts even without the possibility of parental instruction.[3] The implication is that much of this must be inherited, passed on genetically; however, the complexities of discerning exactly what is so inherited become increasingly problematic.

For example, as the animal brain becomes more complex, so the inherited, hard-wired information interacts with greatly enhanced abilities to learn and act with spontaneous intelligence. Mary Midgely speaks of the new situation in higher animals in terms of the presence of 'open' instincts, that is, where the inherited predisposition to act in a certain way is complemented by intelligent activity in its performance. This results in the whole behaviour pattern being less determined and more open

---

[1] Lorenz, *On Aggression*, chap. 5.

[2] Tinbergen, *The Study of Instinct*.

[3] Eibl-Eibesfeldt, *Love and Hate*, chap. 2.

to adaptation.[4] Others have noted that behaviour patterns that appear to be inherited are not simply determined by genes alone, but rather their expression is dependent on stimuli that appear through life. An obvious example is the maternal 'instincts' of a woman. Most might naturally presume that maternal behaviour towards a child was wholly inherited and simply elicited through childbirth, yet mothers whose own upbringing was unusual may fail to develop normal maternal behaviour, so demonstrating a necessary 'learned' component to this activity. These sort of complexities have left most biologists unwilling to speak of 'instincts' at all for fear of being misunderstood.[5] Nevertheless it is hard to deny that all of us have a great deal of inherited information in our brain, that this forms part of the structure of our motivations, and that the more that we can learn about it from other animals the better.

Working with deep-level motivations

For animals themselves, greater brain complexity leads to new problems. Deep level motivations need to be co-ordinated. Aggression, for example, has both an important positive role and great destructive potential. Konrad Lorenz reported how a turkey hen has the ability to show aggression and that this aggression is of immense value in driving predators like polecats away from her chicks. She will lash out at anything that comes near her nest, but the question arises, 'Why does she not kill her own young?' The answer is that they make a cheeping sound. This simple signal acts to regulate aggression and allow proper nurture of her young. It is proven by the fact that a deaf hen kills her chicks while a polecat with a cheeping device on its back is allowed to raid them.[6]

---

[4] Midgely, *Beast and Man*, chap. 3.
[5] Ridley, *Animal Behaviour*, p. 73.
[6] Lorenz, *On Aggression*, chap. 7.

Similarly night herons form an anarchic society; parents do not know their chicks from any others, and all are aggressive to each other. In this context the young appear to protect themselves by particularly ostentatious infantile behaviour including begging calls, wing flapping, seizing the parent's beak and pulling it down to 'milk' it. This seems to prevent them being subject to aggression.[7]

So here we have two simple examples of aggression being directed away from the young by means of particular signs of infancy. Irenaeus Eibl-Eibesfeldt has continued this line of thought to consider infantile expressions in adult animals.[8] He notices that a typical part of courting ritual in birds might include one animal begging for food like a juvenile. Similarly strange, dogs or wolves will appease one another by pushing their nose against the corner of the other's mouth in the manner of a pup asking for mother to regurgitate some of her food. So do humans act likewise?

Many people will have noticed the importance of baby features in eliciting our own sympathetic social feelings. We naturally respond to the chubby cheeks, high protruding forehead, small mouth, large head and rounded body that signify 'baby' to us. Dolls are deliberately designed with these features to elicit the caring response. Women are sometimes illustrated so as to exaggerate these features. A macho male might refer to his partner as 'baby'. A couple may use baby talk in their private banter, particularly at moments of incipient tension. So Eibl-Eibesfeldt makes the case that in fact the care of infants lies behind the development of all social sympathies. Consider, for example, how many news reporters or charities will use a picture of a child to publicise the plight of a people. The signs of the child elicit our social sympathy.

---

[7] Ibid.
[8] Eibl-Eibesfeldt, *Love and Hate*.

Eibl-Eibesfeldt even speculates that the offering of food to a stranger might be an outgrowth of infant feeding mimicry. Just as the dog might pretend to be a puppy asking for food, so perhaps some of our food rituals bear relation to this behaviour. Consider how often we use food to begin a relationship with someone. We invite people to 'a meal'. We offer the ritual coffee. It is part of making friends. We do it naturally without thinking. Food is used for peacemaking throughout the world. Eibl-Eibesfeldt tells an extraordinary tale of a head-hunting tribe in New Guinea. A visitor to the tribe was just finishing a meal when his host proclaimed, 'I should like to have had your head, even though it is not as beautiful as it once was, but now we have eaten together and you are no longer a stranger.'[9]

Scientific problems about motivation

I wonder what you make of that sort of story? Some scientists are deeply nervous about this sort of approach. They will say this is not science. And I think they are right. At least it is not a traditional scientific approach. The mind of a complex animal is hidden from analysis. We just cannot know for sure what is going on in it. Traditional science works within a theoretical framework that understands the organic world like a machine whose parts can be disassembled, examined and put back together again. A complex mind cannot be treated like that. It functions as a whole that is greater than the sum of its parts and any attempt to discern its components involves the dissolution of something of its essence. This means that the study of motivations, as described by Eibl-Eibesfeldt, is viewed with suspicion by many scientists. Motivations are a function of the inner and hidden workings of the mind. Nevertheless an attempt to understand motivations may still be of value. In fact you may be quite convinced by his general argument about infant behaviour and

---

[9] Ibid., p. 139.

its role in generating sympathetic social feelings. Yet we must face the fact that such knowledge is not certain. Aspects of it are probably wrong. As I shall try to show later, this sort of uncertain, but still valuable, knowledge is actually that which underlies all that we call the humanities. The humanities proceed by way of imagination. We critically imagine the world of the other. We imagine what is going on in other minds, even those of other animals, on the basis of similar processes going on in our own. We can be wildly adrift. Someone else might come up with another far more plausible thesis, but the project is far from worthless.

Denying that the study of motivations is a 'science' has left students of animal behaviour unable to deal adequately with the problems they face. How are they to discuss the behaviour of complex, social animals? The issues are far from settled. One group of particularly rigorous scientists have confined themselves to making lists of what particular animals do. They say this is all that we can truly know about them. Anything else is speculation. They end up with masses of statistics of action. In order to make sense of all this they then refer the statistics to a logical evolutionary base by asking, 'Can these behaviours be explained in terms of each animal always seeking out the best way to propagate their genes?' This is the rational framework of the discipline of socio-biology. The extraordinary thing is that it has proven remarkably fruitful. A considerable amount of animal behaviour does seem to conform to the essential logic that animal behaviour can be understood by reference to gene propagation. So many of their competitive behaviours, food gathering, and even social structuring make sense according to this logic. Nevertheless this method of study is inadequate because none of these scientists really believe that the animals are calculating such genetic consequences in their minds. The deep level mental motivations of the animals are largely ignored for fear of not being rigorously scientific. We cannot know what is going on in their minds with scientific certainty, so we effectively ignore that part of the process. Sadly this results in seriously limiting our potential for understanding.

Mary Midgely believes that a great deal of animal behaviour is actually discounted by socio-biologists because it cannot be explained by their theory.[10] She argues that animals have all sorts of behavioural patterns that are in no way linked to biological success at the genetic level. Such behavioural complexity would be the expected conclusion of any serious thinking about the mind. When it comes to human societies, most people would agree that we have the ability to reflect on ourselves and so seek higher goods than that of mere biological effectiveness. Very few people live solely to pass on their genes. Yet if we are going to know any of this, we have to escape the constraints of strict scientific doctrine and explore the language of motivation. The crucial question then becomes, 'How can we do this and still genuinely claim to be seeking the truth?' Chapters four and five will consider this further.

Conflict resolution and culture formation

The socio-biologist Robin Dunbar wrote *Primate Social Systems* to illustrate how much primate behaviour could be predicted from the logic of gene propagation. Yet he was immediately confronted with the problem to which we have alluded. How could the language of science be used to adequately describe the relationships between animals in a hierarchy? 'Relationships that animals have with one another are essentially cognitive [that is they derive from their own knowledge and understanding] ... they are not directly susceptible to observation by conventional scientific means ... We need, in effect, to develop new ways of describing primate societies that break the old moulds within which our thinking has been constrained.'[11]

---

[10] Midgely, *Beast and Man*.

[11] Dunbar, *Primate Social Systems*, p. 11.

Dunbar took an important step forward. He dared to 'imagine' the relational hierarchy that exists in primate colonies. He found this language of relationship to be an extraordinarily powerful means of explaining primate behaviour and his book became a classic. Nevertheless his break with the rigorists was only partial and his explanation fell short because of his failure to engage seriously with the mental motivations of the animals. For example, he notes that the Barbary macaque monkeys have an extraordinary peacekeeping strategy. If two males are about to get into a potentially damaging fight, one may rush and snatch an infant and hold it between themselves and their disputant. What are they doing? Dunbar's logic is at a loss to explain it.[12] Perhaps they are enlisting the mother of the infant as an ally? he says. Yet I find if I tell this story to lay folk, they come up with a far more obvious answer. The infant elicits sympathetic feelings which distract from the conflict. Dunbar cannot think in these terms. Discussing such inner motivations is a step too far.

Of course such lay opinion might be wide of the mark, but it may not. Perhaps the situation is rather similar to a certain teacher from Nazareth who, when his disciples were squabbling about who was the greatest, went and got a child and presented it to them.[13] Or again it might be related to why we put those funny signs 'Baby on board' in our car? In the antagonistic and threatening world of the road, is this sign an attempt to raise our sympathetic social feelings, to get us to back off from any potentially damaging confrontation? Just like the macaque or the disciples. What about Christmas? Why is it so popular? Why is a Carol Service so renowned for generating sympathetic feeling. Is it something to do with the crib and the baby?

---

[12]   Ibid., chap. 11.

[13]   Luke 9:46-48. The disciples were arguing. Jesus took a child and said, 'Whoever receives this child in my name receives me, and whoever receives me receives him who sent me; for he who is least among you all is the one who is great.'

Here then are examples from primates, from the Bible, from a traditional festival and from car travel. They are separated in time, culture and even species. Yet might there be a connection? Could it be that all are instances of the profound connection between infants and the generation of sympathetic social feelings that we have been alluding to throughout this chapter? If this is the case, then it suggests the possibility that the study of this type of deep level motivational behaviour might yield insights into human societies that are general in form and cross time and the particularities of culture. This book will continue to explore this possibility.

Such connections should also cause us to reflect on our minds and the motivational structures they contain. The mind is a system of inordinate complexity, consisting of hard–wired, inherited elements, complemented by a vast stock of learned behaviour and with the capacity for considerable spontaneous intelligent activity. It may be impossible most of the time to isolate any of these elements from the other, yet it is important to acknowledge that they each exist. It is largely the inherited elements that will give rise to behaviours that genuinely relate to those of other animals, yet they may express themselves in very different forms as they find expression in the complexity of our minds and human culture. In a sense the ancestral elements in our brains bear analogy with the calendars of computers which caused such a threat as the millennium ticked over. The calendar is a primitive part of the system of a computer, yet one on top of which a whole host of other functions has now been laid. Much of the time the computer can be worked without reference to this primitive part of itself. Occasionally, like at the millennium, its role becomes crucial. Our minds likewise have primitive functions and these need to be recognised if we are to work for the most fruitful society in the future.

The experts at tapping into our deepest motivations are, of course, the high priests of the advertising world. 'Size matters' says the car advert. We may laugh but the connection is deep –

sex, the phallus and male power. The advertisers know how to push the right buttons in our psyche to draw out our most basic motivations.

This whole discussion raises a darker question that can no longer be avoided. The hesitancy of biologists to talk this language stems not only from scruples on the basis of science, but also from a deeply held fear that knowledge about 'instincts' has the potential to be abused. Those who make simplistic equations between human behaviour and instincts all too easily see humans as genetically-determined beings who can be manipulated. If instincts are genetically inherited then this easily leads to proposals that humans should be bred with particular characteristics. It can be used to justify approaches to the design of master races and, indeed, Konrad Lorenz, the pioneer of ethology fell into exactly this trap early in his career.[14] For this reason, among others, the eminent biologist Stephen Jay Gould effectively refuses to talk the language of instinct, seeing it to be inevitably linked to fascism.[15] Such pervasive political correctness may not, however, best serve the cause of human understanding. Instead I would suggest that the quite proper fear of abuse might be adequately assuaged by stressing the openness and so the indeterminacy of expression of instincts in the complex mind and also by acknowledging that genetic contributions are almost impossible to isolate in any rigorous manner from learned behaviour. This should lend a proper agnosticism to all talk of inherited motivations, but nevertheless allow that such thinking may still be of great explanatory value.

Mary Midgely's work is of particular interest because she is a philosopher who has turned to biology and has not been slow to expose some of the sloppy thinking about the mind and animal

---

[14] In 1940 Lorenz wrote in a scholarly journal decrying racial impurity and applauding the Nazi state. See Konner, *The Tangled Wing*, p. 445.

[15] Gould's position on this is actually quite complex. It is reviewed and effectively critiqued in Midgely, *Beast and Man*, pp. 66–7.

nature.[16] She contends that our minds are not structureless. They are not 'infinitely plastic'. Instead human beings do indeed have predispositions to behave in certain ways. These can be modified or elaborated within a human culture, but they will not be done away with, at least not without continual effort. They act as some constraint upon us. They are part of what is given by our natural inheritance. Within our minds these predispositions are frequently in conflict with one another. In the conversation above we illustrated the potential conflicts between aggressive and sympathetic feelings and how they are brought to a fruitful synthesis. In fact our brains carry not two inherited elements in competition, but a host of these, interacting at different times with different force. Midgely proposes that the resolution of these internal conflicts and the external conflicts they produce in animal society, is one of the principle purposes of rationality. Rationality is not something that is abstract and free floating. It is rooted in the conflicts within us. Immanuel Kant proposed that the best sort of human being would be one that could rise above their passions and consider the world rationally. TV's *Star Trek* plays with that idea in the person of a Mr Spock or an android like 'Data', a fully rational being with no emotions. If Midgely is right, such conceptions are nonsense, for rationality actually takes its origins from our passions and the need to mediate between them. Part of this mediation is to prioritise these conflicting messages within us. Our character might be said to be the 'set of long lasting preferences'[17] that we have set up within our minds to deal with these struggles.

Midgely's analysis suggests that one of the fundamental tasks of the human animal is the mediation of conflict, such conflict originating in the mind and expressing itself in the way we form our societies. The recognition of these conflicts and the search to find the best means of their resolution may be an essential

---

[16] Midgely, *Beast and Man*.
[17] Ibid., p. 259.

ingredient of wisdom. It may also be the primary driver of culture. This is an idea to which we shall return repeatedly during this book, but first let me illustrate it with some simple examples.

Greeting rituals

One of the most rudimentary elements of culture formation may be the greeting ritual. As two animals meet, there can be a need to diffuse potential aggression or predation. To do this they typically develop rituals of greeting.

For example, the little fish, known as a cleaner wrasse, has a problem. It exists by cleaning the parasites off much bigger fish. These bigger fish eat little fish, yet the wrasse is scarcely ever touched. Why? The answer to this conundrum according to Lorenz is the little dance that the cleaner fish does as it approaches. The seesaw-like dance is thought to have derived from the opposite motivations of the fish as it wants to both flee and draw close to feed. When it sees the dance, the big fish knows that it is best to let this one near.[18] It seems that little rituals frequently arise at moments of potential conflict.

Similarly wolves and dogs have a very sophisticated set of teeth and they cannot afford to fight unnecessarily. In response to this they have developed a greeting ritual, familiar to anyone who takes a dog for a walk in the park, in which the dogs do their characteristic approaching and sniffing. Some dogs fail to develop these rituals and regularly get into fights. The vets now offer socialisation classes to puppies.

Likewise we have seen how parents with young can be spontaneously aggressive. A cormorant returning to its nest replete with partner and young brings with it a gift of nesting material. Eibl-Eibesfeldt observed a situation whereby when he removed

---

[18] Eibl-Eibesfeldt, *Love and Hate*, chap. 3.

the nesting material from a returning bird, it was attacked by the female as it landed on the nest. The bird then went to retrieve the nesting material and returned to the nest unmolested. It seems that the ritual bringing of the gift was a peace offering.[19]

Here then are three examples where animals develop rituals to deal with moments of meeting, in the face of potential threat. The rituals appear to be specifically oriented towards a peaceful rapprochement. But do human beings also develop these rituals?

The smile is interesting. It is found universally.[20] Even blind people, who could never copy it, smile. It is a ritual of reassurance. Similarly many cultures develop forms of touch in greeting, a non-violent touch that reassures. It may be a hug, a kiss, a handshake or something else but it signifies friendship, the absence of threat. Sometimes the touch may be deliberately to diffuse aggression. 'Kiss and make up,' we say or 'Shake hands on it.' The importance of such gestures in public life is regularly demonstrated.

Nelson Mandela and F.W. de Klerk were to debate on television just prior to the crucial South African elections. Reporters had descended on South Africa to cover the civil war that so many expected. Mandela's minders gave orders that the tables, behind which they would sit, should be angled to part face each other. The producer ignored their request. They were both to face the cameras. The debate took place and went largely as expected except at the end Mandela rose, leant awkwardly right across to F.W. de Klerk, and offered his hand to shake. De Klerk took it and the picture went round the world. It was a sign, a sign that there could be peace. So that was why he wanted the tables at the funny angle![21]

---

[19] Ibid., chap. 7.

[20] Ibid., chap. 9.

[21] This story is story told by John Simpson in *Strange Places, Questionable People*, p. 526.

Similarly when Chris Patten was governor of Hong Kong, there came the moment when he was to set foot in China for the first time for serious negotiation. The Chinese are very sensitive to ritual signs of acceptance or rejection. The newspaper reporters watched as he was greeted. The Chinese delegate failed to shake hands! It was a snub and the press loved it.[22]

Other signs denote submission or dominance, such as the bow or curtsy, or the doffing of the cap. The eyes are tremendously important. Staring eyes are predatory. As you pass someone in the street, you will be very careful about eye contact. You must not meet their gaze for too long or it will be interpreted as aggression. Eyes down indicates submission or non-aggression. Saddam Hussein is a particularly short man and is very keen that his visitors demonstrate due respect. As he greets a visitor, he holds out his hand particularly low. They take his hand and he pulls them forward just slightly so they begin to topple forward. At this point his cameramen shoot and capture a picture of another western leader bowing to the great Saddam.[23]

Likewise the words are important. We develop a whole set of greeting words. Like the gestures, it does not matter much what they are, so much as that they convey friendliness. 'Hallo.' 'How are you?' 'Poor weather today.' It's all nonsense or utterly trivial at one level, but at another it is absolutely vital.

This summer I went on holiday in Greece and set out without one word of the language. I rapidly discovered that if I could just use the friendly words, the please, thank you, good morning and the like, my relations with the Greek people were transformed. Without these people were uneasy, even hostile. With these words we were accepted everywhere. Perhaps this is why children are taught please and thank you at such an early age. Greeting rituals are important.

---

[22] Patten, *East and West*, p. 68.

[23] Simpson, *Strange Places, Questionable People*, p. 382.

In human culture, of course, we have learnt to communicate, by various alternative means. Interestingly, greeting rituals have developed as fitting for each new mode of communication. For example, secretaries have traditionally had to learn a whole string of etiquette in regard to the forms of greeting in letter writing. More recently there has been a tendency in society at large to let forms of greeting slip, to consider them unimportant. In particular they have come under attack because they are thought to unhelpfully underline power differentials. Yet some form of greeting is generally necessary and if it does not happen naturally, then it will be imposed. Supermarket queues are notoriously stressed places. It is not uncommon for tempers to fray. It all seems so anonymous. I have therefore been particularly interested to note that the check-out assistants in my supermarket have recently been instructed to greet every customer with definite eye contact and a 'Hallo' or some such, before they start processing the goods. I suspect that is a very wise move.

Similarly new forms of communication make new demands. I have a friend who works for a telemarketing company, whose members are spread over a large distance. Most of their internal communication is by email, but she confided in me that emails were regularly causing misunderstandings. People were falling out through this method of communication. Emails are also currently working with the most trivial of greeting rituals. I suspect we will find this form of communication inadequate, or perhaps will need to complement email relationships with other forms of communication.

This same friend went on to speak of how disputes were settled within the company. There was a hierarchy of communication. If e-mail did not sort it out, they would phone. If more was required, they would video-conference. Finally, for the really major issues they would meet face to face. This hierarchy can be understood in terms of sensory perception and the different strengths and weaknesses of the different forms of communication. Each abstract form loses something from the face to face interaction. The situation most likely to engender trust and right understanding is the face to face meeting because then all the spoken and unspoken signals of communication are present in their 'normal', i.e. natural, manner.

The greeting ritual is then perhaps the first and crudest form of culture, and it derives from the need to co-ordinate our deepest motivations and channel them to fruitful ends. In the chapters that follow we shall see that this fundamental need to work with and integrate deep-level motivations drives culture even more profoundly than we have yet realised. It is also an explanatory tool with which we can understand many aspects of our own public life.

2

The difficulties of being sociable

Social animals like ourselves have particular opportunities and particular difficulties. In addition to all the challenges that animals always have to face, we have to negotiate our way through relationships. The social animal's most fundamental belief is that working with others is going to be a better strategy than working on your own. In strict socio-biological logic, these animals are committed to working with others because it is a better means of passing on their own genes than being on their own. This raises an interesting conundrum for the animal. The most basic organising principle of their existence revolves around passing on *their own* genes, but to do this they work in a society of *others*, who have their own 'gene' interests. We might therefore predict that at the heart of any social animal's existence there is a conflict of interests. On the one hand they would be primarily concerned with their own success. On the other they would recognise the importance of the society as a whole in achieving this. The challenges that this places on the social animal may be at the heart of the development of what we call human culture.

The power hierarchy

The most basic way of resolving the above conflict of interests is through the power hierarchy. All primate societies are based on some form of power hierarchy and so, arguably, are human ones. The basis of the life of a hierarchy is that it is a system that limits outright violence through the use of aggression and reconciliation to form a social order. A war of all against all is prevented by the establishment of a hierarchy of power, which is itself a partially fluid structure, open to challenge, but maintained by threat, such as shows of aggression. Aggression is important as a means of reinforcing the social order without often having to resort to actual damaging violence.

At the heart of the system is the most basic tension between the individual and collective interest. Every individual animal is looking for opportunities to rise in the hierarchy. Socio-biologists would link this to the principle that the key ingredients of biological success, namely food, safety and sex, are all more abundant and reliably obtained at the top of the hierarchy than at the bottom. This translates into deep mental dispositions towards status seeking. At the same time they value the social order, because they need it to prevent outright and continual violent competition, which would be damaging to all. Frans de Waal, who has studied primates and their psychology most of his life, puts this essential tension like this:

> The significance that monkeys and apes attach to dominance relationships and their jostling for positions and connections, mean that group life encompasses two conflicting strategies. The first is to probe the social order for weaknesses and look for openings to improve one's standing. In as much as this strategy subverts existing social structures and creates chaos, one might regard it as antisocial. Yet from the viewpoint of the parties knocking down the old walls, there is nothing antisocial about it; for them it is pure progress.

The second strategy is a response to the first: conservation of the status quo. Although very much in the interest of the parties with the best positions, the resulting stability also benefits the young and weak, who are the first to suffer in the case of all-out war within a group. Hence the potential of a pact between top and bottom in which the lower echelons back the reigning powers, provided these guarantee their security. Society results from the equilibrium between these contradictory strategies.[1]

I have quoted this at length, because it seems to me to contain vital insights that are applicable to human, as well as primate societies and we shall continually refer back to it during the book. Most of the statement is of a simple logical form. Granted it begs many questions about how this logic might express itself in mental processes, but fortunately de Waal is well able to escape the constraints of rigorist methodology and imagine the thoughts of the primate mind.

We noted the potentially important role that aggression plays in both challenge and imposition of order, but this is not the only dynamic that one might expect to be present in these societies. There are other potential means of supporting a peace, which might complement or mitigate the need for aggression. For example, in chapter one we looked at a body of evidence which suggests that sympathetic social feelings arise in animals and take both their evolutionary and immediate social origins from the care of infants. Frans de Waal views this development as the brain of animals evolving through mere helping of others in distress through to a full cognitive empathy, present only in apes and humans and in which the animal is able to imagine the situation of the other.

Alongside this psychological development there are other important bonds for the social society. Kinship is obviously a major determinant. On a logical basis, your kin share some of your genes, so special relations between kin are very likely to

---

[1] De Waal, *Good Natured*, p. 102.

have developed. Any cursory inspection of animal or human society would show the extraordinary bonds of loyalty that can be generated through blood, or rather, genetic, relationship. For our purposes, however, as we consider public life, it is most important to think about bonds between non-kin and how they are formed and develop.

Frans de Waal notices that primates are capable of very different forms of society. Rhesus monkeys tend to form a notoriously vicious and despotic hierarchy. In contrast, stump-tailed macaque monkeys have a relatively harmonious society. Interestingly if you mix the two monkeys together such that the rhesus join a harmonious macaque colony, rhesus behaviour markedly improves. So here we are into something that can clearly be learned. What is the difference between the two?[2] Studies have shown that more egalitarian primate societies tend to have better peacemaking strategies and include more grooming, which in primate terms is relationship building. The ability to leave one colony for another also appears to affect the society. If animals feel they cannot leave, then the worst aspects of power tend to be exercised upon them. We might reflect on our own policies with regard to asylum seekers in this light. The ability to flee makes for kinder societies.

Tit for tat and the development of trust

One further important difference between primate cultures is their tendency or otherwise to form alliances. More harmonious colonies form alliances between animals of all sorts, kin and non-kin and this results in balances of power, in subtleties in the hierarchical structure, that work to prevent each individual simply ruling over the ones below. The importance of this to human politics will be drawn out in chapter nine. But the question needs

---

[2]   De Waal, *Good Natured*, pp. 127ff.

to be asked: if alliances are so important, what encourages their formation? It seems that alliances tend to form between animals of similar interest. For example, females of a particular year group may band together. In like fashion human societies exhibit a plethora of such interest group alliances, including Trades Unions, Mother's Union, Craft guilds, professional associations and many others. The reason for their importance seems to be that similarities of interest give a platform on which tit for tat behaviour can grow. If you are bound together in common concern then you will naturally work together on the same agendas and come to do each other favours, expecting a return.[3]

Robert Trivers has made a vital contribution to the logical understanding of this process. His original essay 'The Evolution of Reciprocal Atruism'[4] has been an inspiration to those, such as Matt Ridley and Frans de Waal, who have thought more widely as a result about human culture and the role of tit for tat behaviour.[5, 6] 'It seems that tit for tat behaviour that has an immediate payoff is relatively common in animals. So, for example, herons may work together to corral fish and will all benefit from that co-operative behaviour at the same time. But what particularly exercised Robert Trivers was the situation in which the return of the favour was delayed – when an animal did a favour for another, knowing that it will only be repaid sometime in the future. This situation is fraught with risk. It demands a certain sort of trust. He concluded that, from a strictly socio-biological perspective, such 'delayed tit for tat' behaviour could only be a successful strategy under certain conditions and could only develop among certain sorts of animals. To paraphrase de Waal and Ridley on this subject, one might say there are three conditions necessary for such 'delayed tit for tat' or 'trusting' behaviour to develop in

---

[3] Ibid., pp. 26-7.

[4] Trivers, 'The Evolution of Reciprocal Atruism', pp. 35–57.

[5] De Waal, *Good Natured*, p. 24.

[6] Matt Ridley, *The Origins of Virtue*, pp. 63-84.

an animal colony. Only if the animals had *stable relationships, good memories and effective discipline* could such behaviour logically be expected to be successful. The animals had to know each other individually, remember favours done and returned and have the capacity to discipline those who tried to take unfair advantage. The occurrence of delayed tit for tat behaviours at any stage of the evolutionary process would depend on the development of animals with minds and associated social systems that could meet these challenges. Primates and humans were obviously prime candidates for demonstrating this type of behaviour and Frans de Waal discovered a host of examples of it in primates.

So, in his primate colony at Arnhem zoo, there was a situation where a ruling alpha male, Luit, was overthrown by a partnership. The partners Nikki and Yeroen appear to have done a deal. Yeroen supported Nikki as leader in exchange for mating rights with the females. On occasion, Nikki would grow arrogant and deny Yeroen this sexual access. Yeroen's response was simple. He withdrew his political loyalty. Luit then fancied his chances of regaining the top spot and would grow in boldness, until Nikki and Yeroen made up. The deal between Nikki and Yeroen was a system of trust, sexual access in return for political solidarity. It was built on their relationship. It contained its discipline, through the challenges of Luit, and thereby it was effective.[7] In human societies such delayed tit for tat mechanisms are everywhere and of vital importance to human culture.

I spent the nineties as vicar of a working class community in inner city Bristol. This community had its roots in the Industrial Revolution. The Great Western Cotton Factory had been built and workers imported from Lancashire to work it. The community grew to number about ten thousand, most of which lived in the quarter of a square mile around the cotton factory. Their tiny houses had no piped water or adequate sewage system and the graveyard was soon full of people who died from typhus and

---

[7] De Waal, *Good Natured*, pp. 172–3.

cholera. Most of the deaths were those of children. Despite the hardships, a community life grew of tremendous solidarity.[8] Similar communities have been recorded in many working class districts. Fundamental to their life was the mechanism of delayed tit for tat and the conditions of its formation were that vital threesome, stable relationships, good memories and effective discipline. Here were people bound together by a strong platform of similarity of interest. In this context they naturally developed tit for tat behaviour and learnt who could be trusted to return a favour. 'One good turn deserves another' was not just a pleasant saying; it was at the heart of life. If you were temporarily without means you were truly dependent on the mercy of another. The bags of sugar lent this week must be reciprocated when you were short. The relationships were stable enough and memories strong enough to keep track of what was going on. Reputation was of vital importance. Social ostracism was a most effective discipline for those who offended against the community norms. Although ostracism presented an element of threat, the harshness of life for many was generally offset by such acts of reciprocation and the kindness that often went with them.

Beyond these especially personal encounters, there likewise grew structures of trust at a larger level. There would be pawn shops to buy and sell in a semi-formal manner as a means of tiding you over the lean period. There would be savings schemes, like Christmas Clubs, and there was the natural growth of insurance that would lead to Friendly Societies and such like. All these can be seen as natural developments of a basic 'delayed tit for tat mechanism' or as we shall call them a system of trust.[9] They depended on stable relationships, good memories and effective discipline and they were a means of co-operative gain, providing

---

[8] Details of this community have been recorded in Jennings, *Societies in the making.*

[9] Matt Ridley, *The Origins of Virtue.*

aspects of social life that were not accessible to the individual alone.

As systems of trust like this grew to encompass more people, then systems of accountability greater than those of the face-to-face encounter needed to be put in place. A person would not only have a face but a number in a passbook. They might carry a passport. A car driver would have, not only a name, but a licence and a number plate. The system was still essentially the same, but the mechanisms by which people were kept track of and were disciplined would change and become more abstract as the number of people embraced by the system grew. Such systems of trust are the substance of western society. We need to understand them.

Conditions for sensible co-operation

To further our understanding, I offer an imaginary game. This is adapted from a similar situation expounded by Matt Ridley in his seminal book *The Origins of Virtue*.[10] Consider the situation. You are put in a cubicle. In front of you is a button. You are told that there are twenty other people in similar cubicles being given exactly the same instructions. They are these. If none of you presses the button for ten minutes, you will each collect £1000. On the other hand if one of you does press the button in that time, that person will collect £200 and the others get nothing. What would you do? It is a hard decision. If no one presses for the whole ten minutes you will get £1000, but if any of the others do press, you will be left with nothing. People have different responses to this game, but many agree that the logical thing *is* to press the button as fast as possible. Not to do so will in all

---

[10] The original situation derives initially from Dougls Hofstader who called it the Wolf's dilemma. It is quoted in Matt Ridley, *The Origins of Virtue*, p. 55. I have added the structural variations on the basic theme.

likelihood just lead to you being the sucker who sits there while someone else walks off with two hundred pounds. After all, what reason do you have for thinking the others will not press?

Now repeat the game, but with you all in the same room. The buttons are now underneath the arms of your chair. The rules are the same. If no one presses you each get £1000. If anyone presses they get £200 and you get nothing. What do you do? Now you can *see* them. You are aware of the reality of the others. Button pressing, though still hidden from view, is likely to be more of an issue for the person who presses. Yet if they can do it without being seen, my guess is that they will still press and if you don't press before someone else does you are a sucker.

Now instead of pressing a button, how about if you had to raise your hand? How would that feel? I suspect that people would generally be much more reticent about the individualist option of raising their hands to take the £200, leaving everyone else with nothing. Others can now see them acting and significant social pressure can be exerted towards the co-operative strategy of inaction for the prescribed ten minutes. This would be further accentuated if the game were repeated and conferring between games allowed. The group could then easily bind one another to an agreement that no one should raise their hand and that cheats would be punished between rounds. The sensible strategy would then be to keep your hand down and go for the gains of co-operation.

The situations offered by this game are at the very heart of human society. The question which it raises is, 'How can we reap the rewards of co-operation?' Under what conditions can we safely trust our well-being to a co-operative venture in the hope of greater reward? The point is to demonstrate that the conditions under which the game is played are vital. To take a practical example, think about how the miners were broken. One simple change in the law shattered the miners: the introduction of the secret ballot. In times past they played the game by putting their hands in the air. Often management would make offers of large redundancy payoffs to the men in an attempt to break their co-operative long term view that their welfare lay in sticking together and keeping the mine open. While they met in a public meeting, their community solidarity was such that people would rarely raise their hand for the redundancy money. Yet as soon as voting was in secret, there was little sense in solidarity. It was every man for himself or you were a sucker. And the pits were closed. Depending on your point of view, you might see that change as a good or a bad thing. What I want us to realise is that the structure of the situation mattered. The way society sets up its public relationships is of crucial importance to the sort of society that is generated. The example also shows the connection between this game and our earlier account of delayed tit for tat. The miners' community is a classic example of stable relationships, good memories and effective discipline. People do not like to be called scabs. Under these conditions co-operative systems of trust easily develop, but as we can see, the structure of the system matters crucially as to whether or not it is wise to go for the co-operative gain by committing yourself to working with others.

Human cultures as systems of trust

This game and the basic conditions for delayed tit for tat set us up to understand a vast number of aspects of human culture. Human culture depends crucially on systems of trust, whereby we gain the fruits of co-operation by developing conditions where it is genuinely sensible to trust one another. Traffic, for example, is an extraordinarily effective system of trust. We hurtle along the tarmac accompanied by tons of steel, inches from one another. We pass cars in the opposite lane going in the reverse direction at enormous speed. One error in the system and fatality is likely. Yet we use it every day, with little worry or concern. It is all a system of trust and it has been developed very carefully. The vast numbers of people involved cannot make for conventional relationships in terms of face to face interaction, but we have produced an abstract form to replace stable relationships, good memories and the social ostracism that was effective discipline. Now each car has a number plate. There is a highway code and tests of car roadworthiness. There are driving licences and traffic police. The system as a whole performs the basic function of keeping tabs on people and administering effective discipline when they break the trust. The result is that tolerably reliable cars driven by tolerably reliable drivers, are put on a substantially reliable road system. Things do go wrong. When they do, people are disciplined. By and large it works. Yet it is fundamentally a system of trust. This becomes all too clear at a psychological level when we ourselves have an accident. Suddenly we develop a new anxiety about driving. Some even give it up. They can no longer trust it.

Traffic, of course, is a very specific example. What we need to appreciate is that the fundamental organs of human society, namely the law, politics, commerce, religion and morality are themselves systems of trust.

Commerce owes its origin to barter. It is about an exchange of goods. Where this is a favour immediately returned, we have minimal trust. Hold out the goods with one hand, take his with the other. Perhaps some street dealer exchanges might be an example of this lowest trust scenario. The money and the goods are exchanged together and there is little chance of any comeback if anything is wrong. This essential vulnerability is met by the development of trading standards, a form of discipline that works to discourage traders from shifting shoddy or dangerous goods. Their presence is a sign that there is real risk implicit in most processes of exchange – hence the need for trust. Building projects are likewise fraught with risk, because the transaction occurs over a long period. How can the builder be sure they will be paid? How does the buyer know that the building will be built and be sound? So a law of contract develops to mediate such an exchange. And it all adds up to a system of trust. Money itself is, of course, a system of trust, and chaos breaks loose when confidence in money crashes. So in general terms we can see that commerce develops realistic mechanisms of trust that enable the fruits of co-operation to be realised. Chapter seven will elaborate further on this.

Law, likewise, functions in a similar manner. Any system of laws is dependent on most of the people obeying the law most of the time. This is a trust. Any law that the majority of people regularly disobey would rapidly bring that law into disrepute. It would no longer be effective. The laws against theft are based upon a fundamental respect for private property. If that respect is lost, there is no way that attempted enforcement of the law would bring it back. The special arena of law is the arbitration of dispute. It provides a focus for issues about what one person owes to another or to society as a whole. This is, of course, the language of tit for tat and it is perhaps the most fundamental root of our sense of justice. Law continually develops in its role as mediator as society itself changes. One particularly obvious example of this concerns the present situation of unmarried cohabitees. For years many people shrugged their shoulders about marriage and described it as just a piece of paper. Now cohabiting couples are discovering that they need to make arrangements about pensions, about the care of children and the division of their material goods in the event of their splitting up. A whole new tranche of law is in the making to manage the very real conflicts that such situations provoke. Far from just being a 'piece of paper', marriage is, and was, a trust and it has had its own disciplines in terms of laws that covered just the areas that cohabitees are now finding they need help with. I can imagine in a few years that couples will have a special time when they go along to the solicitor to sign their legal agreements. Perhaps they will invite a few friends to celebrate the occasion afterwards. A new form of marriage will have evolved. Until someone says again that it is just a piece of paper! Of course there is more to be said on that issue, but the principle it highlights is general, namely that law evolves as a mediating system of trust. Conflicts between people are contained and managed within a system whose basis is that of delayed tit for tat, such that there need be no recourse to violence.

Politics has two faces. Any society has an external politic with which it confronts the *other* societies. It also has an internal politic which mediates the power structure of its own society. The external aspect is situated at the margins of culture. It frequently has to do with finding some basis for resolving conflict between societies that have little or nothing in common. Violence is often close to the surface. Yet the name of the game is to develop some basis for trust. At its crudest level international politics is about playing tit for tat. It is about finding some platform on which you may exchange favours and, from there, develop some feeling about each other's existence and value. The development of commercial relations, for example, is a crucial political strategy. The reason that France and Russia are so friendly towards Saddam Hussein at present is simple. He owes them money and they want it back. They are tied up in a commercial relationship that affects their political regard for one another. The reason the west was so slow to recognise the horrors of Indonesia's treatment of East Timor was largely because Indonesia is playing the commercial game with us and we do not want to alienate them and risk a communist take-over of that area of the world.

Similarly internal politics depends on systems of trust. Alliances of all sorts form in any healthy society. These alliances have power through their solidarity and can render the formal governmental structure accountable, forcing it to be subtle in its outworking. Healthy politics is about the balancing of such powers in systems of trust. One of the crucial challenges facing western society at present is the continued weakening of all our intermediate institutions. They are the life force of a healthy politic and the place where we learn the art of politics as a system of trust. More about this in chapter nine.

From the above we can see that overarching systems of trust like law, politics and commerce, all interact with one another, while each retaining their own distinctive function. This is characteristic of what we call a culture. These systems actually develop over centuries. Their manner of working becomes a vast storehouse of learned behaviour, which we absorb into the background of our lives. Over time we have simply accumulated practices that work, means of co-operation that we can tolerably trust. We can justify very little of it at a propositional level. Most of it is inherited knowledge, passed on from one generation to another in what we call culture. Michael Polanyi called it 'tacit' knowledge, implying that it is real knowledge that we rely on in our everyday lives though assumed by us such that it now forms the background to our lives.[11] Of course there must be room to challenge such knowledge, but the basis of such a challenge is very important. For example, Enlightenment thinkers relied on applying reason and reason alone to society, attempting to find a platform of strict logic on which to cut away the false accretions of the past and build a glorious future. Unfortunately their method had no way of valuing the accrued 'how to' knowledge on which society is based. The French Revolution was the logical outcome – in general terms root and branch revolutions tend to give rise to violence, simply because they cannot immediately replace all the tacit knowledge which co-ordinates a society and which grows over centuries.[12] The sad result is that a Napoleon or a Stalin is then required as the tyrant who imposes social order without the subtleties and accountabilities implicit in a good society.

Morality is a bad word for many people today. Yet a discussion of its origins may clarify its positive purpose. The imaginary button pressing game above points to the importance in any society of being able to discern who is trustworthy. If you can

---

[11] Polanyi, *The Tacit Dimension*.

[12] We will return to a discussion of this point in chapter nine.

accurately tell whom you can trust, then you know when work with others is likely to be fruitful. If you grow to know the group of button pressers you are with and one is an unconscionable rogue who will always let you down, then you would be wise not to take the trusting option. Press the button and get out. Yet the fruits of co-operation tend to be greater if people can be trusted, so it is very reasonable to imagine that moral systems might develop that give value to being trustworthy. It is highly likely then that whether a person had a reputation for trustworthiness or not would become a serious matter of public life. Even the reputation of a company or institution might be valued on this basis.

Here, say Frans de Waal and Matt Ridley and a host of other recent analysts, lie the true roots of morality. For the first time the logical connections have been made as to how an animal living solely on the basis of its own genetic interest could have developed a moral system. It therefore becomes highly probable that societies would employ systems of thought that work to enhance trustworthiness and all that goes with it. Furthermore it becomes quite reasonable to consider that our brains might develop a moral capacity. So a person's own sense of self-worth might include a concept of reputation with trustworthiness at its core. Although this might have originated in the pragmatic consideration that society works better on this basis, the importance of trustworthiness might now have become a predisposition of our minds and part of the 'deep, lasting system of preferences' that constitutes our character.[13] A person of such character might therefore be able to withstand an immense amount of pressure to act falsely, to betray someone, or to be dishonest. Of course, such people are also prone to be taken advantage of in a society. They will sometimes be the sucker who trusts while everyone else takes advantage of a breakdown in the system. Yet here is the positive originating source of moral development; trustworthy people are of great value in any society.

---

[13] Midgely, *Beast and Man*, chap. 11.

Morality is itself a system of trust for obvious reasons. The moral code confers expected modes of conduct upon people. These are like the law but now imposed internally, through the strictures of conscience and disciplined by the approval or otherwise of the society which holds them. The moral consensus is itself a trust that the society works with. Its details evolve continually and it is based on stable relationships, good memories and effective discipline. Here again western society faces certain serious challenges. The sheer mobility of people in our global world means that it is hard to keep track of people in the way that an informal system of trust like morality requires. If I only see someone occasionally, I can hardly keep track of their reputation. I simply do not know whether I can trust them. Similarly people now inhabit all sorts of different life situations. They may be tempted to play different parts, aware that no one can really keep tabs on their behaviour. For example, many acts of infidelity occur when a partner is in a strange environment, like a conference. On a more surreal level, we have now a host of false identities being played out on the internet. Morality as a system is under threat not only from the intellectual challenges of reason but mostly from the practical challenge of technological change.

Finally, I believe that religion has a particularly important part to play in human society and that religion itself is also a system of trust. That must be the subject of the next chapter.

3

The mainsprings of religion

The complexity of the situation faced by social animals has been briefly described in the previous two chapters. Like all animals their lives can be seen to have been organised by the processes of evolution around the propagation of genes. In more complex and social animals this takes on new characteristics as mental motivations arise, whose first organising principle in evolution may have been the dictates of biological success, but which have a new complexity and possibility. The development of the mind presents a social animal like ourselves with the possibility of questioning whether biological success adequately defines our ultimate goal.

Although we cannot know the workings of the mind with scientific certainty, the foregoing account might lead us to believe that within the human mind there lie certain deep level motivations. First, we might expect a striving for success. This will be related to our most basic biological motivations. Since food, safety and sex are key to the organising logic of evolution, we should expect them to have at least some part in our developed human motivations. Similarly since success in these areas might be associated with rising in the hierarchy, we should not be surprised if humans were naturally status-seeking. Of course we can balance these motivations with others, developing different types of characters, but who would deny, for example, the importance of power and the desire to advance in status? Frans de Waal has written that 'The desire to dictate the behaviour of others is such a timeless and universal attribute of our species that it must rank with the sex drive, maternal instinct, and the will to survive in terms of the likelihood of its being part of our biological heritage.'[1] This in itself would be enough to give rise to competitive behaviour.

At the same time the social animal has a deep level awareness of the importance of the social order. This might be expected to give rise to relational sensibilities, empathy, and an appreciation of the role of peacemaking strategies. Robin Dunbar notices how primates can give over twenty per cent of their time to grooming activities, this being not just an hygienic function, but primarily a way of making relationships.[2]

Similarly power would be perceived ambivalently. At one level power is a problem. It prevents us rising in the social order. At the other end it is the force which holds it all together, giving cohesion to a society that might otherwise descend into violent chaos. So on that basis it is valued. All these contrasting and yet vital motivations within us find their expression in religion.

For example, religion is employed the world over in the search for success. As the Mongolian steppe people make their tents, they get to a stage when they wrap the felt around a log and drag it behind a pony to roll it. As they do so, they ceremonially anoint the rump of the pony as a prayer of blessing for the felt. They want the tent making to be successful. It is vital to their lives. They pray for success. In fact everywhere you go in the world, the same phenomenon can be observed. Beside the stall in India, there will be a shrine with lights and a picture of a god, to whom prayers are offered for success of the business venture. As an army goes to war, so there will be a priest offering prayers for success. It is everywhere.

---

[1] De Waal, *Good Natured*, p. 98.
[2] Dunbar, *Primate Social Systems*.

Our search for success at an individual level will frequently clash with others. There will be a need for adjudication. In part this may be by the growth of a system of morality, law and custom, but very often it is tied into a system of religion. The priest will be the ultimate arbiter. When all else fails, the priest will be called in to give a verdict. In some cultures, the conflict will be resolved by resort to spiritual condemnation. The 'guilty' party might be termed 'witch' and sent away or worse. Lucy Mair notes how frequently such 'spiritual' accusations are made to settle a conflict when the culture has no other resource.[3] Religion is often used to settle conflicts. How it does so is of vital importance. And it all relates to the social animal striving to succeed.

As the social animal values the social order at a deep level, so this also is expressed in religion. We have a tendency to 'love' the social order. I recall watching the last night of the Proms a year or so ago. It is really an extraordinary event. The time-honoured ritual replayed its way through Elgar's *Pomp and Circumstance* complete with 'Land of Hope and Glory' in which everyone sang about the 'mother of the free' and 'God who made thee mighty make thee mightier yet'. Then came the sea shanties including 'Rule Britannia' and finally they sang Blake's 'Jerusalem' and 'God Save the Queen'. 'Rule Britannia' was particularly interesting that year as it was led by Willard White, an opera singer of some renown and a black man of Caribbean extraction. There he stood, a Union Jack bandana round his head and a Jamaican flag as a cummerbund, singing 'Britains never, never, never shall be slaves'. I thought, really how bizarre! Here is a man whose close relatives were made slaves by us, leading us in this song. How do we make sense of all this?

I think the last night of the Proms is a quasi-religious phenomenon. It is actually all about celebrating and upholding the social order. This is such a deep level motivation that it can be

---

[3] Mair, *An Introduction to Social Anthropology*, pp. 238ff.

expressed in terms that defy simple logic, yet still truly expressed
and so appreciated that tens of thousands of people will turn out
to take part. It makes the bridge between deep level appreciation
of the social order and religion. It is really not very far from those
psalms that celebrate the permanence of the temple or which see
the mountains around Jerusalem as signs of the permanence of
the social order under God. 'How lovely is thy dwelling place O
Lord of hosts!' exclaims the psalmist about the temple.[4] Or again
'Those who trust in the Lord are like Mount Zion, which cannot
be moved, but abides forever. As the mountains are round about
Jerusalem, so the Lord is round about his people.'[5] Upholding the
social order also implies upholding the power structures implicit
in that order. Religion specifically takes on roles in this area also.
The Yako people of Nigeria are unusual in exemplifying 'head-
less' politics, that is they do not have one king over all. Even so
their religion plays a major part in upholding the social order. For
example, Lucy Mair writes of many groups claiming the author
ity of spirits to punish people for particular offences like stealing
crops. Punishment might be meted out by a specific organisation
of priests who imprisoned people by planting stakes in front of
their houses, threatening attack by the spirits if they left their
home. More commonly, African countries with a head of state
and with a majority of their populations involved in tribal religions have justified the appointment of that head by reference to
the tribal religion. So a dynastic succession might be legitimated
by a myth concerning the original ancestor.[6] In all these
instances religion is being used to legitimate and uphold power
structures.

---

[4]   Psalm 84.
[5]   Psalm 125.
[6]   Mair, *An Introduction to Social Anthropology*.

Religion as an integrating focus for life

The background to the role of religion in the social order may be deeper. On one level its role is simply to explain why things are as they are, in particular why the power structures are as they are. Generally it is also to give a certain confidence to people as they go about life and to provide an explanation when things go wrong. It can, however, under certain circumstances become much more than this. It can become part of the essential search to try to make sense of the world as a whole. In my view, this is when religion becomes truly significant. In this form it can become an attempt to unite all our conflicting motivations, and the struggles in society that result from them. Appealing to that which is transcendent, it provides for the possibility of both uniting our inner tensions and reaching beyond the biological definitions of success that we have inherited. It can therefore, at its best, become a vision for society and the common good.

Part of the 'glue' which keeps any society together is the relational sensibilities that develop. Human beings have become most truly individuals–in–relationship. They need *individual* 'space' and they need *others* at a psychological level. Others are the sounding board for the formation of our own identities. We need others to affirm us and challenge us. We search for relationship. Have you ever considered the extraordinary way we treat our pets? We approach animals searching for relationship, naturally imagining them to think and feel like ourselves. Is it therefore so unreasonable that we should search for a relationship with a greater being? Perhaps it is 'natural' for us to do so. In human beings the mind has developed to such a point that it now naturally searches for relationship. This impulse is not unknown among other animals. Take the goose for example. A newborn goose searches for a greater being. As soon as it is hatched, it searches for its mother and in doing so it fixes on almost anything that might do. It can imprint on an orange ball, on a human keeper, on almost anything during that particularly susceptible phase when it is searching. It may be controversial, and it does not matter to the rest of the book if you disagree, but I think it is possible that our search after God is similarly part of our basic search for relationship, the search for a greater being. I am reminded of some words of St Augustine about the human longing for God. He said, 'thou hast made us for Thyself and our hearts are restless till they rest in Thee'.[7] I suspect that this statement is most deeply true of the human condition.

It is hard to define any one characteristic that truly differentiates us from other animals, but religion is clearly ubiquitous among the human species. From the earliest cave drawings to today's most convoluted formulations of the Trinity, human beings have been religious. What is so interesting, as we have noted over the last few pages, is how religious motivations seem to relate so well to our basic motivations as social animals. It seems that the most deep-seated motivations of the human animal quite naturally give rise to religious expression. Leaving the 'truth' question aside for the moment, it is also quite clear that religions vary in their potential to be helpful. I would suggest that a religion that is most helpful should be one that does indeed integrate our various conflicting motivations into a fruitful whole. It should be a religion that can form a focus for all our social institutions and all our private desires, causing us to seek a vision for what is good for all.

Studies of world religions have indicated that many contain some concept of a 'High God'. Such a being is often envisaged as all knowing, all good and all powerful. In some situations the being is even addressed as 'Father'. For example, there are such supreme beings evident in the Vedic hymns of Hinduism, in the ancient Chinese religion of 'Shang Ti', and in many African religions. Where do such beliefs arise? Is it natural for human beings to respond to the search for relationship, as well as to the sense of all that is tremendous, fascinating and mysterious, by believing in

---

[7] Sheed (tr.), *The Confessions of St Augustine*, p. 1.

a God? The prevalence of this type of belief among so many different cultures of the world would suggest that it may be. You might also say that, if there were a creator, such an idea might be intended to arise. Yet in many religions this belief is overlaid by other myths and rituals such that the monotheism breaks down and the integrating focus is lost.[8]

The Judaeo–Christian scriptures have offered the world an influential example of monotheism. The experiences described and understood by the 'Old Testament' of the Christian Bible serve as the foundation for Judaism, Christianity and Islam. The Bible as a whole can clearly be interpreted in a large number of ways, but there is the potential, I believe, for this Scripture to meet the demand for a vision for that which is good for all. Let me explain.

If the religious quest is something deep within us, a search towards which we are naturally inclined, then the Hebrew injunction to 'make no graven images' or to 'have no other gods before me' has a particular purpose. As the goose may call the rubber ball mother, so humans may have the capacity to fix their religious search for a greater being on all sorts of objects. I think a cursory inspection of all sorts of religions would confirm this. Witness for example the notorious 'cargo cults' where tribal people responded to the aeroplane that dropped goods as to a god. Or the people in the First World War who developed superstitions about rainbows as a sign of their survival. These things are commonplace. Yet the Hebrew tradition deliberately forbade people from fixing their religious hope on anything material. This *via negativa* was different from that of certain eastern religions in that it did not seek to deny the material per se or to limit God to an inner contemplative sphere. The God of the Hebrews was a God who interacted decisively with the world, but could not be constrained to any particular image. This had the vital function of keeping the vision of God transcendent and so

---

[8] Schmidt, *Primitive Revelation*; Richardson, *Eternity in their hearts.*

essentially out of reach of human manipulation, and also to encourage a vision of God that was always open to new understanding and to the search for a greater good. Any 'fixing' on an image would collapse the integrated vision rather like the bursting of a balloon. God would become partial, aligned with a particular faction of people, a particular type of operation or whatever, but no longer the One who embraced all. The integrating focus of life would be lost.

In this way the Hebrew understanding of God could lead naturally to the big search to make sense of the world with which we are presented. It could become the search for truth, for goodness and for beauty, that is for all those fundamental integrating visions of human beings and their purposes. As such it could reach beyond the starting point of evolution, namely the requirements of biological success. The Scriptures record the progressive understandings of the people of faith as they sought to do just this. The search itself had a certain structure to which we must now give attention.

Characteristics of biblical faith

The first five books of the Bible set up biblical faith within a simple theory of life. This maintains that life is a system of trust between God and people. The story of this society in its relationship to God develops in precisely the same way as illustrated for human systems of trust in the last chapter. The great themes of the Pentateuch are fascinating in light of our previous discussion. Abraham sets out in faith believing God for a blessing that is about the propagation of his genes. What could be closer to the socio-biologist's rationale! The blessing of God is that God will make of him a 'great nation'. He is told to 'Look toward heaven and number the stars, if you are able to number them.' Then he (God) said to him, 'So shall your descendants be.' And he believed the Lord and he reckoned it to him as righteousness.[9] As Abraham's tribe makes the transition from the nomadic pastoral life to a settled existence, so the scriptural account becomes concerned for territory. As they understand God to have rescued them from Egypt, so they are given a 'Promised Land', where there will be abundant provision for their needs. It will be a land of milk and honey. It will be theirs. They will be free from intruders upon their territory. God will empower them to see off all challengers. This again relates to the most fundamental needs of biological success. The concern for propagation, the need for land as a source of provision, the need for safety, all these things are the legitimate concern of every territorial animal. They relate to our deepest motivations and their associated concept of biological success. Yet the interesting thing about this conception is that all this 'blessing' is perceived as given by the grace and mercy of God, who lives in a certain trust with his people. The implication is that things will go well for them as long as they do not break this trust.

The book of Deuteronomy tells the story of the people as they are about to enter the promised land. It is set up like an ancient near eastern treaty between a king and a vassal state that the king is going to leave to rule itself, yet who requires that it remain loyal. In this case the king is God. These verses describe the system of trust envisaged:

> See, I have set before you this day life and good, death and evil. If you obey the commandments of the Lord your God which I command you this day, by loving the Lord your God, by walking in his ways, and by keeping his commandments and his statutes and his ordinances, then you shall live and multiply, and the Lord your God will bless you in the land which you are entering to take possession of it. But if your heart turns away, and you will not hear, but are drawn away to worship other gods and serve them, I declare to you this day that you shall perish.[10]

---

[9] Genesis 15:56.
[10] Deuteronomy 30:15-18.

Just like the systems described in the last chapter, their trust is dependent on stable relationships, good memories and effective discipline. In this situation the memory is predicated of God. The people remember their relationship with God through their tradition and rituals. They recognise themselves as subject to effective discipline if they err. Yet this system of trust is special because it embraces the whole society. The books of the Pentateuch contain provision about law, politics, economics and morality. All these come within the 'covenant', as it is known, the great system of trust with God and each of these parts of society are the concern of God.

This system of trust is also a process, it is not a completed theory. Just as the other systems of trust continually grow and adapt, so this trust with God grows and adapts. God's ultimate authority renders all human authority potentially accountable. The keys to this process are the prophets. According to the earliest versions of this understanding, when things go wrong for the people, then something must *be* wrong.[11] Such moments of crisis become moments of ferment in the Hebrew vision. Conflicting voices arise, proclaiming the 'word of God' that makes sense of the situation. There are several possible interpretations of what is wrong and searching questions can be asked.

Sometimes these questions go to the heart of the justifications for the social order itself. In the face of great cruelty, Amos questions even the 'election' of Israel as God's special people. "'Are you not like the Ethiopians to me, O people of Israel? says the Lord. Did I not bring up Israel from the land of Egypt, and the Philistines from Caphtor and the Syrians from Kir? Behold, the eyes of the Lord are upon the sinful kingdom and I will destroy it utterly.'"[12] Similarly when exile is looming all the traditional

---

[11] Later this link between obedience and success would be found wanting (see chapter eight) but the essential ingredients of their belief as a system of trust would remain.

[12] Amos 9:7–8.

justifications are brought into question. Does God really want all the sacrifices at the Temple? 'Thus says the Lord of hosts, the God of Israel: "Add your burnt offerings to your sacrifices, and eat the flesh. For in the day that I brought them out of the land of Egypt I did not speak to your fathers or command them concerning burnt offerings and sacrifices. But this command I gave them, 'Obey my voice, and I will be your God, and you shall be my people.'" '[13] Jeremiah maintains that God is really more concerned with the unjust greed of the powerful than with the sacrificial cult. For him, the injustices and corruption of the society are the key issues that need to be addressed to avert the coming disaster.

It was by asking just these sort of questions that the people of the Old Testament tested their experience, trying always to make sense of their lives in terms of their relationship with the God who was all good. In so doing they were also searching for what was good in itself and for the good society. Along the way they developed insights into market activity, political power, the role of law and morality. All of these are important to public life and the following chapters will consider some of them.

In summary then, the true role of religion may be to integrate our conflicting human motivations into a fruitful whole. It may be to provide a vision and a practical method for going about the business of being people. In the course of the development of this vision it may also provide the means to transcend the limited views of success with which humanity entered the world. Our biological constraints remain with us, but religion can, at its best, both help us to acknowledge them and to reach beyond them to a greater vision of what life can be. The reason that this is so may be because it was intended to be so.

---

[13] Jeremiah 7:21-23.

4

Why science is not adequate

Mad cow disease they called it, but if you had followed the public debate that ensued, one might be forgiven for questioning who exactly was mad. BSE has been a roller coaster ride. Then there was the GM debate. It still rages, quite unresolved. Before that we had Chernobyl and Three Mile Island. All these issues have something in common. They involve important debate about the proper role of science in human society. How far can science solve our problems for us? How much should we trust the expert on genetics holding forth about the great advantages of a new form of disease resistant tree or the microbiologist who waxes lyrical about the safety of beef? These issues are now at the centre of the public life of western society and we need a way of thinking about them.

Great hopes for science

For several centuries we have had great confidence in science. We have dreamt of being able to order our human society according to reason and logic. It seemed a laudable enough aim. As the methods of science caught hold of the public imagination, so people naturally began to dream of the scientifically ordered society. In D'Alembert's view science was revealing the 'true system of the world' and would sweep away all previous pretensions to knowledge.

> Spreading through nature in all directions like a river which has
> burst its dams, this fermentation has swept away with a sort of vi-
> olence everything along with it which stood in its way. Thus
> from the principles of the secular sciences to the foundations of
> religious revelation, from metaphysics to matters of taste, from
> music to morals, from the scholastic disputes of theologians to
> matters of trade ... everything has been discussed and analysed.[1]

At heart it was a new method for the production of knowledge and it promised results of far greater certainty than any that had been used before.

The scientific method sought to break every problem down to fundamental components which could not themselves be doubted and then to attempt to rebuild the system using only these components. Descartes offered four laws that should be followed in the pursuit of all knowledge:

> 1. the first was never to accept anything for true which I did not
> clearly know to be such; that is to say carefully to avoid precipi-
> tancy and prejudice, and to comprise nothing more in my judge-
> ment than what was presented to my mind so clearly and
> distinctly as to exclude all ground of doubt.
> 2. the second to divide each of the difficulties under examination
> into as many parts as possible, and as might be necessary for its ad-
> equate resolution.
> 3. the third to conduct my thoughts in order that, by commenc-
> ing with objects the simplest and easiest to know, I might ascend
> little and little, and as it were, step by step to the knowledge of the
> more complex... .

---

[1] Quoted in Cassirer, *The Philosophy of the Enlightenment*, p. 3.

> 4. and last, in every case to make the enumerations so complete
> and reviews so general, that I might be assured that nothing was
> omitted.[2]

Descartes actually found his initial certainties in the ideas inherent *within* his own mind and was profoundly sceptical about the reliability of interpretation of sensory experience. This proved quite inadequate to the new science with its need for embedding itself in observation, but these four principles for the pursuit of knowledge remained in use right through the Enlightenment. Indeed Locke was later to use phrases such as 'clear and distinct ideas' in abundance, which demonstrated his indebtedness to Descartes. The ultimate aim would still be complete rational explanation, though the empiricists' starting place would be the data of sensory experience. The necessary corollary of the new approach would be the sweeping away of all that derived from previous, inferior approaches to knowledge.

Evidence of failure

It was a heady vision, one that would captivate the western mind, affecting not only our thought forms but also the shape and rationale of our institutions. Yet it was profoundly inadequate. Science had its place and has its place, but it is not an adequate means of knowledge for a whole human society. Consider the BSE crisis for example. At first in the UK there was considerable public anxiety. The new killer disease, new variant CJD, was just emerging and no one knew how many would ultimately fall victim. The government tried to reassure, but the public suspected that they were in league with the farming lobby and not telling the whole story. Deep public suspicion then led to rigorous government measures with the aim of restoring public trust.

---

[2]   Descartes, *A Discourse on Method*, p. 15. (First published as *The Principles of Philosophy,* 1637.)

The most extreme of these was to ban beef on the bone. Gradually the public mood changed. The plight of the farmers was becoming evident. Then the French refused to lift the ban on British beef. Now the public was incensed. 'How dare they? Our beef is fine,' we declared. In this new confidence, the ban on beef on the bone began to look like overkill, playing too safe. France had its own problems. Its fear had little to do with beef and again everything to do with public confidence. They had suffered from a scandal regarding AIDS. The government had not acted rigorously or quickly enough in response to the science showing the dangers of transfusion with contaminated blood. The government felt a need to rebuild public confidence. They did so by perpetuating the ban on British beef.

So we see that public policy is not driven solely by science, but by an interaction between the politicians and the level of trust prevailing towards them. Central to this trust is the debate about the proper role of science. How far can science really settle these issues?

Sometimes the scientific debate can be over and essentially closed and yet the society not react. Such was the case with smoking. It was quite clear to the scientific community in the sixties that smoking caused a raft of health problems and that it was a major cause of lung cancer. Yet governments did not react. It took decades before the changes in public policy occurred so as to provide smoke-free workplaces, 'No Smoking areas' in restaurants etc. Some cancer researchers considered resigning. What was the point in going on researching into a cure for a cancer when a major part of it was preventable? As the millennium turns, it is only now that tobacco manufacturers are accepting their responsibilities for these health problems. Why has it taken so long? Because science does not exist in a vacuum. It is part and parcel of a society which has a host of other purposes that can readily conflict with a proper response to its findings. In this case, the tobacco lobby has fought a long and powerful battle to prevent the truth about smoking being acted upon.

Humans and their purposes

It is to the credit of the postmodernists that they have shown how science does interact with a society and that the vision of cold, detached rationality is far from the truth. Institutions need funding. Scientists crave recognition. Both people and institutions have purposes over and beyond the pursuit of propositional knowledge.[3] These things need to be recognised and come to terms with. They affect both what is studied and how it is interpreted.

As governments seek to minimise public expenditure, it is all too easy for them to force universities into a position where they must go cap in hand to large multinational organisations for funds. The story of the power of the tobacco lobby should cause us to worry about this. There has recently been a rash of major donations to UK universities. BP Amoco is establishing a new institute at Cambridge costing £25m. It is one of the largest donations ever to Oxford or Cambridge. Its aim is to co-ordinate work that includes the earth sciences, engineering and the like. No doubt its professors will publish on the matter of global warming. Oil companies have a serious interest in the global warming debate. Their products are the main cause of it. To recruit the best university professors is an astute political move. It will seem to the public that the researchers are offering unbiased and well-founded opinions. Yet their views will undoubtedly be influenced by their paymasters. Their choice of experiments, their interpretation of data, all will bear the marks of the sponsoring opinions. Who will know that they are in the pay of BP? These are important questions as more and more of our universities accept private finance.

The battle over GM foods illustrates another side to the problem. Many important questions are actually outside the

---

[3] See for example Lyotard, 'The Post modern condition; A report on knowledge'.

reach of science. Humans have been selectively breeding plants and animals for thousands of years, but the new techniques of genetic modification give us a whole new set of powers. The genetic components of organisms have developed over millions of years through the dynamic interaction inherent in complex ecosystems. Certain genes often occur together in an organism. Others never do. Our technology now allows us to put genes together in organisms in a completely artificial manner. Growing such modified organisms on the planet carries a continuing risk of unforeseen interactions with the established ecosystems that support life on the planet. We simply cannot predict all the ramifications of this. There is much about the interactions of life forms on the planet that we do not understand. The presence of such new disturbing influences may wreak havoc. Or may not. We do not know. But it is not an experiment we can repeat. Once we have messed up this planet we are done.

A report by the Economic and Social Research Council (ESRC) entitled *The Politics of GM food – risk, science and public trust* argued that science could not settle the most fundamental questions about GM foods. The authors suggested that the central issue for this and other related issues like BSE or nuclear power was 'how to make decisions in the face of uncertainties while at the same time implementing precautionary approaches under fierce commercial and trade pressures. We will suggest that science cannot provide definitive answers in these cases, so the policy of relying on "sound science" may, ironically, itself be unsound. Ethical issues are central. Building the legitimacy and accountability of political decisions on GM food requires a much more participatory style of decision-making...'[4] The conclusion that one may draw from this is that the problems of human societies are irreducibly complex. Aspects of them are understandable by scientific endeavour, but this will not account for

---

[4] Economic and Social Research Council, *The Politics of GM food – risk, science and public trust*, Special Briefing no. 5 (Oct. 1999), p. 4.

the whole or solve the problems of the whole. What is needed are appropriate methods for appropriate types of knowledge.

For example, the ESRC report noticed that scientific studies involving a certain risk were inevitably bound around by 'framing assumptions' about the uncertainties. Such assumptions will give widely different interpretations of what risk is acceptable. This is evident in the story of the BSE crisis. The public's assessment of the degree of the risks involved varied dramatically over time. Science has nothing to say about these assumptions. They concern people's own assessment of human behaviour, the degree of real political accountability and the quality of the public debate. In general terms, where science interacts with deep-level human motivations and purposes, it needs to allow other processes to play their part in the pursuit of truth. These may be less certain than the conclusions of science but they are a necessary part of human activity.

Such 'framing assumptions' actually encompass all of science as it applies to human society. The assumptions exist around the science. They allow its expression and interpretation into the society. Take 'red lining' for example. Insurance companies have a method whereby they assess the premium of a person according to the area in which they live. Some areas are particularly prone to crime and may be 'red lined', that is, a particularly high premium may apply. Now in one sense, this is a purely scientific procedure. Teams of actuaries will consider the past history of the area, carefully calculate risk and set the premiums appropriately. What could be more scientific than that? It looks like a total explanation. Yet underneath lurk other ideas.

The original purpose of insurance was in mutuality. People would put a sum together aware that the risks of life struck at random. The sum would be administered so that if any of them suffered misfortune, they could be helped. Since no one knew who would suffer, insurance was a sensible system of trust. Anyone paying into the system knew they would be safe from that risk. Fair enough, but who should be allowed to join such a society of risk sharers? What the postcode or 'red lining' system does is to effectively divide an insurance company into areas, which are treated separately. The people within each area are held responsible for the criminal activity around them. If you happen to live in a poor area where there is much burglary, then the structure of the insurance holds you responsible for the criminal activity in your area. Is that proper? Some say it is not. They argue that criminal activity is the responsibility of the society at large, that if any are to be held responsible it is the rich that uphold the structures of power, alienate the poor and are ultimately responsible for the crime. Therefore the insurance risk should be spread across the whole society.

It is evident that what looked like a cold rational calculation, a pure scientific and certain deductive process, is not actually what it seems. Its very structure has implications for much deeper questions of justice and accountability that have to be dealt with at another level. All science finds itself embedded in such 'framing assumptions'. This is also true of rational processes in general. Important as they are, the processes of reason simply explore connections between things. If they are to find expression in human societies, these connections must ultimately find a reference in the deep motivations and purposes of the human animal. Discussions of human purpose need to be managed in a different way.

Towards a more adequate view of knowledge

The starting place has to be with knowledge itself and how we go about obtaining it.

As social animals such as ourselves go about life, we have seen that we naturally develop an array of systems of trust to co-ordinate our activity. As this is done, so we also work at making sense of the life we are constructing, seeking truth about the world. Our cultures consist of complex, interlocking systems of customs, mores, institutions and laws, which we continually reflect upon. These systems of trust contain a vast amount of 'how to' knowledge which we absorb into the background of our lives. For much of the time we are unaware of all that we know. We take it for granted how we greet one another or how we should behave in a queue. It is part of what we assume about life. Michael Polanyi proposes that this 'tacit' knowledge about life is also the background to our search for truth.[5] In addition, as we try to make sense of our lives, we naturally construct big, overarching views of the world. These become part of our ongoing commitments which we use to test and so refine our knowledge. Justice might be an obvious example of this. We develop a natural sense of justice through tit for tat behaviour. We go on to test and refine this understanding through the development of a system of law that mediates conflict. In this way a society continually works at a theory of justice and is committed to it, but may never be able to expound it in precise, detailed and fully rational terms.

The pursuit of science should therefore be understood as a subset of this general search for truth. For example, the first scientists tacitly assumed that the world was particulate. They did not always state this, but it seems it was there, in the background.[6] It was an understandable assumption to make: those parts of the world we did not understand were likely to be similar to those parts of the world that we could see and understand. The first centuries of science explored the corpuscular theory. It was and remains enormously fruitful. The fundamentals of atomic theory underlie all chemistry, biochemistry and all the life sciences. Few

---

[5] Polanyi, *Personal Knowledge*, or for a simpler account see *The Study of Man*, or *Tacit Knowing*.

[6] For a discussion on this see Urbach, *Francis Bacon's Philosophy of Science*, or for a more general introduction to the role of theory and experiment see O'Hear, *An Introduction to the Philosophy of Science*.

would doubt the truth of atomic theory. Yet the worldview within which this knowledge was originally conceived was ultimately shown to be inadequate. The particulate theory was useful under certain conditions, but when you considered the subatomic, or the intergalactic, then paradigms about relativity and quantum theory were in order. These gave us an entirely new way of looking at the world and could account for the original data of mechanics as a special case of the new, much more subtle and beautiful, relativistic universe. Such is the pursuit of knowledge. We have knowledge only as a result of our commitments to particular overarching theories. It seems established, even irrefutable, but is always somehow contingent on the next discovery, always open.

Knowledge as a whole turns out, according to Polanyi, to have an asymmetric structure. At one end we have the fundamental forces of the universe, giving rise ultimately to the probabilities that construct our laws of physics and chemistry. This inorganic world seeks truth in terms of *force* and *law*. It is the domain of Galileo as he sought to reconstruct the path of the cannonball using equations of motion. It is likewise the domain of the astrophysicist today who works with the most complex mathematical transformations to predict the behaviour of a star. Yet beyond the inorganic lies the organic. This domain of knowledge has to do with relating structure to function. It is a world of far greater diversity and complexity and is concerned with how atoms and molecules work together. Here is the great and wonderful molecule of hemoglobin. What does it do and how does it do it? That is the question. In this world the quest for knowledge concerns *function*. Organic systems are treated like machines whose working parts are to be understood. Yet there is another domain of knowing that also should not be overlooked. As soon as the mind of an animal develops the sort of complexity such that it acts to integrate the experiences of life into a whole and so act with a degree of creative spontaneity, then any study of such a being must be of a different sort. Such a study has to take into account concepts of *purpose* which the mind of such an animal might construct to give a 'reason' for its actions.

This has become evident already from what we have noticed about animal behaviour. Ethologists have been in a quandary. The methods of analysis appropriate to other forms of science simply do not make sense of animal behaviour. To understand creatures with minds, you have to have a new method. You have, in Frans de Waal's words to use a 'critical anthropomorphism' whereby you bring together all that you know about the animal's activities and then imaginatively enter its world and try to make sense of its behaviour.[7] To do this one must, of necessity, use the language of purpose. That animal is being aggressive toward the other in order to challenge for the top spot in the hierarchy. This is purposeful language. It is also error-prone language. We cannot know in fact what is going on in its mind; but we can make an intelligent guess. Moreover such intelligent guesses may make sense of life in the colony in ways that rigorous scientific approaches cannot. Indeed using such language may be the *only* way to make sense of their behaviour.

In tackling any human problem, all three of these domains of knowledge may be important. To return to the GM debate for example. Any proper consideration of the subject must be fully aware of the latest understandings about genetics. There must be a familiarity with what we know about ecosystems and their interrelations. There are controlled experiments that can be done to assess certain issues like the spread of pollen. Yet there are also fundamental understandings about people, their purposes and behaviour that must be considered. The latter are far less easy to determine nor are they certain in their conclusion, but they are vital. It is essential to have some feel for the real motives of a government that is reassuring about things that are implicitly uncertain. It is essential to come to some judgement as to how much the tangle of political and scientific opinion may be

---

[7] De Waal, *Good Natured*, p. 64.

influenced by commercial pressures. Yet such knowledge will be a 'judgement', that is, a carefully considered, uncertain assessment, involving knowledge of human behaviour patterns and of the likely purposes that are being followed. Knowledge of purpose is outside the reach of traditional scientific method.

So we have at least three domains of knowledge, the inorganic world of fundamental forces and law, the organic world of functional, machine-like relations, and the holistic world of the mind and its purposes. A proper understanding of issues in human society will need to consider the relevance of all three domains of knowledge. For the last few centuries, we have worked for a society totally ordered by scientific rationalism. This has necessarily excluded a proper consideration of human purposes. It has not only proved inadequate, it has also been highly dangerous. A brief review of our attempts to scientifically order society will illustrate the problem.

The dangers of using only scientific rationalism

The Enlightenment set itself to consider as true only that which could be proven with certainty by building from clear and distinct ideas using chains of reason. The method was to determine the outcome of the enquiry. There were only two results possible from such a 'scientific' approach to the question of how we should organise ourselves as a society. One was individualism. The other was totalitarianism. It all hinged around where you found your clear and distinct idea.

One group of thinkers took the view that the individual was the most obvious unit of society. All that was then required was to think how these individuals should behave. Scientifically speaking the best description would be one that acted like a law, they thought, because these individual people must act predictably if certain knowledge about society was to be obtained. The earliest social thinkers spoke of discovering 'laws' of human

behaviour. Adam Smith is a prime example. His classical theory
of economics is built on the individual motivated by self-interest.
It was a model he developed in conjunction with the earliest
utilitarian theories of morality whereby the individual could be
understood solely by reference to the inner antagonism between
pleasure and pain. John Stuart Mill summed up the approach of
the economists, Smith and Ricardo in these terms. He said economics was a theory based on an 'arbitrary definition of man, as a
being who invariably does that by which he may obtain the
greatest amount of necessaries, conveniences and luxuries with
the smallest quantity of labour and physical self-denial with
which they can be obtained in the existing state of knowledge.'[8]
If this is taken as true says Mill, then the 'science' of economics
can be drawn up with accuracy. The fact that the writings of
Smith and Ricardo were already having such an impact pointed
to the relevance of this view of humans, at least when acting out
of certain situations in certain sections of society. But Mill
thought this view of people inadequate. Economics was an
abstract science because the people it conceived of did not actually exist. People were in fact far more complex. Economics, says
Mill,

> is concerned with him (a person) solely as a being who desires
> wealth, and who is capable of judging of the comparative effi-
> ciency of means for obtaining that end ... It makes entire abstrac-
> tion of every other human passion or motive, except those which
> may be regarded as perpetually antagonising to the desire of
> wealth, namely, aversion to labour, and desire of the present en-
> joyment of costly indulgences ... Not that any political econo-
> mist was ever so absurd as to suppose that mankind are really thus
> constituted, but this is how science must proceed.[9]

---

[8]   Mill, J.S., 'Political Economy' (1884), pp. 321ff.
[9]   Ibid.

It was both an absurd and a dangerous idea to limit humanity to this psychological caricature, but the method demanded such an approach. Today we have largely forgotten the assumptions that underlie the prevailing economic dogmas offered in the name of science.

One feature of theories of life based on the individual is that they inevitably end up valuing the individual and give no ultimate value to collectives. When Mrs Thatcher declared 'there is no such thing as society' she was actually following a long tradition of thought. For example, both classical and neo-classical theories of economics see the collective organisations of society in deeply ambivalent terms. Families, local communities and suchlike are ignored by Smith. The bonds between people in these situations simply cannot be considered on his model because his method only values what can be exchanged in the market place. For example, Smith cannot understand why people will not move freely to places where there are better paid jobs. People will move *goods* to places where they can get a better price for them. He says despairingly, 'man is of all luggage the most difficult to be transported'. [10] He could not conceive of the bonds of communal and family loyalty that bind people to a place. We find it difficult to value these things too, only we now move house with abandon unaware of the bonds of community that we are tearing asunder. So, local communities are withering to nothingness. Families are weaker than ever. We now expect the whole adult populace to take their place in the market, doing paid work. We have no way of valuing those who contribute in ways that have no simple exchange value.

On the other hand, those collectives which arise through the market are valued, but are always contingent realities in the sense that they are seen as infinitely adjustable according to the dictates of the market. The company must downsize, or be taken over. Six

---

[10] Smith, *An inquiry into the nature and cause of the wealth of nations (1776)*, p. 178.

thousand will be made redundant. That is what the market demands and no other value system should intervene. So says the 'science' according to someone like Freidrich Hayek.

The other 'scientific' model used to analyse society was to see it as analogous to a functioning organism, using the language of biology. Auguste Comte began the discipline we now know as sociology with this type of model. He thought of society as a whole, perhaps not fully realising that this functional, biological approach implicitly thought of systems as machines. It therefore naturally leads to a totalitarianism which overrides a proper and subtle view of individual human purposes.

Comte was to set the ensuing agenda for sociology. In his wake came many who would take up his basic analogy of society as an organism. The functionalists and structural-functionalist schools of sociology use this basic methodology. Emile Durkheim attempted to frame an objective analysis of society around the forces in society which impose an inherent constraint to action upon individuals. Durkheim held that 'A social fact is to be recognised by the power of external coercion which it exercises or is capable of exercising over individuals and the presence of this power may be recognised in its turn either by the existence of some specific sanctions or by the resistance offered against every individual effort that tends to violate it.'[11]

More recent structural analysis has centred on structural-linguistic concepts as the foci of social data.[12] All such approaches, however, suffer from the basic flaw that they attempt to be purely objective in a field which must deny pure objectivity. The role of the individual is always compromised in such descriptions. The chains of reasoning that describe the system are so strong and certain that they become chains of oppression upon the human individual. Most importantly, the methods employed to describe

---

[11] Quoted in Nisbet, *The Sociology of Emile Durkheim*, p. 59.
[12] Reviewed in Best and Kellner, *Postmodern Theory*, pp. 18–20.

society necessarily rule out concepts of *purpose* and so fail to give an adequate place to the reality of human will and intention.[13,14]

These quasi-scientific views of human beings in terms of the collectives have the other notorious property of regularly being associated with a concept of 'scientific' progress.[15] So Comte thought of human societies as progressing from a theological view of the world, through metaphysics to pure rationality. This led him to devalue the arts and to denigrate women as being apparently less rational. Even worse in its effects was the progress rationale of Marxism. This 'scientific' view of society propounded that all societies were inevitably heading towards a classless society. It led some of Marx's disciples to the view that how you achieved this did not matter. It was inevitable and therefore 'right', and therefore could be achieved by means that overrode all previous moral considerations.

In summary then this chapter has tried to show that any problem of human society can be examined in a number of different ways. Some aspects can be addressed by using the

---

[13] See Giddens, *In Defense of Sociology*, chap. 4 for a critique of functionalism pointing out this intrinsic methodological problem, whereby inadequate consideration is given to purposive human action. In the light of these problems, Giddens seeks to redefine social knowledge to include that which is non-propositional and to redefine the structures of society as coming into being at every moment in a process of 'structuration'. The role of purpose in the structure of knowledge will be taken further in chapter 5.

[14] For a review of structuralism see Best and Kellner, *Postmodern Theory*. The structural linguistic approach pioneered by such as Levi-Strauss, Althusser and Lacan attempts a holistic approach, revealing underlying rules which organise phenomena, e.g. culinary rules in a kitchen or sacred/profane distinctions in traditional societies. In this method the very existence of the subject is questioned, becoming merely an effect of language, culture or the unconscious.

[15] Popper, *The Poverty of Historicism*.

traditional methods of scientific enquiry. Others can be explored by making the connections possible through reason. Yet no understanding of human society is adequate without consideration of that knowledge that derives from the domain of purpose. Attempts to derive the whole of human knowledge from scientific rationalism will always result in individualism or views of the collective that tend toward totalitarianism. Knowledge about human purposes is implicitly uncertain. It requires that we make judgements. Yet it is a knowledge that all peoples have always worked with. The pursuit of truth in the realm of purpose requires a different means and it is to that we now turn.

5

Storytelling and the pursuit of truth

Stories are central to public life

At 10p.m. on 16 December 1998, Tony Blair appeared outside No. 10 Downing Street and told us a story. It was Christmastime. The Downing Street Christmas tree framed the background, but this was no story of 'peace and goodwill among men'. Tony Blair told the story of Iraq as he perceived it. He spoke of the end of the Gulf War and how conditions had been agreed for the inspection of the country and the elimination of weapons of mass destruction. He told how great quantities of such weapons had indeed been found and yet how the work of the UNSCOM inspectors had been repeatedly delayed or interfered with. This was a sign that the regime could not be trusted. He spoke of lies and people who were evil. They must be shown that the rest of the world would not stand idly by while these promises were broken. Finally he announced that he was sending the bombers in.

Other people would have told the story differently. No doubt Saddam Hussein would have told a story about a country suffering under punitive sanctions, of children starving and people lacking access to basic healthcare. He would have told of the arrogance of UNSCOM inspectors who marched into any and every place demanding access with no notice. Such foreign inspections were an implicit violation of his sovereignty. No western power would have allowed it.

More cynical western journalists would have told yet another story. Their story would be about the process of President Clinton's impeachment trial. They would tell how that very week there were to be crucial votes taken in the US that might decide the President's future. They would suggest that the bombing of Iraq was simply a useful distraction that would concentrate minds and hearts on national defence, raise patriotic zeal and help to prevent any impeachment trial.

These are all very different stories. Yet they have certain characteristics fundamental to all stories. First of all they are attempts to make sense of human behaviour. They try to take the experiences of life, pull them together and present them as a coherent whole. This necessitates talking the language of motivation and purpose. Most importantly each story gives reasons for actions taken. Tony Blair's story told why he thought it right to bomb Iraq. He may have been right; he may have been wrong: but he laid out his argument as a story. This is characteristic of storytelling. The construction of a story is a natural way that we try to make sense of the experiences of life. Stories give us reasons for action. We need reasons for behaviour because we believe that human beings act purposefully. Stories give those reasons. This is particularly obvious in politics.

Of course it is possible to form an account of an experience that is more sceptical. For example, consider this account of a sea battle from a novel by Thomas Pychon:

> What happened on the 9th March 1864 … is not too clear. Popov the Russian admiral did send out a ship, either the Corvette "Bogatir" or the clipper "Gaidamek", to see what it could see. Off the coast of either what is now Carmel-by-the-sea, or what is now Pismo beach, around noon or possibly toward dusk, the two ships sighted each other. One of them may have fired; if it did

then the other responded; but both were out of range so neither showed any scar afterward to prove anything.[1]

The subject matter of such a sceptical report might have become a cause for international antagonism and even war. Consider our own struggles about the sinking of the Belgrano at the outbreak of the Falklands conflict. Yet this sort of account is useless to someone who has to make a decision about how to act. Politicians have to commit themselves to a story in order to give reasons for their actions. In many situations action is necessary and the failure to do anything may have just as important repercussions as any positive action. The decision whether to intervene in acts of ethnic cleansing in Kosovo or East Timor has recently exercised our politicians. In these sort of situations, inaction is itself a political act with terrible consequences. So a politician *must* construct a story in the fullest sense and commit themselves to it. This is not to imply some artificial and self-conscious act of storytelling on their part, or that they are being disingenuous. It is simply that they must act and in the process of doing so they will be committing themselves to a story that gives reason for their actions. Sceptical accounts like Pychon's may be of interest in universities but they are useless in public life. Even if we are wrong, we have to act, and in order to act we need to commit ourselves to a story.

Stories are hard for rationalists to swallow, partly because of their implicit moral content. Underlying each of the above stories of Iraq, there are moral arguments. The story does not elaborate on these, they are simply there. 'This is evil.' 'They are arrogant.' 'They lied.' 'Children should not suffer like this.' These sort of statements appeal to the listener saying, 'You accept this sort of behaviour is right (or wrong) don't you?' This shows that storytelling is actually a relational act. It implies that there are listeners who may or may not agree with the construction on life

---

[1] Quoted in Kermode, *The Genesis of Secrecy,* p. 107.

given by the author. The story appeals to them, effectively saying, 'This is how I make sense of these experiences, join me in seeing the world like this.' In a face to face encounter, a negotiation would then typically take place as someone else told a similar or related story that shed a different light. Such responsive storytelling is the hallmark of the pursuit of truth. The three stories of Iraq then should be seen as arguments about truth, appeals to the world, about people's behaviour, about purpose, and therefore about how we should act. Their fundamental differences point to the seriously inexact nature of this process. Yet storytelling is the means we have for the pursuit of truth when human purpose is on the agenda. We shall discover later that its very uncertainty is also its strength.

Noam Chomsky takes an extreme view of the western media, but it is also an important view.[2] He notices how our media carry deep and systematic biases. Media corporations are public companies. Many of their shares are held by the big financial institutions. They will hesitate to say anything that will affront such institutions. Similarly the media are dependent to varying degrees on advertising. A significant proportion of their revenue will come from advertising and they will be keen to cultivate their own identified niche market of readers so they can more easily sell their advertising space. Finally the leading figures in media companies now have business interests worldwide. They have fingers in many pies and are powerful people. No editor would want to seriously upset them. Each of these considerations gives a certain bias to the way the stories of the world are told by newspapers or on television. Not that this is often exercised consciously. It might be rare for a Rupert Murdoch to phone the editor and demand a particular policy, but generally there will be certain things that a newspaper will not say. It will be subconsciously aware of the opinions and interests of people who back the paper. Editors will be aware of the depth of criticism that is

---

[2] Herman and Chomsky, *Manufacturing Consent*.

permissible and will restrain anything that seems beyond the pale. These constraints may even lie deep in the mindsets of the employees. Yet evidence of such bias is not hard to find and Chomsky is a master of such revelation. For example, what was the substantial difference between the activity of the US in Vietnam and of Russia in Afghanistan? In both cases a major foreign power installed a puppet regime in the country which was in keeping with its ideology. Then, when the puppet regime was threatened with being overthrown, the foreign power stepped in to uphold 'their' government and its ideology. Despite this the media were basically hostile to the Russian 'invasion' of Afghanistan, while initially they wrote up Vietnam as a crusade of righteousness. The real difference of course was the prevailing opposition to communism in the west. In a similar way opposition to communism has dramatically affected the way that conflicts in Central America have been reported over the years. The media has been only mildly critical of US involvement in Chile, El Salvador, Nicaragua and Guatemala. Their stories were told through the blinkers of political bias.

The purpose of that is not to make a point about the rights and wrongs of the communist ideology or the ideology of the west that has opposed it, it is only to show that stories carry implicit moral and ideological assumptions. The struggle for truth must be acutely aware of these assumptions and our truth seeking must include deliberately trying to hear the story of the other, the one whose perspective is most opposed to our own. We can never be unbiased. We can never be a detached observer of life. Each of us has commitments that we need to own. What we can do is expose ourselves to the story told by the one whom we perceive as the enemy.

This approach naturally overlaps with history. A few years ago the Emperor of Japan visited Buckingham Palace and the people of the UK listened with great attention to see how he would interpret the Second World War. Columns and columns of newspaper were devoted to the issue of whether or not he used the phrase 'deep sorrow' about the victims of the war. People were acutely aware that Japan still told stories about the war that masked any sense of corporate wrongdoing on their part. There was a battle going on for truth and justice in the telling of the history.

During the late nineties there was recurrent concern about Drumcree in Northern Ireland. The Protestants wanted to retell history, as they are accustomed to do, by means of a march. This was to be a public, powerful and quasi-military retelling of the story of the massacre of Protestants in 1641 during an Irish uprising. Banners would depict the scene in which a hundred men, women and children were herded onto the bridge at Portadown and thrown into the river beneath. Other banners would proclaim the day when things were finally 'settled' at the Battle of the Boyne. Yet this was part of a wider history. A history that would include the planting of Protestants into Ulster under James I and their systematic stripping of land and power from the Catholics. A history that would include Cromwell's invasion to put down Catholic rebellion, how he likened himself to the army of God entering Canaan to rid it of its idolatrous inhabitants, of how he put Drogheda and Wexford to the sword and much more. What happens at Drumcree and has prevailed in Northern Ireland for so long, is that different communities tell different stories and refuse to listen to each other. The whole peace process might be summed up as the attempt to facilitate each side truly hearing the stories of the other. Such a process might be said to characterise the pursuit of history and to be the subtext of the political process.

History is storytelling with a particular type of debt to the past. Historians collect their sources and then imaginatively enter the world of their study, telling a story about what happened and why. Although novelists have a freer hand to construct scenes and instances of behaviour, most still place their stories in real life and try to imagine real human characters and their behaviour. Their form of story can also be of vital importance in the search for truth. A lady was once brought before Abraham Lincoln. 'Ah,' he said, 'so you are the lady who made the book that made the great war.' The lady in question was Harriet Beecher Stowe and her book was *Uncle Tom's Cabin*. It is a story about a runaway slave in the United States in the 1850s; a simple tale, romanticising the slave so that he became a sort of Christ figure. Some would be highly critical of it for that reason, but it did something. It made the slave real. Throughout the northern states of the US, people had their consciences raised about the treatment of slaves and, rightly or wrongly, Abraham Lincoln considered that the book had provoked the civil war.

Uncle Tom's Cabin had really addressed the more fundamental question of who matters. One of the deepest biases in our own storytelling comes from the simple moral perspective given by who 'matters to us'. Consider how the western media report instances of tragedy around the world. If a westerner is involved, then it will be a front-page story. By contrast almost any amount of mayhem among Africans will produce few lines. Foreign nationals are becoming increasingly aware of this and African movements are now taking western hostages as a deliberate ploy to get their struggle into our headline news. Ransom money for western hostages has played a pivotal role in the financing of the Chechen resistance to Russia.

Of course in one sense it is quite natural that we should value those closest to us rather than others. Moral formation begins from the self, extends to the family, to neighbourhood, nation and beyond. Of course we value our own most highly, but history shows us that our moral sympathies can and should be extended as far as possible. The campaign to abolish the slave trade used a picture of black men and women under the slogan, 'Am I a man and am I a brother?' or 'Am I a woman and am I a sister?' That was the question. It was simply, 'Is this person real?' If they are real, then they must be treated as such. Similarly Martin Luther King's civil rights demonstrations in the States often proceeded under banners proclaiming, 'I am a man'. One way that we become sensitive to other's reality is through stories that make them feel real. Dickens, for example, told stories of the nineteenth century through the eyes of the poor. He thereby made them real to us and helped precipitate social change.

Of course, it can work the other way. A story can desensitise us to the reality of others. During the recent NATO bombing of Serbia, there was a film called *The Knife* showing in all the major Serbian cinemas. It was enormously popular. Based on a book by the politician Vuk Draskovic, it contained appalling scenes in which a pious Serbian family were humiliated, the women raped, the father and priest burnt to death in the church, while the Muslim perpetrators of this horror laughed mockingly. It was a familiar tale to Serbian people. They have told tales of Muslim atrocities for so many years that they have a mindset about being victims. Yet this story merely massaged that sense of being a victim. It failed to challenge it. It confirmed their antagonism against Islam and in so doing deflected from any sensitivity they might have otherwise felt towards their own maltreatment of the Muslims of Kosovo. On the day I read of this film, the fleeing Serbian army had laid waste to an estimated 85,000 Muslim homes.

The importance of story to the whole community

It is not only on the big public stage that these things matter. Stories are fundamental to the life of every individual and the function of the story in the public arena mirrors its function for individuals. So it is that each of us is continually trying to make sense of the experiences of our lives and incorporate them into our 'story'. Our stories help constitute our identity and give reason for our actions, and they implicitly contain our deepest commitments about life. These commitments are negotiated as we converse with others. Let me try to explain further how this happens.

As we noted in the last chapter, each of us carries with us a vast amount of tacit knowledge. This includes all that we inherit as animals from our deep level motivations. It includes knowledge that is built up as skills. It includes 'how to' knowledge about what works in society in terms of relationships and institutions. It includes the inheritance that we call culture. Very little of it is accessible to us in logical, propositional terms. It is the assumed background of our lives. The principle way in which we work with and refine this tacit knowledge is by storytelling.

As stories are shared between people, an implicit negotiation takes place around the knowledge held by the two parties. Questions like 'Does this person see the world like I do?' or 'Do we share the same view of justice?' are all there, but hidden deep in the conversation and unspecified. This process of negotiation through story is crucial to the formation and sustenance of our sense of identity, to the establishment of culture, moral understandings and of theology.

If someone challenges us as to why we are doing something, our reply will be to give reason for our action by relating it to the story of our lives in some way. 'Why were you driving that car so fast?' 'Because I have to get my wife to hospital. She is in labour.' Without a story, we cannot give account of our actions. We call people mad who cannot give account of their actions. Our stories integrate the experiences and intentions of our lives so as to make them a unity. Otherwise our lives would be just a disconnected blur of experience.[3]

Traditional societies have been principally oral communities formed around the telling of stories. Konrad Kottak has given an account of Arembepe, a fishing village in Brazil, which until the

---

[3]   The best account I know of the role of story in individual lives and in forming self-identity and tradition is in Macintyre, *After Virtue*, chap 15. Macintyre himself builds on the work of Paul Ricoeur, *Time and Narrative*, though has a different view of fiction as opposed to non-fictional stories.

1960s had remained essentially cut off from western type societies and continued as a community sustained by sail-powered sea fishing.[4] Central to this traditional society was storytelling. Each evening as the men finished fishing they would gather on the chapel steps and tell their stories. Similarly the women would converse by the lagoon as they washed. The process of storytelling was the continual making sense of life together. It drew the individual's lives into the experience of the community. Each story implicitly contained a worldview, assumptions about mutual obligation, about people's character and actions, the difference between accident and intention and all those features by which we make sense of the world. All this tacit knowledge was daily renegotiated and affirmed in the sharing of stories.

In an earlier chapter I described how systems of trust were built up in a traditional working class community like the one I know at Barton Hill in Bristol. What also needs to be said about this community was that the community life was sustained and negotiated by means of story. It was essentially an oral culture. People met daily at their corner shop, pub or club and interpreted the world to each other in stories. So the community was bound together – a myriad of face to face relationships sustained by story. The effect of such storytelling is to bind people into the world of which they are a part. So the people of Barton Hill may have been desperately poor but at least they felt they had a place in the world. Consider, for example, the following statement made by sociologist Hilda Jennings who made a study of the area in the 1950s: 'The children ... gave the impression of the security which comes from a sense of belonging and of the acceptance of affection as the natural and normal background of their lives.'[5] The old community has now largely disintegrated in the face of modernity and with it went much of the storytelling.

---

[4]   Kottak, *Assault on Paradise*.

[5]   Jennings, *Societies in the Making*, p. 58.

The police now spend much of their time attending to difficult children. I strongly suspect these things are related.

In this sort of situation the stories of the individual blend in with those of the community. These two aspects mediate the individual and relational poles of our being. A further dimension is added by our inherited stories from history and fiction. These too help to shape our understanding of the world. Alasdair Macintyre put it like this:

> Man is in his actions and practice, as well as in his fictions, essentially a story-telling animal. He is not essentially, but becomes through his history, a teller of stories that aspire to truth. But the key question for men is not about their own authorship; I can only answer the question 'What am I to do?' if I can answer the prior question 'Of what story or stories do I find myself a part?' ... Deprive children of stories and you leave them unscripted, anxious stutterers in their actions as in their words. Hence there is no way to give us an understanding of any society, including our own, except through the stock of stories which constitute its initial dramatic resources.[6]

In this way storytelling can be understood as the most fundamental way in which we negotiate and absorb meaning and purpose both for ourselves and our communities. Storytelling may be the very foundation of culture.

It is also vital to our sense of well-being. Frequently, as a vicar in inner city Bristol, I would meet those in the grip of some compulsive addiction. In fact many such people became my friends. I struggled to try to understand what was going on. In so many lives, there was a deep grief, some terrible incident, betrayal or abuse, and it seemed that the addiction was formed somehow in response to this. Could it be that the addiction is linked to the failure to be able to construct a meaningful story? Perhaps the bottom line was that these people were unable to incorporate the

---

[6] Macintyre, *After Virtue*, p. 216.

awful thing that had happened to them within a concept of the world as in any sense good or meaningful. Macintyre says this about suicide:

> When someone complains – as do some of those who attempt or commit suicide – that his or her life is meaningless, he or she is often and perhaps characteristically complaining that the narrative of their life has become unintelligible to them, that it lacks any point, any movement towards a climax or a *telos*.[7]

This is broadly Giddens's view of addiction in general. In the following quotation he notes how one of the fundamental roles of the group work in Alcoholics Anonymous is the rewriting of the narrative of the self; that is, helping people to make sense of their lives, restoring meaning and purpose through the telling of story.

> As with psychotherapy and counselling, those who attend meetings find an atmosphere in which criticism or judgement are suspended. Members are encouraged to reveal their most private concerns and worries in an open way without fear of embarrassment or an abusive response. The leitmotif of these groups is a rewriting of the narrative of self.[8]

If this analysis is fair, it points to the tremendous importance of story in the life of every individual in western society. Storytelling is the means by which we pursue truth about ourselves and about our societies. It is a process with intrinsically less certainty than traditional science yet it is the proper way, indeed the only way, to pursue truth about purpose in the humanities. Storytelling is different from science. It is a holistic method. It does not break a problem down to clear and distinct ideas and then seek to rebuild certain truth; rather it recognises the necessity of a holistic approach to the study of beings whose minds necessarily work in a holistic fashion and who use those minds to frame concepts

---

[7] Ibid., p. 217.
[8] Giddens, *The Transformation of Intimacy*, pp. 74–5.

of purpose and hence give reason for action. Yet it does have some interesting parallels with the traditional scientific method.

Testing truth by experience

Science has built itself around real experience as a principle reference point. I spent a considerable part of my professional career as a research scientist. I vividly recall my doctoral supervisor, Alan Williams. He was a down-to-earth Australian, who was widely respected in the field of immunology. It was a fast moving, complex field and there was a great temptation to draw up wonderful theoretical schemes. If Alan walked in on any of these discussions, his behaviour was quite predictable. He would listen for a while and then say, 'Do the experiment.' Alan was a true scientist. He was really only concerned with doing and thinking things that were sure and certain and that others could build on. The way to do that was to keep rubbing your nose in what actually happened, testing your theory by experimental practice. His spirit was much like that of the pioneer Francis Bacon who said,

> Men are to be entreated again and again that they should dismiss for a while, or at least put aside, those inconsistent and preposterous philosophies which prefer theses to hypotheses, have led experience captive and triumphed over the works of God: that they should humbly and with a certain reverence draw near to the book of Creation; that there they should make a stay, that on it they should meditate, and that then washed clean they should in chastity and integrity turn them from opinion.[9]

Experience was the essential reference point for science. I believe it should also be so in the humanities. The goal is to make sense of the real experiences of life. Elaborate theoretical treatises,

---

[9]   Quoted in Faringdon, *The Philosophy of Francis Bacon*, pp. 54–5.

whether they be in sociology, theology or any other -ology are only of value if they impact on our lives and how we make sense of the world. Experience should be their arbiter. Now I believe this is actually the case in storytelling as I have described it. The story is always trying to make sense of the real experiences of life. This we share with science.

Furthermore there can be little doubt that scientific investigation proceeds by some sort of interaction between theory and experience. Many believe today that some sort of theory is a precondition of science. Just as the earliest scientists assumed a particulate theory and explored within that, so all science proceeds by interrogation of a theory.[10] The key question about good science then becomes how to do the crucial experiments. These are those particular experiments that will most rigorously test the theory – the most important of these may be those that can clearly falsify it. Similarly the story is like a primitive theory. It is the first attempt to make a theory about human experience. Furthermore, conversation with others is the analogue of doing the experiment, testing the theory. 'Does it make sense to you?' the storyteller is implicitly saying. Again the best tests of the theory will be by exposing it to crucial conditions and this will mean trying out the story on the person with the most different perspective from our own. It is to listen to the enemy, to hear the person of the other race or culture.

This overlaps with another classic concern of science, that of objectivity. Objectivity was originally conceived by philosophers in terms of being able to stand back from a subject and view it rationally. Our ability to do this depended in turn on whether we could really be sure that the constructions of our minds in response to sensory stimuli truly reflected the situation of the world. This led philosophy into a form of psychological investigation. Much ink was spilled over the problem, but the world yawned. Most people were quite happy to trust that the

---

[10]   See O'Hear, *An Introduction to the Philosophy of Science.*

impressions of their minds reflected reality. Since that time postmodernists, like Richard Rorty, have concluded that such certainty is impossible in this area anyway.[11] Others, such as Karl Popper have suggested that scientific objectivity is actually guaranteed not through our mental processes at all, but simply because an experiment done by one person in one part of the world can be repeated by another person somewhere else.[12] That is objectivity. If he is right then this concept again overlaps with storytelling in that the story does actually appeal to others like the scientist appeals to others to repeat the experiment. So a story says to the other, 'Does this make sense to you?' Of course the story functions at a much lower level of certainty than the scientific experiment, but still the method offers some real accountability. Again, it is of course easy to find lots of like-minded people who may see the world as you do, but the crucial test for the 'objectivity' of the story is how it negotiates truth with those of opposing perspectives. Agreement may sometimes be impossible, but some real engagement and appreciation of the position of the other is certainly a realistic possibility in the pursuit of truth. Both parties may be changed by such an interaction. I recently heard of a psychotherapist storyteller who is trying to arrange for Palestinians and Israelis to tell their stories to each other. It is highly unlikely that such a process will produce immediate harmony, but there is every prospect of real change and increased understanding.

Truth in all its aspects is about the attempt to make sense of the world by appropriate means. Scientific methods are appropriate to physical realities, but not appropriate to purposeful aspects of the study of beings with minds.

At this point I think I should declare that I do not want this to appear as if rational deduction has no place in the humanities. On the contrary, I believe it has every place. There has been a huge

---

[11]   Rorty, *Philosophy and the Mirror of Nature.*

[12]   Popper, *The Logic of Scientific Discovery,* chap. 1, sec. 8.

amount of fruitful study during the Enlightenment period in which rational enquiry has been used to probe the purported connections between aspects of life. What I would maintain though, is that such rational enquiry typically proceeds by reference to certain bigger stories containing purpose. For example, we are all familiar with statistics. We are also aware that statistics are very difficult to use well, that statistical proofs in human affairs are notoriously difficult, rather like pinning jelly to the wall. The reason for this is rather simple. Statistical data is gathered to prove something or to test something. In human societies this almost always involves some aspect of human behaviour and so purpose. This means that statistical enquiry always has stories lurking underneath it that are determining which particular things are measured, how they are measured and how the results are portrayed. The objectivity of much work in statistics is actually an illusion. The statistics merely test the connections between different stories. The stories themselves contain implicit assumptions and have to be evaluated on a different basis.

To summarise the argument so far: stories are a first attempt to theorise on human experience. A story is constructed by trying to draw together experiences of life into a coherent whole, utilising overarching theories with which we are making sense of life. These include our deepest moral and religious commitments. The constructed story is then used to give reason for action, appealing to others to see these events as we do. The truth of such a story is tested in conversation with others who have different perspectives. The most crucial of these tests is in conversation with those of the most extreme alternative perspectives. This procedure of construction and testing stories is the proper means of pursuing truth in public life and is the only means of adequately considering human motivation and purpose. It bears some similarity to traditional scientific method, but is significantly different. From such a perspective, science becomes merely a subsection of the overall human quest to make sense of the world.

Stories and the biblical community

If the foregoing discussion is accepted, then there is absolutely no reason why stories of religious faith should not be examined on precisely the same basis as other forms of truth in the humanities, that is as stories seeking to make sense of the world. I come from the Judaeo–Christian tradition. I am a Christian and it is that perspective that I feel confident to expound. I would not like it to be thought that in doing so I had no interest or concern for those of other faith traditions. My silence should be interpreted more as an admission of incompetence than any value judgement. I look forward with interest to seeing how those of other faith traditions react to the sort of approach I am taking.

Theology is notorious for losing touch with reality. The medieval scholastics would idly chatter about how many angels could dance on a pinhead and were rightly castigated by the first scientists for their stupidity. A truly practical theology needs to engage with how the Bible was formed. The Bible was formed by people who tried to make sense of their lives in terms of an overarching story about God. They had simple, but profound assumptions about this God. Such a God would be the focus of all good, of all that was true, of all that was beautiful. Such a God would be in authority over the world. Such a God must be personal and be known personally. These were the sort of assumptions made by the people of faith. They then tested these assumptions by reference to life, to their real experiences. And they did so by telling stories. How can God be good if this happens? How do we deal with leaders who behave like that? How should they be accountable to us and to God? These were the questions that the community tussled with as it framed its stories about its relationship with God. It was nitty gritty stuff. Their understanding of God grew with their experience. As time went on, so significant shifts would take place in their theological understanding. Different theological factions would evolve reflecting different tensions in their community. Yet the overall commitment to the one God would hold the community together through it all. The pursuit of the knowledge of God would become the pursuit of all that was actually good for people, a quest that would embrace their law, politics, economics and their moral development. At many points the stories would be in tension. The community would be in tension. A resolution would be found and the understanding of God would grow.

In the coming chapters, we shall see examples of precisely this sort of conflict as the biblical community progressed in their understanding of what was good about the market, how life should be ordered politically or how people in authority should behave. All these issues are immediately relevant to our own pursuit of what is good in our society today. The Bible contains stories seeking truth and has precisely the characteristics summarised above. In particular these stories were in conflict within the community just as we have noted that stories need to come into conflict if they are to be part of a genuine search for truth.

Ultimately the big question for them, as for us, was 'Does this understanding about God make sense of life?' Or in other words, 'Is it true?' This needs to be answered in conjunction with other questions about whether this community demonstrated any special resource. Is there any evidence that their purported relationship with God was real in the sense that it made a difference? If so what difference did it make and does that tie in with the basic assumptions that are being made about God? These are all questions that demand an answer, but which I intend to leave until the end of the book. First we need to look at the evidence.

Of course many have argued that the Bible has no relevance to modern life because it is set in an ancient civilisation and the world has changed so radically as to make its words irrelevant. I hope to convince you in the course of this book that that is not true, but my theoretical justification for its relevance is really rather simple. The point is that human beings are really much the same as they were in biblical days and the way we seek truth by means of story is also the same. For example, human beings have deep level motivations. We have explored some of them. They have not changed. We are substantially the same animals as we were thousands of years ago. We have the same human nature. Furthermore, that human nature still impinges on our lives as people. The most basic problems involved in forming and progressing human societies derive from our nature and remain issues for us just as they were in biblical times. In this light the vast range of experiences recorded in the Bible become a storehouse of knowledge about human life and society.

For now, I would like to summarise the basic method for seeking truth as it concerns human motivation and purpose. It is a method that applies to the biblical people of faith in precisely the same way as it applies to the humanities in general, to times past and to times future. The method has three essential components. First it begins from *human nature*. We have deep level motivations and these affect our lives. They are complex, susceptible of a number of resolutions, but they are there and form the background of our lives. Second it centres around *human experience* and the basic animal response to make sense of that experience. We are faced with life. We are faced with how people behave, with the real world, in all its ugliness and beauty, in all its despair and hope. We have nothing else but human experience to found our knowledge on. Finally we make sense of life by *telling stories* in the pursuit of truth. This is how we test and refine our fundamental commitments about life. Our own lives are an ongoing story. This is how we are making sense of life ... so far. It is an open and intrinsically uncertain process, deeply exciting and yet also very threatening.

I do not like diagrams. They suggest mechanical formulations and are always simplistic. But for those who do, this is a diagram concerning the method for the pursuit of truth about purpose as it affects the members of all human societies.

The story so far

Human Nature ⟷ Human Experience

Part two

Working it Out

6

Striving to succeed in the commercial world

The street children of Lusaka have plenty going against them. AIDS has decimated families in Zambia leaving vast numbers of orphans. The traditional extended family networks cannot bear the strain and many are left on the street. At the same time the debt issue leaves the government in the hands of the International Monetary Fund. There is little hope of any welfare system adequate to their need.

Which all leaves the street children to shift for themselves in whatever way they can. Survival is the name of the game, and the sewage plant is where it is played. The edge of the great stagnant pond turns out to be the best place. There you will find children scooping out half-formed faeces with their bare hands and ramming them into bottles. The bottles are then sealed and shaken. In about half an hour, they become filled with a gas, which will be sold to teenagers for about twenty pence. That money is precious. It means another day's survival. As for the gas, the teenagers sniff it. They are addicted to the stuff. Desperate to escape the harsh realities of life, they live for the 'jencon', as it is called. This is economic reality at its harshest. It is spontaneous. It is about survival. It breaks all our civilised codes of hygiene and ethics, but these are luxuries when you are faced with starvation.

I heard about the street children from *Radio 4* as I was driving my car. It was Sunday morning at 9.30a.m. Suddenly there were cars everywhere, all jockeying for roadside places. At this time on a Sunday, I thought, 'What's going on? There are no shops near here.' As I drew near the heart of the congestion, I saw a giant football field swarming with people around parked cars. It was the monthly car boot sale, that new form of unregulated market activity, immensely popular, with everyone in search of a bargain and keen to trade without restrictions or overheads.

As I pondered these two activities, one amongst the poorest of the poor, the other in the affluent west, it seemed to me that they were both examples of the same thing. They were both about striving to succeed and about channelling that deep-level motivation into commercial activity. These sort of activities are spontaneous. They arise from deep within us, from our most basic animal motivation towards success, and they find their expression in trade.

The Entrepreneur

One young lad at school found himself shut out from the academic world through dyslexia. He took to sport and was very successful, winning everything in sight. But then he broke his leg. What was he to do? He hit upon the idea of running a student newspaper. He put a huge amount of energy into making it work. His headteacher said of him when he left that he would either become a millionaire or go to prison. He did nearly go to prison, and he did become a multimillionaire. His name was Richard Branson.[1] Here was a man with a huge amount of natural creative and competitive energy. If one channel for it was closed, he sought another. Business became the focus of his efforts, but the mainspring of his life appears to be simply the joy

---

[1] These stories derive from Branson's autobiography, *Losing my Virginity*

of facing the challenge. He has publicised his companies through his own exploits in fast boats and in balloons. Frequently he has been right on the edge of life, and death, but that is how he wants it. He launches an aviation company on a minimal budget, against established and powerful competition. As the maiden voyage is just hours away, his own major partner is seeking an injunction to stop him taking off. Then an engine explodes costing £600,000. The bank refuse extra credit. The company hangs on a knife edge. But this is all how this adventurer wants it. The balloons and the companies are all about the same thing. He says after recounting a harrowing escape from tragedy in a balloon. 'Both the series of balloon flights and the numerous Virgin companies I have set up form a seamless series of challenges which I can date from my childhood.'[2] And later, 'My interest in life comes from setting myself huge, apparently unachievable, challenges and trying to rise above them.'[3]

Richard Branson may be an extreme case, but I wonder if he spells out something basic about the entrepreneur? The entrepreneur is essentially a challenger. They are challenging the social order. They do not need to do that as aggressively or explicitly as Branson does, but that is what they do. Some may simply dream of how the world could be, as Bill Gates did, and then seek to make it so. Another might face the challenge of finding new technology for the vacuum cleaner as James Dyson did. But in each case the very creativity of these people was subversive. They are about changing things. Some may be out to make an impact in simple retail activity. Jack Cohen started as a barrow boy. He looked for the main chance. He looked for the good deal and he put energy and creativity into what he did. The story goes that in his early Tesco stores, he was not always quite sure what he was buying and selling. There were these plummy looking things in cans that he had brought in from South Africa. They were part of

[2] Ibid., p.12.
[3] Ibid., p.195.

a deal, but what were they? The managers of his emerging Tesco stores did not know which section to put them in. They put them in 'fruit'. The next week they received thousands of complaints. It turned out they were peppers! I guess the pies that weekend had tasted rather odd! But for Jack Cohen it was the deal that was important. That is where his creative, entrepreneurial energy went.[4]

Creative challengers have an interest in maintaining their freedom to continue to challenge. This means they fight to remain at the top of the tree. This is the constraint-free position. In the sixties Richard Branson was running his newspaper from a hippy dive in London. One of his closest colleagues and friends who had helped set up the newspaper, began lobbying to make it a co-operative. This threatened Branson's freedom as leader. In his autobiography, he acknowledges that at this point he stooped to bluff and deceit to keep his power. He took his friend aside and told him that everyone was against his plans for the co-operative, but they hadn't the heart to tell him. He had better leave and it would be best not to speak to anyone about it as he went. His friend fell for the bluff and went.[5] Later when Virgin was a public company, again Branson felt the constraints of public accountability too much to bear. He did not want non-executive directors telling him what to do, nor shareholders, with their short-term view, dictating policies. His only option was to stage a management buy out. Although Ian Maclaurin may be a biased witness, his account of Tesco in *Tiger by the Tail*, suggests that Jack Cohen was not exactly keen to hand over control of Tesco either. Maclaurin records one moment when things became so heated in the board room that two board members reached for the ceremonial swords on the wall and threatened each other! Freedom of action is important for the challenger.

---

[4] This story is told by MacLaurin in *Tiger by the Tail – A life in business from Tesco to cricket*.

[5] Branson, *Losing my Virginity*, pp. 67–9.

These instances are extreme examples of course, but they may represent basic motivations that are present all over the commercial world, albeit mostly in much more benign forms. Commercial activity in general may be tied in to our most basic motivations to succeed. If we refer back to the discussion in chapter two, we will recall that the social animal has two conflicting strategies. On the one hand they are committed to a strategy of working with others so they recognise the need to uphold the social order. On the other hand they are naturally challengers of that order. Here we see entrepreneurs in human culture as creative challengers of the status quo. We see their need to maintain their position in the hierarchy not just for its greater assurance of biological success, but because it is also the most constraint-free option and the best way to maintain their creative freedom. As entrepreneurs grow in influence so greater forces are unleashed toward them so as to discipline their behaviour and prevent damage to the sizeable number of people whose lives are now in their hands. So we generate a whole tranche of company law, rules about employment, accounting, boards of directors and the like, all intending to place limitations around the entrepreneur and protect those under their power. It is a primal struggle.

Evolution as a model for business

The overall behaviour of the market is also interesting to reflect upon. How should we describe the human behaviour made manifest in the business sections of our newspapers, the rise and fall of companies, the struggles to be the first to embrace new technologies, to make gains in efficiency and market share? I believe the process bears a striking similarity to biological evolution.

Businesses inhabit a market niche, just like a particular species inhabits an ecological niche. A beaver has a lifestyle of cutting down trees and building dams and lodges to protect its young from predators. That is the way it has found to successfully carve out its place in the natural world. Likewise a company seeks to find a niche in the market, producing a particular saleable product in a new way, or to a new standard, so that it will be able to survive. Any beaver colony will be in competition with other beavers in its locality for the best locale, and all the other requirements of successful reproduction. The best ones will be more successful in populating the landscape and come to dominate the gene pool. Similarly a company will test itself against its competitors, those doing the same sort of thing, occupying the same niche, and seek to grow in its market share.

This very process of competition will force the development of new technologies. In biological terms new technologies develop over thousands of years. The beaver took many generations to develop its particularly fine incisors that are so well adapted to its tree-cutting lifestyle. By contrast new technologies break into human culture continually. A new press at a car plant may be up and running in a few months. One process depends on genetic change, the other on much more rapid cultural adaptation, but there are remarkable similarities between the market and nature in this harnessing of new technology. They are both developments forged in the heat of competition. Without such a competitive environment there would be no effective spur to their deployment. Likewise both developments are fundamentally concerned with maximum efficiency. The competitive situation forces a continuing search for efficiency. Whatever it is they do, in both biology and the market, they want to do it better and more efficiently and so win in the competitive game of life.

In fact there are a whole group of words and phrases, like 'survival', 'competition', 'multiplication', 'maximum efficiency', 'new technology', 'exploiting any available niche', that apply both to biological evolution and the behaviour of the market. Business people regularly employ this sort of analogy. Richard Branson, for example, has spoken of the importance of small businesses to a healthy market by describing them as 'blooded in competitive tooth and claw'.[6] When asked the secret of his recent strategic success, Mr Walker of the company Iceland said, 'What you have to do is fight your corner' – and went on to speak of the need to 'compete and differentiate'.[7]

These parallels are so striking that one needs to consider whether the link between the market and evolution is more than an analogy. I believe that in fact the true relationship between the two lies at the deepest level of our animal nature. The link between the market and biological evolution is the simple animal motivation to succeed. The drive to be successful is a principle organising feature of all animal life and it has been taken up, transformed and re-expressed by humans in market activity.

Measurement and competitive processes

If, then, both biological evolution and the market are competitive processes, a further parallel is worth exploring. Every competitive process needs a system of measurement, implicitly agreed by all competitors around which the competition turns and by which winners are identified. So, for example, animals of the same species frequently compete with one another for access to reproduction. The reader will be familiar with the sort of ritual trials prevalent in the animal world to decide the contest for reproductive rights. Animals frequently fix on particular signs to decide the contest. The Irish elk apparently measured antler size. Those that had the finest pair of antlers won the females.[8] Birds frequently use other signs, like the length or colour of a tail feather or some form of courtship display to decide who gets to mate. We shall think about this some more in chapter eleven, but what it shows is that animals measure things, using fairly

---

[6]   Ibid., p. 469.
[7]   *The Independent,* 8 Sept. 1999.
[8]   Barnett, 'Hey, big spender', p. 36.

simple signs to co-ordinate their lives and decide their competitions.

Similarly the whole 'discipline' of economics, if that is the right word for it, might be seen as an attempt to reduce human behaviour to a limited system of signals. We are familiar with chancellors instructing us sagely on the changes that will be necessary in order to fall in with macroeconomic indicators such as inflation and interest rate. Economic textbooks try to write life into formulae that can predict economic activity. It is all an extraordinarily inexact 'science', but it is clearly of some explanatory value. The fact that it works at all suggests that commerce does actually run on these sorts of lines. It works by a limited system of signals. Of course, this is not news. Any company studies its balance sheet and takes every measure it can of its market position. Shareholders likewise monitor profitability, ready to bale out at the first sign of trouble. The whole commercial system exploits such systems of signals as measurements of success and failure. They are the framework within which the struggle takes place. It is no good moaning about companies being concerned about profit. It is central to their whole activity. It is the measure, above all, of their success. Without the measures there could be no competition, the impulse towards improvement would be broken and new technologies would not be sought or efficiently used. The economy, which is vital to human prospering, would grind to a halt.

Yet the problem with such limited systems of signals is that they fail to take into account important aspects of life. They set up a process that is intrinsically myopic and cannot take any sort of overview. Animals have very little choice about this. Their whole life is co-ordinated by such signalling and frequently these signals are subverted and exploited. Take the cuckoo, for example. The cuckoo is known as a brood parasite. The mother cuckoo lays her egg into another's nest. The young cuckoo hatches out before the eggs of the host bird and one of its first actions is to push the other eggs out of the nest. The host bird brings up the cuckoo as if it were its own. Typically the host might be a reed warbler, a tiny bird, which ends up feeding this enormous cuckoo fledgling. When we see pictures of this feeding going on, we think, 'Stupid bird, can't it see that the young one is not its own.' But it cannot. The host bird works on a limited system of signals. A gaping beak at that angle means 'feed it'. The reed warbler cannot spot the enormous incongruity before their eyes. It can take no overview of the process.

If business is like an evolutionary process, might it not suffer from the same sort of myopia? Might business also be unable to take an overview of its activity because it works to a limited system of signals? I think screen traders in the modern stock market are rather like cuckoos. They exploit a limited system of signals and get fat on it. Sitting in front of their VDU, they play a sophisticated game with numbers. The game works by careful calculation of odds and mathematicians rise to the top, but really it is all just playing a game according to a system of signals. This stock falls. That pattern of activity means this. Buy! Sell! Do it all at the right time and soon there will be a fat bonus winging its way into your bank account.

So the signals of commerce are not a problem to be weeded out of the system. They *are* the system and without them the process would grind to a halt. The problem is whether such a system is adequate in itself or whether it needs other aspects of human culture to correct it and constrain it. Without such constraint perhaps business is fundamentally vulnerable to the same sort of myopic behaviour as exploited by the cuckoo. As a reed warbler is deficient in not being able to take an overview of its position, just so is commercial activity unable, by itself, to take an overview of its activities. Animals regularly multiply so well as to destroy their habitat. Humans are currently facing the possibility of destroying their planet. Human commercial activity can destroy rain forests, choke the atmosphere and melt the ice caps and there is nothing in the system to stop it. It is intrinsically blind and haphazard in its process. We need to face this and face the desperate need for some system outside of commerce that can provide an overview of commercial activity in the light of a broader search for the good for us all, including the planet and the rest of creation.

It might be thought that one answer to the problem would be to redefine the signals. Much work has been done in recent years on an 'Index of Sustainable Economic Welfare' as an alternative to Gross Domestic Product.[9] While these aims are worthy, they run the risk of promoting the idea that the issue is a technical one. Get the signals right and the rest follows. In fact we are dealing here with a behavioural issue that has deep-level human motivations at its roots. No rational, or technical re-definitions can address this effectively. We have noted the fundamental link between market activity and the search for success. The other great taproot of motivation is power.

Power and the market

Evolution is a power struggle and many of its processes depend on interactions to assess powerfulness in one form or another. Territorial behaviour is an obvious example. Your robin in the garden is not quite the benign little fellow he appears. David Lack discovered that if you put a bunch of red feathers in his patch, he will attack it ferociously. In his limited system of signals, 'red feathers' indicates the red breast of another robin intruding onto his territory. He must defend his territory.[10] A large number of vertebrate animals defend territory in some form. The beaver colony defends its elaborate constructions against intrusion by other beavers. Male deer will fight over territory and the consequent access to females. Such behaviour sometimes appears to be for the purpose of mate selection,

---

[9]   See, for example, Daly and Cobb, *For the Common Good*, pp. 401–55.
[10]   Based on an account by Ardrey in *The Territorial Imperative*.

sometimes for ensuring adequate food supply, but the question needs to be asked, 'Do humans also fight over territory?'

Consider the typical Mafia scenario. The Mafiosi work a patch, offering 'protection' to those who have businesses within it. If another operator intrudes on their patch, they will put the frighteners on. If they continue to intrude, they will suffer violence. Is this deep-level animal behaviour? It certainly looks like an expression of power and territoriality. Of course humans have the ability to translate their deep motivations into all sorts of forms. Some may remember Glasgow for its ice cream wars. The ice cream vans worked territories and they achieved notoriety for the vigour with which they defended these territories. This might suggest the possibility of a cultural transition from defended geographical space to defence of a group or a company. What about the company analysing the impact of their competitors on their market share? As they assess the strength of the opposition, seek to exploit possible weaknesses and gain ground, surely this also is territorial behaviour?

The advent of cyberspace has produced a whole new 'ground' to fight over. It may be very abstract, but the fight for territory in cyberspace is manifest. The year 2000 saw the UK government auction territory, in terms of frequencies, to potential suppliers of the latest generation of mobile phones. The fight was spectacular. This peculiar form of real estate fetched twenty-two billion pounds. Likewise there has been great fascination with the new dot.com companies. Many thought their new cyberspace territory important and stocks rocketed in value. Gradually questions were asked. It was all too easy. People could set these things up in a flash. Then it was pointed out that as soon as any of these companies raised their prices enough to make a reasonable profit, another would set up alongside them and take their market.[11] They had no way of protecting their territory. People are now

---

[11] I am grateful to Peter Warburton for this insight offered long before the fall in dot.com stocks.

much more suspicious about backing the dot.coms. Nevertheless it is all the same game. It is at root a power play.

Power in one form or another is endemic in business and part of its driving force. It cannot be otherwise. Imagine the scene of the hostile takeover. Two boards clashing like two giant stags, powerful people and powerful corporations, assessing the other in minute detail, considering their chances of success in various kinds of assault. Here is power. The adrenalin rushes. The news breaks. The clash of the titans is over. Until the next time, when the next challenger arises. Such is life in business and such is animal life, linked together by deep-level appreciations about power and its role. Of course this can be civilised. Systems of trust can grow, as we shall see in future chapters, that modify its effects, but underneath there is still a system of power.

One of the key issues facing the western world at the moment is the possibility that large corporations will subvert the power of governments. According to Davidson and Rees-Mogg in *The Sovereign Individual,* this is both inevitable and desirable. Their book is an unashamed polemic in support of the rich of the world and analyses human civilisations entirely on the basis of a power struggle. The absence of any moral constraint in their predictions is frightening, particularly since one of them is a former editor of *The Times* and still a regular columnist. Their take-home message is that international companies and rich people will subvert nations by choosing which nation they will formally locate in. Our mobile world allows the company to make a product in one country, keep its money in another and locate its head office somewhere else. So companies will locate according to which government gives them the best deal for their taxes. The corporations will hold the governments to ransom according to their own version of the good, or in other words according to their own advantage in the power game. Davidson and Rees-Mogg end their book by advertising a club for rich people and their own off-shore banking facilities.

An interesting example of just this type of behaviour arose in October 1999. Glaxo Wellcome have produced a new drug called Relenza for the treatment of flu. Government advisors looked at the evidence for the efficacy of the drug and decided that on balance it would not be a good use of funds to offer it for prescription on the NHS. Glaxo's response was remarkable. They sent a veiled threat to the government effectively saying that if they did not use the drug, the company would relocate. This behaviour caused very little comment. Yet it was in effect saying, 'I do not care about your democratic institutions. I do not care about your arguments. This is a power game and if you do not play along with us we will withdraw from the country and find a more sympathetic host nation.' Commerce works by processes of power.

A wholly similar perspective needs to be applied to the issues of debt release for the heavily indebted regions of the world. This matter cannot be treated as a rational argument about the best way to encourage development. The system is upheld by power. The G8 countries control the world. Debt is a means by which the poorer countries of the world are kept in control. No amount of pure logic will adequately address this and the environmental issues that loom. What is required is new means of moral engagement. The system of values promoted by the commercial world needs to be brought into proper tension with other human values.

Working for the bigger picture

First of all, it must be acknowledged that the commercial world can only give a partial perspective on human existence. Its limited system of signs is inadequate. It has been common for UK governments to make statements to the effect that the economy is *really* what matters to our society. Everything else hinges on the health of the economy. Therefore the value system derived from the market must be our dominating value system. This totalising view of the market can be presented by neo-capitalist economists with a quasi-religious fervour. Yet it is plainly and disastrously inadequate.

In the period after Adam Smith wrote the *Wealth of Nations* a similar and even more pervasive dogmatism descended on society. The market should not be controlled. It must be left alone at all costs. The market would see to the prosperity of all in the long run as long as no one interfered. His logic was profound and marvellous to many. Yet his prescriptions for the poor were devastating. Hear this:

> Every species of animal naturally multiplies in proportion to its means of subsistence and no species can ever multiply beyond. But in civilised society it is only among the inferior ranks of people that the scantiness of subsistence can set limits to the further multiplication of the human species: and it can do so in no other way than by destroying a great part of the children which their fruitful marriages produce.[12]

This sort of statement reveals the horror. The market actually only *measures* that which can be exchanged in a market transaction. This means that it *values* only that which can be exchanged in the market place. Human society is rich and diverse. Its cultures take centuries to build. The bonds between families and nations are strong and powerful. Humans value the beauty of the land and the wildlife it contains. They value the air they breathe, the stability of the planet and the relationships they work with. Yet none of these things are exchangeable in the marketplace. None can be given a value in sterling. They simply cannot be measured by the market system. And if we are limited to the market's system of signs, all of these things can and will be swept away.

---

[12]   Smith, *An inquiry into the nature and cause of the wealth of nations*, p. 182.

Yet it does not have to be like this. We are storytelling animals. Storytelling is a powerful medium for the pursuit of truth and right and can offer the means to reintegrate our lives. It can engage with our partial views, with their limited systems of signals, and open up a bigger view of the good for us all. In the wake of the Industrial Revolution, many were not content with the new economic logic. They brought their stories powerfully into the public arena. Folk like Dickens and Kingsley wrote fiction, but fiction that made the poor real. Others brought the story of the poor forward into public life. They told of the children dying from sheer exhaustion in the mills. They told of the hideous mangled bodies that resulted from industrial accidents. Workers themselves combined, in the teeth of furious opposition, to form unions and bring their story into the public arena. So the process continued and the society heard and changed. Factory Acts were passed to limit working hours. Health and Safety at work became a real issue. Unions attained recognition and organised themselves politically. Such is the power of storytelling in the pursuit of what is right and true.

The story of the Industrial Revolution actually mirrored another older story. This was the struggle of the emerging marketplace in the Bible. As we saw in chapter three, religion has often been aligned with the search for success. People naturally look to God to provide for their needs and even for their prosperity. It was a fundamental strand of early Old Testament theology that people expected that if they lived well by God, then they would prosper. So the blessing of God was readily interpreted in terms of material success.[13] This also expressed itself, at least in part, in the concept of wisdom. Solomon is described as 'wise'. This attribute essentially meant 'skilled in living'. Most particularly, Solomon was skilled in trade and made a fortune by it.

Reading the account of his life in the first book of Kings introduces us to a world where Israel had suddenly been

---

[13] Deuteronomy 28:1–6.

catapulted onto the world stage. The gradual consolidation of Israel into a nation had now come together with relative weakness in the surrounding peoples. Israel was placed on the major trading route and took the opportunity to capitalise on market freedom. Solomon rose to international stature. He built magnificent buildings, traded far and near and made political alliances through his many marriages. A civil service grew up around him in the capital city. These were new cosmopolitan people, open to new cultures and new understandings and generally quite well-off. The school of wise men who wrote Proverbs and Ecclesiastes descended from such an environment. They no longer told the particular stories of Israel, but looked to a generalised, abstracted human being, to the properties of human character that would bring success in this new world for whatever person. They were mildly critical of aspects of their world, but their words were clearly from the privileged perspective of the Royal Court. We can imagine the easy-going surroundings and rather boringly predictable life that surrounded the philosophic writer of Ecclesiastes as he decried the meaninglessness and vanity of life. Similarly the writer of Proverbs might be imagined as an equivalent of today's public school chaplain, full of good and godly advice for young people, but inevitably limited to a particular privileged perspective.

The problem was that there was another side to this success story. Solomon was in fact undermining the tradition of monotheism and through that producing a fragmentation of the society that was to beset it for centuries. His foreign wives worshipped foreign gods and drew people after them. His fine buildings were built with forced labour. Social division between rich and poor was growing. This 'success' culture was set to disintegrate. This begs the question whether Solomon was really wise after all.

It would be false to equate the economy of Solomon's time with the neo-liberal economies of today, yet they do have a common theme. They both give prime value to that which can be exchanged in the market place. This emphasis on materiality leads inexorably to the undervaluing of the non-material goods essential to so many aspects of human relationships and cultural development. Such societies inevitably fail to integrate themselves adequately and are continually susceptible to fragmentation and social unrest. This is precisely what happened to Israel after Solomon. The country split in two on account of the social tensions that he had generated.[14] Solomon's approach was both highly successful and profoundly debilitating for the emerging nation. Yet that was not the end of the story. In the period that followed a critique of Solomon and his 'wisdom' arose.

Of those who were alienated from the successes of Solomon's legacy there arose spokespeople, known to us as prophets. One of the magic ingredients of the biblical faith was that there was no respect for pretended monopolies on hearing the word of God. People like Amos could arise, the shepherd of Tekoa, and roar at the government of the northern kingdom in the name of God. To the rich women he said, 'Hear this you cows of Bashan, who are in the mountain of Samaria, who oppress the poor and crush the needy ... The Lord has sworn by his holiness that behold the days are coming upon you when they shall take you away with hooks, even the last of you with fishhooks.'[15] He denounced those who traded unfairly and who treated people as commodities to be bought and sold,

> Hear this, you who trample upon the needy and bring the poor of
> the land to an end, saying, 'When will the new moon be over,
> that we may sell grain? And the sabbath that we may offer wheat
> for sale, that we may make the ephah small and the shekel great,
> and deal deceitfully with false balances, that we may buy the poor
> for silver and the needy for a pair of sandals, and sell the refuse of

---

[14] This story is told in 1 Kings 12.
[15] Amos 4:1–2.

the wheat?' The Lord has sworn by the pride of Jacob: 'Surely I will never forget any of their deeds.'[16]

Some prophets would approach the king directly. 'Do you think you are a king because you compete in cedar?' said Jeremiah to Shallum, and he told him to behave like his father Josiah and remember the poor.[17]

In general terms the prophets worked by making an appeal to those sympathetic social motivations of people that are so easily crushed in the culture of material exchange. They also made direct challenges to power. Their work was to result in forcing a bigger view of life than the one dominated by the market agenda. Their words would forge explicit links between success and justice, declaring that there could be no success without a proper concern for all the members of the society. Micah, for example, would declare, 'Hear this, you heads of the house of Jacob and rulers of the house of Israel, who abhor justice and pervert all equity, who build Zion with blood and Jerusalem with wrong … Zion shall be ploughed as a field; Jerusalem shall become a heap of ruins.'[18] And of course they got into trouble for their words. The establishment did not like them.

This was the real world which made the Scripture. It was a tough world of conflicting ideas and perspectives. It was a world in which powerful stories came into conflict and forced a growth in the understanding of God and of what was good for the society. The context for this struggle was the belief in the one God who was all good. This overarching commitment, expressed practically in the rituals of the community, was the holding context for the great struggle that was to further their conceptions of just and right behaviour.

---

[16] Amos 8:4–7.
[17] Jeremiah 22:15.
[18] Micah 3:9, 10 and 12b.

So we see how the people of both the nineteenth century and the biblical world both managed to put justice on the agenda of success. In a sense they could be said to have questioned what success truly was. If it was at the expense of the poor, the foreigner or anyone else, then it was not truly success. Or alternatively we might say that what they achieved was to force an engagement of the deep striving for success with sympathetic social feelings, so contributing to our own inner integrity.

In both instances the process was to put questions of overall purpose back on the centre stage. It was to force an overview onto an intrinsically myopic process. A materialist success culture so easily loses contact with the big questions of purpose. Think of how many Chancellor's speeches talk about 'rising this and falling that', about 'jobs' and wages, but so rarely does anyone talk the language of what it is all for. A job is not just a job. It matters *what* you do. It matters whether this is a real contribution to society. It matters how it is done, what people are trampled on in the process. Similarly the particular people matter in and of themselves, who they are and what they have to bring. All these things are lost to the conventional material analysis. There are three big questions that any business can ask itself to begin this process of engaging with purpose in a proper holistic manner.

1. What good does this business do?
2. What does it mean to be doing this business well?
3. What sorts of people are required to be doing this business well?

The answers to these questions are not all obvious. They become even more interesting when we consider what business really is in the human context. The conventional material analysis, reflected in this chapter, does not really do justice to the commercial world. It is actually far more subtle, even if it does not want to admit it. It is really all a system of trust.

7

Commerce as a system of trust

The art of exchange

One understanding of the commercial world might be set up like this. Imagine it is Christmastime. You are making a list of presents for family and friends. After several hours' hard imaginative labour, you get down to those people who you are least close to. How do you think about your present giving to such people? Most likely you will consider precedent. What did they give us last year? And in the back of your mind you will be weighing the actual cost of last year's present. You then will suggest something of similar value to give to them this year. It is quite natural. Present giving to those we least know comes closest to tit for tat.

Studies of traditional societies across the world come up with similar findings. Present giving can be extremely fraught. The head of the tribe will closely inspect the present offered by the chief of the neighbouring tribe, its value will be the subject of serious analysis and strict tit for tat behaviour is likely to be the order of the day. By contrast, within the close community or family, gifts will vary in value. They will be mere signs of other greater loyalties that are dependent on a long time period and on many goods that cannot be exchanged materially.[1]

Gift giving between strangers may be the root of commercial behaviour. In behavioural terms, the simple act of barter may be very close to such gift giving. Because the givers are relative strangers then there is a tendency to empty all of the mutual obligations into the act of material exchange. After all they may not meet again. This is the basis of commercial exchange. You do the deal and walk away. The material exchange is the total obligation. The absence of other obligations can be important to the system working properly. This report of shopping in Hong Kong illustrates the problem:

> One old lady carefully avoided shopping at the mixed goods shop run by her sister's son because she would feel obligated to buy once she went in. If she wanted a blue thing and all they had were red ones, she would have to take a red one. So she went to the shop of a non-kinsman where she could carefully look for something that exactly suited her taste, walk out if she didn't find it and bargain fiercely if she did.[2]

So commerce is a system of material exchange designed for strangers, people who have no other deep-level obligations to each other than the actual exchange. The transaction is envisaged as a simple, immediate and complete version of tit for tat.

Such is the theory and it has a great deal going for it. It certainly makes for neat and tidy economics textbooks. Nevertheless the relationships between people in the commercial world are actually more subtle and complex than this model would imply. The theory probably comes closest to its perfect expression in the simple act of shopping. We give the money and they hand over the goods. Nevertheless in reality even this

---

[1] Matt Ridley, *The Origins of Virtue*, p. 119. Ridley himself is using ideas drawn from Marcel Mauss and Marshall Sahlins.

[2] Fukuyama, *Trust*, p. 76.

situation is considerably more complicated. For example, we have discovered that such simple exchanges still need the protection of trading standards and sale of goods acts which act as a discipline over those who would abuse the system. In the modern shopping environment there are in fact a host of controls that effectively police the transaction. Immediate tit for tat exchange is actually rarely achieved. For example, many transactions have some aspect of the exchange that extends over time. It may be about the long-term performance of a product. So we have a system of guarantees. It may be about the construction of a building over a period of time. So contracts are drawn up which specify the obligations of each party over the period and the anticipated outcome. In each case there is some real degree of risk implicit in the relationship and the transaction is covered by some form of discipline in case it fails to deliver the anticipated goods.

Searching for systems of trust that work

From this we begin to see that commercial relationships are generally a function of what we have called 'delayed tit for tat' behaviour and are actually systems of trust. Commerce is crucially dependent on wise structures that are implicitly aware of both the potential gain in co-operating and of the need to effectively discipline the one who would exploit the situation for their own ends. In some situations it is genuinely sensible to trust. There is real potential for greater success this way. In other situations one is almost certain to be ripped off. The wisdom is to know the difference. Such systems of trust are everywhere in commerce. Wherever people need to work together with others, they need some system of trust to mediate their relationship, even in the commercial underworld.

It might be thought that a criminal fraternity is the last place where one would find trust exercised, yet criminals need to co-operate with one another and to do so they need to have a system of trust. It may be very crude, and potentially violent, but it is there. Loyalty between criminals is upheld with a frightening discipline. If something goes wrong in a racket and there is a suspicion that they may have been double-crossed, the Mafia have a saying that either there must be a 'body in court or a body on the floor'. That is, either someone must have been caught or there has been betrayal, punishable by death. It is rough justice but necessary for those who have opted out of the subtleties of developed culture.[3] Yet here we have a system of trust, that is a co-operative venture dependent on favours done over a period of time, and still more deeply on the relationships between people and on effective discipline when one betrays the trust.

A more benign example is money. Money is one of the most basic means by which economic systems develop. Money is itself a system of trust. Through the late nineties, Somalia has been run by 'barons' without any centralised authority. They have consumed vast resources with their feuding and some have been printing money. This is certain to lead to rampant inflation and cause serious suffering to the poor. Observers are predicting an increase in the popularity of Muslim fundamentalism to arise out of a concern to re-establish the social order. Maintaining a workable monetary system is a basic responsibility of government. The monetary system is a trust that holds the commercial world together. When the rouble crashed, Russians queued outside their banks to convert their money into durables. They could no longer trust the money supply.

Banking arose as a way of managing money. It was a trust, whose roots are in the simple savings club. Money deposited in a bank could be used more efficiently than money stored under the mattress, but that efficiency depended on the bank behaving

---

[3] A fascinating account of underworld activities and their various systems of trust can be found in Marks, *Mr Nice – an autobiography*, particularly p. 160.

responsibly in its use of money, so various safeguards, or disciplines arose. In the last few decades credit unions have arisen, attempting to find a new low-cost niche in the banking world. Some observers comment that their chronic need to attract high levels of capital investment might be best met by developing a stronger system of regulation so that people would more readily trust them with serious money. Both banks and credit unions are systems of trust.

Joint stock companies arose in the fifteenth century. They were the only means of exploiting the new possibilities offered by transoceanic merchant shipping.[4] No one person could sensibly stand the risk of the long sea voyage with all its imponderables. Yet forty people together buying shares in the voyage could share the risk and reap the benefits of a successful voyage. It was a sensible deal. It demanded the development of new laws to protect this new type of investor. From this there gradually arose stock markets, limited liability protections and the whole gamut of legislation that now surrounds public companies. Yet it was, and remains, a system of trust. It was the contracting together of several people, who could be strangers to each other, in a commercial venture, based upon rules that ensured that if one was to let down the others in payment, or whatever, they could be brought to book. Lloyds of London similarly arose from the insurance needs of such shipping ventures.

In all such cases we see a similar general pattern. Relationships between those involved in the commercial world naturally give rise to new initiatives based upon the development of a trust between people and effective disciplines being put in place against the time when that trust might be broken. Most of our commercial institutions arose in the days when a relationship was principally a face-to-face affair. The commercial community was relatively small and so the basic conditions for a system of trust – namely stable relationships, good memories and effective

---

[4] Fukuyama, *Trust*, p. 47.

discipline – were easily available. In such face-to-face conditions the value of trustworthiness was also clear and a morality that upheld a reputation for trustworthiness could easily develop.

As technological and economic development have proceeded, the relational possibilities of the world have also vastly increased. This has resulted in a world where people are now kept track of by their passport, their driving licence and other forms of abstract identification. People can still be called to account and so systems of trust are still generated, but these systems are far removed from face-to-face relationship and the small communities to which they owe their origin. Such developments in abstract relationship have had profound effects on the commercial world.

Challenges of technological and economic development

Richard Sennett tells the story of the development of the department store in the middle of the nineteenth century.[5] The traditional shopkeeper had stood behind his counter and engaged each customer in conversation as they came in. The conversation itself gave rise to a sense of relationship which in turn generated a commitment to buy. Most people did not leave the shop without buying something. Yet the process was inefficient. It took a great deal of time to serve people. This necessitated a high mark-up and a low turnover of goods. In contrast, the department store deliberately aimed for the mass market. It intended to sell a large volume of goods at a lower price than the traditional shops. The unintended cost of this new approach was a different type of relationship with the consumer. Now goods would be sold through image, not through face-to-face conversation. Much attention was given to the display of goods. Attempts were made to

---

[5] Sennett, *The Fall of Public Man*, pp. 143–5.

associate the goods with other signs that conveyed luxury, status or some other perceived desire of the customer.

It was just this sort of change in means of relationship that began the movement toward 'public relations' which is now such an indispensable part of commercial activity. The advertising industry has grown to gigantic proportions. More money is currently spent on advertising in the world than on education. Perhaps it *is* the new form of education. Yet this relationship is still part of a system of trust.

Take brands, for example. A brand is a highly valuable commodity. It works on a mental association between people and a product. This may be mere association, the bombardment of people with an image so as to raise it in their awareness and increase sales, or it may also have deeper connotations that have to do with trust. If a company has established a reputation for high quality goods, if it has been in the market-place for a long time and traded successfully, if it is renowned for the good treatment of its employees or its concern for the environment, all these things can feed into the valuing of the brand. The Body Shop, for example, will gain seriously from its established reputation for environmental and social concerns. That is part of its brand, part of its image and part of its success. Yet this brand business is actually all intangible. It is not part of the material world. It exists in the realm of story and relationship. And it gives the lie to those who see the commercial world in cold, rational and calculating terms.

In fact much of the value of a company cannot be assessed in any scientifically adequate manner. There are a host of 'intangibles', known best to accountants, that affect their market valuation. For example, the company has a trading history that one can reasonably assume might continue. This will normally be reflected as value in the accounts. But who knows what actually will happen? A new CEO might change things so drastically that all previous synergies are lost and the future is suddenly altogether bleak. Gerald Ratner can make some comments at a dinner, the media can fix on it and the company collapses. The stock market has many such stories and they all point to the element of trust in the valuation of companies.

As communications technology increases in power so the degree of abstraction in relationship increases and there is correspondingly more emphasis on image. The film production company 'Dreamworks' was floated on the stock exchange.[6] It was a new venture. It had nothing in production and no studio, yet its market valuation rose immediately from $250 million to $2 billion. This valuation hinged entirely around the reputation and image of its founders, Steven Spielberg, Jeffrey Katzenberg and David Geffen. Such intangible assets are likely to be of increasing impact in the surreal worlds of future technology.

Richard Branson has claimed that his company was subject to a particularly foul set of tricks from the management of British Airways. One of these was very simple. It was simply to say at any and every opportunity that Virgin Atlantic Airways was about to collapse. 'Didn't you know? I doubt if they will last the month. I've heard that the situation is so bad that their fuel suppliers are asking for payment up front.' Remarks such as these can *of themselves* bring a company down. The stock market gets nervous. The share price dives. Bankers refuse new loans. The fuel companies, who were giving a month's *credit*, consider actually asking for cash up front and immediately the company crashes. It's easy and, according to Branson, it almost worked.[7] It illustrates how important trust and reputation are to the marketplace.

These examples point to a basic instability in the modern commercial environment, which probably derives from the increasingly abstract type of human relationship that it works with. Communication in the whole of public life is now in the hands of the mass media. Image and soundbite are the order of

---

[6] Davis and Meyer, *Blur. The Speed of Change in the Connected Economy*, p.12.
[7] Branson, *Losing my Virginity*.

the day. There is no doubting the power of these methods to influence people, but there is much more room to worry about what a society dominated by this methodology will come to be, particularly in terms of our most basic and vital ability to trust. We shall return to this in chapter fifteen.

In all the instances above, despite increasing layers of abstraction, we are still concerned with systems of trust and the basic conditions described for systems of trust still apply. To note, as we have, that any commercial system carries risk or involves trust is to say that this is a system of delayed tit for tat. People have made a commitment to something. They may have invested money in a ship in the fifteenth century or bought some stocks and shares today, but in both situations they are taking a risk. They are committing themselves to a commercial situation whereby the taking of the risk has the real potential to reap reward. But as a result they are yoked to others. Their future is tied up with others. It is essential in that situation that proper disciplines are in place, in law, morality and in custom, that will effectively prevent free riders from abusing the bond of trust.

Work cultures as systems of trust

The internal workings of a company are a rather different scenario from external market relations. While market exchange is designed to work through strangers, the members of a company have a whole range of relational possibilities open to them. At the lowest trust end of the spectrum, there is the traditional assembly line. Here the workers are assumed to be skivers. They cannot be trusted. For this reason they are paid according to piecework in a quasi-mechanical environment where their jobs are replaced by machines as soon as possible. The workers' own scope for creative imagination is minimal. In response to this distrust, the workers typically react by mistrusting management. They develop strong, confrontational unions and ensure strict job demarcation. Conflicts are frequent and threatening behaviour tends to be the first not the last resort.[8]

This sort of scenario works at one level, but fails to reap the full rewards of co-operation and can cause immense psychological stress. There are a large number of alternative possibilities. A family firm is typically a high trust environment, while it is small. The members of the family give over and above what might be expected. Through the trust implicit in kinship, they co-operate better than strangers in the common task. Most of our large firms today originated as small family concerns. Yet they became large because they were able to adapt. Francis Fukuyama points out that in some parts of the world, there is a cultural resistance towards trusting non-kin. In southern Italy and in some Chinese cultures, there are strong family ties, but firms tend not to grow bigger than the family concern because they fail to make the transition to appointing professional managers when they need them.[9] One way of seeing a firm is as a complete micro-culture in itself, including whole systems of beliefs and norms that affect the relationships of their staff. The variety of such cultures is immense. A new CEO can typically alter the whole culture of a firm. Such is their power.

If the assembly line is at the lowest end of the spectrum of trust, so at the other end there are long established firms inhabiting a continuing market niche that face minimal challenge from competition. These typically develop high trust working relationships. Staff may expect a job for life. It will become hard to get rid of unsuitable people. There may be maximum creative freedom for the employees but little to encourage the development of this creativity. Such companies frequently fail to develop, are slow to adapt and vulnerable to any change in market conditions. So we see the positive role of competition. Competition provides a means of challenge and so a spur to development. It is

---

[8] See Fukuyama, *Trust*, pp. 225ff.
[9] Ibid.

a means of continually calling a company to account. Those who lack such market accountability may ultimately suffer for it. The same applies to individual staff. They can be trusted too much. Barings offer an interesting example. Nick Leeson was given too much creative freedom. His freedom brought the whole bank down. For the sake of everyone who was involved, tighter disciplines on his activities were necessary.

What is a firm anyway? A firm is a system of trust, even, as we have said, a micro-culture. Most particularly a firm is a system of co-operation based around a unitary power structure. So why do firms grow to the size they do? Oliver Williamson is an economist known for his insight that the real costs of commercial activity involve both production and transaction costs.[10] For many years company activities focused almost exclusively on productivity as measured by unit production costs. Williamson showed that any manufacturing enterprise is actually part of a supply chain and that transactions along this supply chain could crucially affect the profitability of the whole process. When the railway was first built in the US, a different company owned roughly each fifty miles of track. Getting goods from one end of the track to another involved a nightmare of negotiation. Each company was totally dependent on the others. One rogue player could bring the whole thing to a halt. In such cases it makes sense to unite the operation into one company. Transaction costs are thereby decreased.

This sort of thinking can be applied to the whole commercial environment. Day by day in the business pages a host of company take-overs, mergers and the like are announced. The rationale for all this activity is that companies are continually searching for the best and most efficient systems of co-operation in the current circumstances. If all the operations of the market were laid out on a grid, the whole thing could be envisaged as one vast supply

---

[10] This discussion is based on Williamson, *Economic Organisation – Firms, markets and policy control.*

network, a mass of interconnected instances of co-operation. The question then becomes, 'Which of these activities are best organised as one structure (that is, within one company), and which are best outsourced? Through the nineties there was a rash of downsizing as each company concentrated on its core business, those activities that it was particularly well placed to do best, and everything else was outsourced. At the same time there was the move to 'lean supply',[11] where different companies explored very highly dependent relationships, holding minimal stocks and establishing high trust relationships with suppliers.

All this juggling with structures can be understood in terms of a fundamental tension that underlies the whole of the commercial world. There are always synergies to be gained from the development of relationships, but such relationships also need to be continually disciplined in order to keep them sharp and efficient. The foremost market discipline is competition.

Synergy of established relationships ◄——► Disciplines of competition

For example, any firm holds a wealth of knowledge in its relationships. Transplanting firms is notoriously difficult for this reason. Oliver Williamson tells the story of a new electric light bulb manufacturer, which tried to copy another established firm to the letter. Yet it failed to produce a single quality light bulb for a whole year. He explained this by the fact that there was much knowledge held in the established firm, but it was tacit knowledge, held in the relationships between people and not easily accessible in any terms that could be copied. There was something of an 'art' to making light bulbs. In this firm as in any firm, people had learnt how to co-operate. They had learnt how to get

---

[11]   Lean supply is a term used to describe a shift in supply management, whereby all sorts of firms greatly reduced the stocks of their raw materials and instead agreed very tight schedules of delivery with their suppliers, who would deliver the required items just in time.

things done, who to go to when something goes wrong and the like. But most of this is not written down anywhere.

If this is so then every company reaps great gains from its established internal network of relationships. At the same time any firm can go stale. It can become bureaucratic or full of internal power struggles that prevent effective co-operation. It can lose touch with the cutting edge of skills and knowledge in its field. It can become too large for effective internal communication. It can fail to adapt. It therefore also needs challenge. Competition will be necessary to keep it on its toes.

The same applies to any supply chain. The proponents of lean supply have noticed that there are gains to be had from good relationships with suppliers. A traditional buyer/supplier relationship is adversarial. The buyer is continually shopping around for the cheapest and best product. He cares nothing for the supplier and blames the supplier when anything goes wrong. By contrast in lean supply, buyers and their suppliers work on building their relationship. They establish much longer contracts. They even share secrets, all with the purpose of seeking new synergies in their supply chain mechanisms to give them the competitive edge.

Yet some companies in supply chains have a pretty tawdry time. There may be much talk of partnership, but the small player dealing with the giant company has few grounds on which to develop a relationship. They can easily be bullied and intimidated with the threat that their business will be withdrawn, or with draconian contracts. In general, supply chain relationships seem to work well where there is a partial, but not total dependence between supplier and buyer. The situation of partial dependence provides a mutual interest within which tit for tat behaviour can be exchanged and trust explored and built up. The big question as always remains, 'Does this system of co-operating work better than potential others?' It is a minefield to tread, but that is what human culture is all about.

The importance of moral and religious commitments

If the commercial world is a specialised system of trust, it is clear that it cannot be separated from the other systems of trust in human culture. We have seen, from Fukuyama, how the strength of family ties can interact with commerce, having an affect on firm size. In fact the nature of commercial activity is affected by the whole culture of which it is a part. Some neo-liberal economists have attempted to isolate the commercial world from other activity and then to claim that this world is really all that matters. This is false. The systems of trust, which make up the whole culture, must be brought into the picture. The difficulty is that trust is a different *type* of thing from other market signs. It is not a commodity that can be given a market value. Some theorists have sought to introduce trust into the commercial equation by calling it 'social capital'.[12] The difficulty is that trust simply cannot be measured on the same scale as the other signals of market profitability. Trust can neither be measured nor exchanged. Once we acknowledge that commerce is a system of trust, then all the other systems of culture must be considered whether we like it or not, and we have to find creative new ways of bringing these disparate elements into a proper tension.

For example, Fukuyama has shown how religion in Japan has a fundamental affect on the life of a company. In their particular version of Confucianism, the father can adopt children who then can even become heirs to the family fortune. Companies reflect this religious ethos in that the manager sees himself as the 'father' of the company. He will take a personal concern for the lives of his staff, attending their weddings, funerals etc. and they in return will give him immense loyalty. I remember talking to a Japanese

---

[12] See for example Coleman, *Foundations of Social Theory*.

scientist at a conference in Japan. He said to me sadly that his six-month-old daughter smiled at his wife but not at him. We talked some more and I discovered that he worked as a medic during the week and at the weekend he did the research he was present-ing at the conference. I was not surprised his daughter did not smile! I then asked him what he would do for the next stage in his career. He said, 'I will go to Professor Sasagawa[13] and he will tell me what to do.' In this country, we wouldn't dream of sub-mitting to a system like that! But it makes clear that moral and religious concerns profoundly affect the nature of all corporate activity.

Fukuyama goes on to point out how damaging litigation and corruption are to a country's system of trust. The US is currently overwhelmed by a storm of litigation. People sue for anything. If you see someone lying in the street, you may think long and hard before helping for fear of doing something wrong and being sub-jected to a lawsuit. Increasing litigation is a sign of the decay of trust. The purpose of litigation is to act as a safeguard in the event of an abuse of the public trust. What I think we see happening in the States is that litigation is being used as a means of free-riding itself. The litigation process, with its no win/no fee structure, has encouraged people to use the law as a first resort and as a means, not primarily to settle legitimate dispute, but simply as a means of making money for the litigant. This is a sign of system failure. Litigation is expensive. Overindulgence in litigation is expensive to the society that supports it and will significantly detract from the overall benefits of co-operation in that society.

In companies too, litigation is a serious issue. Legal action on the basis of contract should be a last resort, but some companies routinely use it to threaten. As soon as the order is placed, the accepted supplier might be directed to the 'contracts officer' who will spell out, in all its threatening detail, what will happen *when* they fail to meet the contract. There is clearly no doubt in

---

[13] This name is fictional.

the contractor's mind that this person will fail to meet the contract. That is a foregone conclusion. Again the contracts officer cares nothing for the real purpose of the operation. He is the bully boy, keeping the small fry in place and wielding the big stick to make sure that *they* suffer rather than his own company. Nevertheless when things do go to court, there is often little to be gained by the defendant or plaintiff. It is the professional lawyers who are kept in business. Legal action is extraordinarily costly.

In the face of this there have been a number of recent attempts to look for better ways of providing mediation when a commercial relationship goes wrong. Jane Gunn has been dubbed by the Financial Times 'The Corporate Peacemaker'. She has launched an initiative to get people to talk *before* they take each other to law. Such a process allows people to tell their story to each other. She finds people are more open about themselves in this situation and more able to use imagination in seeking a mutually agreeable settlement. The adversarial processes of the courtroom on the other hand typically close people down and shrink the imagination. Law is expensive and not often satisfactory. Any society that needs frequent recourse to the law is very inefficient.

This whole discussion leads to an interesting conclusion. When a society can realistically trust its systems to work, and works on that basis, then the maximum fruits of co-operation will be achieved. That is, society works best where people can be trusted and where systems are well designed and reflect that level of ability to trust. The most efficient society is always one where people can be most genuinely trusted.

Similarly, we are aware that corruption itself is inefficient. If bribes are necessary at every level in a transaction, they increase the cost of that transaction in an arbitrary and unaccountable way. The costs of a bribe cannot be adequately linked to the good exchanged, so the process introduces notorious inefficiencies, rather like the railway where you have to renegotiate before using each section of track. Again the most efficient society is the one where people can be most genuinely trusted and thereby do their work for the publicly advertised and accountable fee.

Finally we saw how, in terms of company organisation, the assembly line exemplified minimal trust, offered the least creative imagination and the most hostility and psychological stress. Yet on the other hand we noted that very stable and free environments easily stagnate or become prey to free riders. This dichotomy also has a best solution. A company can best organise itself, giving most creative freedom to its workforce, and so most satisfaction at work, when the workers themselves can be trusted to work well. Trustworthiness is again the crucial determinant of best practice. If people can genuinely be trusted to work well, then a maximisation of spontaneous creativity and efficiency can be obtained. This would imply that if the moral and religious environment of a country were such as to encourage trustworthiness, then the most efficient and most personally satisfying experiences of commercial life would be obtained.

As we saw in chapter three, the Judaeo–Christian tradition is set up as a system of trust. The people live and derive their society from within a commitment to a relationship with God that has all the hallmarks of a system of trust. This has the remarkable effect of automatically reinforcing the value of trustworthiness. The religion itself acts both to encourage trustworthy people and as a source of discipline towards those members of the community who betray the trust of others. In general terms it results in exhortations to people to be 'faithful' as God is faithful. More specifically it leads to core commandments such as 'You shall not bear false witness.' 'You shall not steal.' 'You shall not commit adultery.'[14] All these are actually commands about being trustworthy and act to encourage the development of trustworthiness within the structures of the society. Likewise people are exhorted to keep

---

[14] Exodus 20.

their word.[15] 'Let your yes be yes and your no be no' ... nothing else should be necessary, said Jesus.[16] Furthermore it led to an enforced openness in public life as prophets challenged those in power and brought stories of corruption into the public arena. It also led to the prohibition of bribes.[17] All these derive from the understanding of life as a system of trust. We see that it is extraordinarily in keeping with our search for a good society in commercial terms.

---

[15] It is an interesting reflection on the life of David that, though in many ways a violent man, his felt duty to keep his word prevented some bloodshed and helped to keep the society together during a turbulent period. See chapter nine.

[16] Matthew 5:37.

[17] Compare words about the nature of God in Deuteronomy. 10:17 and instructions to judges in Deuteronomy 16:19. Faithfulness is a major theme of Hosea, see particularly 4:1–2, where the absence of a basic faithfulness is held to be at the root of all sorts of social disorder.

8

Confronting the addictions of success

The child was spotted by a swimming coach when she was five. Since then she has been at the baths five or six days a week. She is just turning fourteen now and approaching the peak of her performance. She spends two, three or even four hours a day in the water pounding up and down the pool. Her parents have organised her life and theirs around her swimming. The school make special allowances for their emerging star. She has very little time for academic work, or for anything else come to think of it. She has few friends or other interests. Swimming is her life.

How do you react to a story like that? To me it is both inspiring and tragic. At one level you have a story of struggle against the odds to be the best, a story of human endurance and dedication. On the other hand it is such a focused life that it appears narrow, cut off from the balance of normal interests that form a rounded human being. It is an example of the search for success, but a search free of restraint and therefore almost addictive in its power. We all struggle to succeed in some way or another. The vicar works to build a large and vibrant congregation. The political activist attempts to build a movement that will influence government. The actor seeks for the lucky break that will result in fame. The drive to succeed is primal. It is deep in us. Yet in a normal life it is balanced by all sorts of other considerations such as doing the washing up, making friends and being constrained by family obligations. Developing quality relationships with others is a vital part of developing a balanced life. Without these things, the striving for success can take on an addictive power.

The roots of addictive behaviour

It may be that western society has become particularly susceptible to such addictive behaviour both corporately in terms of the market and at the level of the individual in terms of our attitude to paid work. At the corporate level there is something about our modern western life that particularly focuses on success in the commercial environment and tends to ignore other dimensions of life. It is reflected in the attitudes of successive governments whose underlying message is always that the health of the economy is the real arbiter of the success of our culture. Economic success is the *sine qua non,* the one thing we must have and the one thing to which all else should be referred.

It is an attitude that stems from the Enlightenment and its pseudo-scientific, rational approach to life. Adam Smith's logic was captivating. Do this and all will be well, he proclaimed. Despite the challenges that the Industrial Revolution brought and the modifications to his theory that our history has insisted on, our essential mind-set has remained unchanged. We still think that the marketplace is where we will find all that is good for us. A.N. Whitehead, the philosopher of science, said that Smith's logic 'riveted on men a certain set of abstractions which were disastrous in their effect on the modern mentality.'[1] One of those abstractions was that the individual was the one who really counted in life. It went together with the Enlightenment's great failure to expound any adequate moral theory which could articulate our obligations to one another. So we were on our own. The greatest struggle of the western persona was to be the

---

[1]   Whitehead quoted in Daly and Cobb, *For the Common Good.* p. 35.

self-project, the attempt to establish oneself while being merely an atom adrift in a great marketplace. It is not surprising that such an environment would mean that vast numbers would identify their own personal struggle for success with how they were doing in the business world.

There was also another side to this market dominance of our thinking. It concerned the structures of the marketplace. All conceded that some structures, laws and systems were necessary for the market to function, that people needed some boundaries within which to compete, but the structures of the marketplace have never been seen in the same way as other social systems. Instead an economist such as Hayek would argue that market structures must always remain contingent upon circumstances and therefore in constant flux.[2] A properly functioning company must continually adapt and change in order to maintain its competitive position. This meant that the company as a social order had no intrinsic value, no value in and of itself. Its structure, numbers and even its existence were continually up for grabs as it sought to adjust to a changing market environment. 'Change is on the agenda. Continual change is the order of the day,' say the market gurus. As technology advances, so does the speed and reach of change. Davidson and Rees-Mogg suggest that the company of the future will be analogous to the film production company that sets up for a moment and then disbands.[3]

This sort of process needs thinking about with reference to our nature as animals. In chapter two we noticed that one of the fundamental tasks of the social animal is to maintain the tension between the individual striving to succeed and the need to value the social order itself. In that light it is questionable whether the modern company is a social order adequate to the role it now plays in human society. The extraordinary nature of the company

---

[2] An in-depth review of Hayek's thinking can be found in Crowley, *The Limitations of Liberalism*.

[3] Davidson and Rees-Mogg, *The Sovereign Individual*.

as a social institution can be illustrated by comparing it with other forms of social group. Consider a village where every now and then lists appear on lampposts of villagers who are required to move out. How would that feel? Psychologically it might bear comparison with those rural villages of wartime France where young men were rounded up at random and shot in response to resistance activity. Or think of a school in which the head teacher was accustomed to read out in assembly the names of pupils the school could no longer accommodate. They were to return and clear their desks immediately after assembly and leave the premises. They would have to find a new school. This is the social environment of the modern company. Psychologically it is bound to accentuate an individualistic, survivalist mentality as the individual struggles to succeed in a hostile environment.

This social deficit is exacerbated by the penetration of the market mentality into almost every area of western life. The introduction of market accountabilities into our public institutions may be a necessary means of reform (chapter eleven will take this further), but 'marketisation' also serves to increase social inadequacy. Health workers, schoolteachers and even local government employees now feel under the same threat as the worker in a company. The threat of redundancy hangs over all. 'You are surplus to requirements. It is necessary,' says big brother. And of course in one sense it is necessary. We must have accountabilities and we need to search to benefit from structural changes made possible by new technology. But efficiency is not the only value in human society. We need relationships.

Large structural change is currently being forced onto the agenda of every part of western society. The market is a major influence in this process, but it is not the only factor. Technological progress has led to far greater mobility for the whole society. Our ability to move around naturally undoes the potential for stable relational networks. We send children off to university. There they mix with people from across the country and are very likely to meet their long-term partner in life. They cannot live close to both sets of parents. They may be hundreds of miles from each other. So they live close to neither. Anyway their career demands that they go here and there. A whole series of career moves prevents them settling in one area. One bank manager said to me, 'I only plant grass in my garden. It's not worth doing anything else, because I know that soon I will have to move.' The career dictates the agenda. Few stay long enough anywhere to establish the routines that lead to trust and delayed tit for tat behaviour, and that ultimately builds local communities.[4]

The consequence of all this is that the solidarity of the extended family is lost and the local community diminishes to dormitory status. We might have all sorts of good intentions to keep up with friends, care for relatives hundreds of miles away and all the rest, but the brute fact is that we will not do so. The nature of society will prevent us. Instead we are prey to a market mentality that does not value relationships in the way that we are built to do. The dominance of the market in western society has led us to a situation where we are being forced to behave in ways that are deeply out of kilter with our psychological make-up. Let me explain what I mean.

It was a fundamental arrogance of the Enlightenment to assume that we could build human society into any shape we liked. We may be very adaptable, but we are fools to ignore our basic psychological make up. The psychology of the human animal was formed in face-to-face relationships. Systems of trust grew up through stable relationships, good memories and effective disciplines. Furthermore, it was in this relatively small world of face-to-face relationships that the most basic predispositions of our minds were laid down. For example, we came to value the social order, seeing ourselves not just as individuals, but as individuals-in-relationship. Relationship with others became the means by which we reflected on our own identities. As a person

---

[4] A fascinating and lively account of the degeneration of relationships in the west can be found in Schluter and Lee, *The R Factor*.

greeted us so they affirmed our existence, our place in the world. As we conversed we negotiated the way we saw life, told stories and sought truth. So human society grew up in such a way that the individual human beings needed quality relationships with others for their own sense of worth and their own sense of identity.

The Independent ran an autobiographical article by Neil Crossley entitled 'The loneliness of the long-distance tele-worker'. It told of a couple who decided to leave a busy life in London and bought an idyllic thatched cottage in Devon. Neil was a journalist and had decided to work freelance from home. After three years he began to suffer serious depression. He sought therapy and was advised that his lifestyle was the issue. There was simply not enough quality human interaction. Professor Michael West, psychologist at Aston University was quoted as saying, 'Work colleagues spend a huge amount of time gossiping and kidding each other and discussing their families or what was on TV. That frequent contact, sense of belonging and mutual concern are fundamental human needs. And you don't get that sitting in front of a TV screen.'[5] Given that home working is pre-dicted to rise from the present 1.3 million to 3 million in 2004, we need to take this issue seriously. It will take a major shift in thinking for us to do so.

Putting relationships on the agenda

In the light of these endemic problems faced by western society, it is not surprising that human beings are feeling under pressure. We consult therapists continually to massage our self worth. 'Hasn't she got any mates?' said Crocodile Dundee, hearing of someone who regularly consulted a therapist. And the awful truth is that many today do not have an adequate set of

---

[5] *The Independent, Review,* 1 Nov. 1999.

friendships and do need therapy to keep them on an even keel. Most particularly, it leads to unbalanced lives. As we have seen, our striving to succeed is properly placed alongside, and held in tension with, other deep-level motivations in the human psyche. These include all kinds of relational responsibilities like care for our family, involvement in our local community, or in global concerns. If all these other responsibilities are subverted by the work environment, then the striving for success at work easily becomes addictive.

'Work/life balance', as it is strangely titled, is a major issue today for many responsible employers. Yet it is notoriously hard to handle. It is now assumed that everyone does, or should take paid work. That means that no one works voluntarily 'in the community'. Unpaid motherhood is replaced by the paid nanny, such a change being an apparent improvement as measured by its contribution to GDP. This in itself is a sign of the dominance of the marketplace. Likewise many are working massive hours. They may have leisure, but it is when no one else is around. I know a young man who works for a major retail chain. He has recently got married. He has also recently become a Christian. Yet he is only allowed one weekend in twelve off work. His wife works as an estate agent. How are they supposed to maintain friendships or keep up with relations, let alone each other? How can he nurture his new faith adequately? His plan is to get out of retail. That means lots of study in the evenings and is yet more pressure on their young marriage. They are not alone in living lives that feel subject to enormous stress.

So how can we break out of the chains that bind us? A beginning can be made by simply putting relationships on the agenda. Even the efficiency of the workplace is dependent on good relationships. Oliver Williamson's transaction cost analysis of companies points to the importance of relationship within and between firms, as a crucial indicator of potential performance. Similarly Coleman, Putnam and Fukuyama and other 'social capital' theorists have all highlighted the need for good relationships within any society that is to have a flourishing economy. Such analyses engage with the idea of the economy as a system of trust which is therefore deeply embedded and dependent on all the other systems of trust that make up a flourishing culture. Nevertheless the social capital story does not quite tackle the root of the problem. Typically an argument along such lines will say something like, 'These particular social institutions or general attitudes are important to the economy. Attend to them and you will do better.' Such analysts are basically in agreement with the dominating theoretical commitment that says the market is what matters. Success is still defined solely by reference to the market. This is the root problem. For as we have seen such a view of success is partial. It needs to be brought into tension with other values or it remains an addiction. An alcoholic is told that they must confront their addiction to alcohol. It is time that we confronted our narrow commitments to success. For these are our chains.

Questioning success

Of course we are not the first society to discover the need to tackle these issues. As we saw in chapter three, striving for success naturally translated itself into religious terms. People expected that if they got it right with God they would be successful in life and a huge amount of religious activity continues in the world on this basis. In the Judaeo–Christian tradition the focus on one God served to integrate the competing claims of individuals or sections of the society into the search for what was good for all. In chapter six we saw how the prophets forced the perspective of the poor into the public arena. In general terms the work of the prophets might be said to have made the connection between success and justice. Since God was good, then obedience to God was going to demand justice. Only if they behaved justly would they be successful. So Micah would proclaim, 'He has shown you, O man, what is good; and what does the law require of you but to do justice and to love kindness and to walk humbly with your God.'[6] So the prophets served to force a bigger story onto the people, one that insisted that the society be treated as a whole. They began to ask the hard questions about purpose and of what success would really look like. Nevertheless, they never quite confronted success itself. In other words they said, sort out your lives, sort out our systems, make them just, fair, merciful and kind and then we shall all do well.

For the Old Testament prophets suffering and failure were almost always signs of something being wrong. This was part of the commitment to a God who was good. If God was good, then people must get what they deserved. If they did right, they would be blessed. They would succeed. If they did wrong calamity would come. It was a powerful theoretical commitment and it encouraged considerable moral development as, when disaster loomed, the people felt the need to listen to all sorts of accounts of what may be wrong with their behaviour in God's eyes and even entertained the painful and offensive words of the prophets. But in the end this whole theory about the link between obedience to God and success was to prove inadequate. At a personal level there were so many examples of apparently unjust suffering. And there were rogues who did well. 'Why do the wicked prosper,' cried Jeremiah, no doubt echoing the voices of many. In response the community let into its tradition some extraordinary stories. It told the story of Job, the righteous man who nevertheless suffered terrible tragedy, who struggled to find out why, and found that there was ultimately no answer. He had done nothing wrong. Likewise the community in exile in Babylon told a mysterious story of a suffering servant.[7] The success theory was under strain. These stories were suggesting the revolutionary theory that God might allow innocent suffering.

---

[6] Micah 6:8.
[7] Isaiah 53.

Finally in the story of Jesus there was what we might call a 'paradigm shift'. This term has previously been used to describe major changes in the overall worldview of science.[8] For example, as the mechanical worldview of Newton gave way to relativity, so people had to come to terms with a whole new way of seeing the world. It involved a mental revolution, or paradigm shift. A similar seismic change in thinking occurred as the community of faith came to modify their success paradigm. The story of Jesus came to demonstrate that God could actually call people to a path of suffering in this life. Success was no longer the necessary sign of obedience to God.

This great change in thinking was made logically possible by the prior commitment to God as good and the different ways that this can be understood. If God is good then God must act justly, but how such justice worked out was open to interpretation. In the Old Testament the prophets largely interpreted this in terms of God acting by means of specific interim judgements in the life of individuals and nations. So people got what they deserved. The exile was God's punishment for a nation that had gone astray.

Interestingly this was often pronounced as a future judgement. It was predictive, not yet fulfilled. Such looking to God for future judgement would occasionally result in visionary statements that transcended the here and now, and appeared to look to a final judgement and a whole new world order. So Micah speaks of the people drawn to judgement around the mountain of the house of the Lord. The language is of justice, 'he shall judge between many peoples', but it is also idealistic, 'neither shall they learn war any more'.[9] Similar considerations apply to third Isaiah where the prophet speaks of 'new heavens and a new earth'[10] so implying that a whole new situation was coming and that justice

---

[8] See, for example, Kuhn, *The Structure of Scientific Revolutions*.

[9] Micah 4:1–7.

[10] Isaiah 65:17–25.

would be done. These visions of hope were a foretaste of the New Testament paradigm, but they never became the focus of life in the Old Testament era. The working paradigm remained that justice would be seen in this life. Blessing was for those who lived rightly.

Jesus lived in a time of particular religious ferment where people readily envisaged the possibility that God would break into the world with great power in a final sense, and so create a whole new situation. Jesus' own proclamation of the kingdom of God built on this and became the new paradigm. But it still had a now *and* not-yet quality about it. Something of God's judgement was actually breaking in on the world through Jesus' own actions, yet much would remain until the final act of God, the coming of the kingdom in all its fullness. At this point the *focus* of the working paradigm changed from justice in the here and now to justice in the form of a final vindication. It meant that you did not necessarily get your just desserts in this life. All would be revealed on the last day, the 'day of judgement'. This change allowed that God could both be fully just *and* allow that his innocent people should have to suffer through their earthly lives, even unto death. Justice would await the final judgement. Jesus' own suffering summed up the new teaching.

Taking a risk for what is right

So what has that got to do with us? If we recap on the story of the market in the Bible as outlined in chapter six, we can identify three stages in the development of the Jewish understanding of what was right and good for humans in this area. A first stage is illustrated by Solomon. In our terms he stands for market dominance of society: the nation's success was measured predominantly by its trade. He failed to consider all sorts of injustices that were to undermine the very integrity of the nation. In national terms he stands for western governments whose policies are oriented entirely around market success. In terms of the company, this stage is exemplified by the dominance of win/win thinking. Such companies see trade as the be all and end all of their purpose. All other considerations, for staff, for the environment, the local community or any other interaction with the wider culture are largely off limits to their minds and their policies. Trade is all there is. This is the view championed for thirty years by the economist Milton Friedman. He said, 'there is one and only one social responsibility of business – to use its resources and engage in activities designed to increase its profits.'[11]

At the next level of development, we have the prophetic era. The prophets forced the stories of the poor onto the agenda of the wider society. We saw in chapter six how this process was mimicked in this country by the aftermath of the Industrial Revolution as a variety of forces in society provoked debate and constrained the activities of the new factories around a larger human agenda. In terms of the companies of today, this stage of development is analogous to those companies that have accepted the need to demonstrate some community responsibility. They may be concerned for their staff at a real and personal level. They may be concerned to hear the voice of all that have a stake in the company and may monitor its potential environmental impact. They may work with the idea of social capital, centring on teamwork and the development of sensitive forms of appraisal. They may seek membership of 'Investors in People'. Yet for all their concern, their bottom line remains the same. We will do all this *providing* it does not materially affect our profits. So all the promotional literature for new socially responsible initiatives will be at pains to stress that actually it is good for the company too. In some way it will feed in to better profitability. It is in their interest to take this socially responsible step. Like the prophets, they have not yet truly confronted the success paradigm. They are still working within it.

---

[11]   Quoted in 'Doing well by doing good', *The Economist*, 22 April 2000.

The final stage and the only stage that could be truly identified as Christian becomes far more problematic. The Christian
position embraces a willingness to do all that the prophets called
for, working for the big vision of society and planet, yet it further
includes the possibility of suffering. In other words there are situations where governments, countries and individual people are
called to take a risk in order to do what is right. I need to earth
this to make it clear. At the governmental level, the slave trade is
an obvious example.

The cities of Bristol and Liverpool owed much of their wealth
to the notorious 'triangular trade' which involved taking slaves
from Africa to the New World, then goods from the New World
back to England. Many of the merchants in Bristol argued
strongly and used all their influence to prevent those who would
abolish slavery from having their way. There was a serious possibility that the economy of these major cities would suffer a
terrible recession in the event of abolition and that this could
even have a knock-on effect on the whole economy. The government of the day took a risk for what was right in abolishing
the slave trade. It was no doubt a careful and calculated risk, but
nevertheless it was a risk and it was based on moral criteria, not
economic ones. This is an example of Christian behaviour.

The countries of the world today face other major problems.
Many of the world's economies are held in the chains of debt.
Dare we take the risk of debt release? If we do we need to do so
wisely and carefully; but to do so would be to take another, albeit
very slight, risk for the sake of what was right. Or again, how are
we to manage the possibility that our economic activity might
destroy the very planet or at least cause damage to our long-term
future? Our current concern is with global warming. Dealing
with it will demand an extraordinary co-operation between the
countries of the world, many of whom have yet to benefit from
the technologies of modernity that have produced the problem.
It will require a new level of moral imagination to confront the
issue adequately and ultimately our being prepared to embrace a

certain risk as countries bind themselves to behaviour that may jeopardise their own economic position. Just like the slave trade, it will be a hard issue. Just like the slave trade, it is also a vital one for our future.

In terms of the company, this Christian position should not be seen as a call to stupidity. Market realities cannot be ignored or any company will rapidly go under. What can be done, however, is for a company to think imaginatively about its relationship to the community around. For example, Auchan, one of France's largest supermarket chains had a store in an area ruled by violent gangs. Disruption of trading forced them to consider closure, but they had the imagination and courage to do something interesting. They took the risk of employing the leaders as security guards. At first it was hard, the gang members were scarcely sociable, late and difficult. Over time it worked. The new security guards became socialised and the store was able to stay open in a difficult area. It was only a marginal risk for a company the size of Auchan, but perhaps it shows the principle. McIntosh and others have recently compiled a book full of examples of this sort of activity entitled *Corporate Citizenship*.[12] The key appears to be the use of *imagination* to conceive of several alternative possibilities to a problem, *engagement* with the moral dimension of these possibilities and then careful and managed *risk-taking* in their execution.

This brings us to the possibility of failure. If there is risk, then that means failure is somewhere on the agenda. Some companies who follow such a path will fail. However careful they are, however well they consider and manage the risk element, some will fail. That is the nature of risk. Yet companies are well used to the language of risk. They take risks continually in search of a

---

[12] McIntosh et al., *Corporate Citizenship*. The authors are in fact at pains not to mention the risk element in these strategies, like the social capital theorists, but the examples they give are very helpful in reflection on this subject.

better return, or greater success. Some companies die. The question is what do they die for? Is it perhaps better to die through taking a risk for what is right, than to die simply through a roll of the dice in the great competitive success game?

Finally we should return to the individual worker. Typically in any company there are usually members less principled than themselves. What responsibilities do we as individuals have in such a situation? I would suggest the principle is exactly the same. We are called to see our own situation imaginatively, to think about what real difference we might be able to make for the good. Are there real and practical possibilities for changing aspects of the work environment, for doing the work better, behaving better towards each other or dealing with the office bully? Engaging with these issues morally will lead to careful consideration of a plan of action. This may entail risk, risk for change, risk for what is right. We might then feel called to take the risk. It may go well. Occasionally it may fail and the person lose face in some way or even lose their job. That is a serious matter and no one can or should try to legislate for that, but, in the end, perhaps even that sort of suffering can rightly be on the agenda for the Christian. A friend of mine was the former finance director of a public company and felt that he had to report the managing director for stealing. He had embezzled £60,000. Unfortunately it backfired, the leaders closed ranks and the finance director lost his job. Was he wrong to do it? Working imaginatively for what is right will occasionally involve suffering, yet its potential fruit is also vast. If thousands of people in UK industry took such a line, working relations in this country would be transformed.

Of course such talk brings us face-to-face with the dread of failure. The whole reason that we pursued success in the first place was to be sure of our place in the hierarchy, to improve our standing, or at least tread water. The one thing no one wants is to be seen as a failure. We have a deep dread of failure. Yet failure can be the key to a new door and a larger vision.

Jesus did not want to be seen as a failure. In the garden of Gethsemane, he cried out to God, 'If it be thy will take this cup from me …' He did not want to be seen as a failure, to endure the humiliation and stigma of a criminal dying on a cross, but he added, 'nevertheless not my will but thine be done.'[13] Such is the attitude of the risk taker, the one who is willing to embrace failure if that should come. Jesus felt called to do this thing because it was right. He was doing it for others. It is an inspiring example. And this attitude is actually the way to freedom.

The ultimate answer to an individual breaking the chains of their work, or any other success paradigm that they have embraced, is this willingness to fail in the pursuit of what is right. All our strugglings for success are actually narrow specialist visions. The swimmer pounding up and down the pool is confined in a very narrow world. The middle manager working all hours is also confined to a very narrow world. The strange thing about failure is that it can open us up to a bigger vision, help us to ask the questions relating to what life is really about, what success really means. These are liberating questions.

I suppose this process is illustrated by what we call the mid-life crisis. People in mid-life typically get to a point where they ask the big questions. Why am I striving away like this? My life is half over. What is life really about? This is a sign of someone breaking out of their confines and looking for the big view. It is an agonising process and it is similar to what happens when the track that we have been pursuing in life comes to an end and we face apparent failure. Providing the necessities of life can be met, it is an opportunity to break out and think widely, to start a new path with a greater vision. So perhaps a willingness to embrace failure is an essential aspect to freedom and a truly fulfilled and integrated life? Such a life is only possible if we are willing to confront the addictions of success.

---

[13]   Luke 22:42.

9

Is there such a thing as good politics?

The year 1999 was a fairly typical one in many ways. Serbia attempted to 'cleanse' Kosovo of its Muslim population. There was much bombing and mayhem. One hundred and twenty thousand homes were destroyed and it was estimated that three hundred and fifty thousand people would celebrate the turn of the millennium in tents or patched up ruins and vulnerable to a freezing climate. In Indonesia, the government continued its long persecution of the East Timorese people, but a referendum on independence brought matters to a head, and a serious attempt was made to forcibly transport or eliminate the population. The year ended in Russia with the Chechen people being killed and driven from their homes by a Russian army purporting to be avenging acts of terrorism. Some houses in neighbouring Ingushetia had to accommodate up to seventy people that winter, and there were thirty thousand in tents or disused railway carriages.[1] It adds up to a bleak picture and should impress upon us that human civilisation has yet to learn the secrets of good politics. Indeed we might cynically ask, 'Is there such a thing as good politics?'

---

[1] Justin Huggler, *The Independent*, 25 Nov. 1999.

The heart of political struggle

In chapter two we saw that any social animal has a fundamental conflict of interest. As an individual it needs to propagate its genes. On the other hand as a social animal it is committed to the belief that working with others is better than working on your own. This translates in human societies into a continuing tension between upholding the social order and protecting the diverse interests of the individuals within it. The simplest way to resolve this conundrum is the power hierarchy.

The power hierarchy is a trust of a kind. Animals accept the dominance relationships of the group most of the time. They will always be looking to improve their status within the group and will make challenges for power, but at the same time they will value the relative order of their life as a group. There are real fruits to the co-operative venture. It is certainly better than the war of all against all. Although there is a power implicit in the system, the actual amount of damaging violence is limited by a careful assessment of power through threat displays. A threat is often enough to maintain the social order, so there will be moments of challenge as individuals or alliances reach out for power, and also there will be peacekeeping strategies to ensure that the whole system does not dissolve and chaotic violence break out. Each of these behavioural tendencies is reflected in deep level motivations, which are shared between humans and primates and include both status seeking and peacemaking.

I would suggest that the simple power hierarchy is the default condition for human societies, that is, it is what happens when all else fails. Human societies are able to develop all sorts of complexities and accountabilities to modify the power hierarchy, but underneath it all a substratum of power remains as the most basic organising force in every human social group. The social anthropologist, Radcliffe-Brown said that politics is 'that part of the total organisation which is concerned with the maintenance or establishment of social order, within a territorial framework, by the exercise of coercive authority through the use, or possibility of use, of physical force.'[2] This is the language of the power hierarchy. And it is most evident when other more subtle systems of trust in a society break down.

Norman Davies has noted the extraordinary similarities between totalitarian systems of society and criminal fraternities. Both operate on strict hierarchical lines, exact slavish obedience and work by fear, spying and brutal terror. He speaks 'of the Nazis special style, where studied bestial ferocity had to compensate for the structural weakness. A high level of well-publicised brutality was required simply because more refined instruments of control were often lacking.'[3] A modern example would be the paramilitary groups of Northern Ireland. Mistrust of external law grew to such a degree among the closed sectarian communities that conventional policing lost its hold on the community and the real political order was upheld by the paramilitaries. In this scenario a 'punishment beating' was an enforcement of law and order. A perpetual thief would be kneecapped. Justice was based on rumour and mistakes of identity were regularly made. There was little subtlety in terms of sentencing. Yet it was an order of sorts, an order re-emerging out of chaos. And it has all the hallmarks of the simple power hierarchy. Groups who need to establish their identity on the edges of a culture are always prone to such behaviour, particularly since their strategy for power often demands a high degree of loyalty. The Luddites similarly had a military character, extracted solemn binding oaths and viciously ostracised those who broke their trust. Framebreaking was a capital offence; it was vital that there were no informers. Those who fell out with the hierarchy were frequently reduced to begging or chose to emigrate.[4] Power is

---

[2]   Radcliffe-Brown in the 1940 introduction to *African Political Systems* edited by Fortes and Evans-Pritchard.

[3]   Davies, *Europe – A History*, p. 975.

[4]   Thompson, *The Making of the English Working Class*, p. 631ff.

always on the agenda of a human society, but the essence of human culture is to develop better and more refined systems of trust to overlay it and mitigate its worst effects.

Making progress through balances of power

Political progress is rather like a game of snakes and ladders. The first square is the simple power hierarchy. Every step beyond that is part of a journey in which the fragile bonds of trust that hold a society together are maintained and developed. If at any time this basic trust fails, then the society slips down the snake so to speak and reverts to the simple power hierarchy.

The first step away from the simple power hierarchy is the development of alliances for power. In chapter two we noted that primate colonies are of different types and that the most benign hierarchies are typically found amongst animals that develop complex alliances.[5] Alliances, as we saw, develop naturally and are particularly prevalent among animals that share a common interest of some sort. The common interest provides a platform for tit for tat behaviour leading to mutual trust. Similarly a healthy human society has a plethora of intermediate associations, each of which can present an appropriate challenge to power.

Clearly many of our lobbying organisations are interest groups. We have trades unions, environmental groups, industrial organisations like the CBI, the Road Hauliers Association, the National Farmers Union and a host of others. At the same time we have established seats of learning, a judiciary and several tiers

---

[5]   I noted in chapter two, and I restate here, that alliance formation is not the only important factor in mitigating the brute power hierarchy. Other relational aspects are important such as the nurture of social sympathy, the development of peacemaking strategies and the ease with which a colony may be left. Any of these make for fruitful reflection on our politics.

of government, all of which add a complexity to our power structure. These all work together to allow for the development of accountabilities between the various groups. Yet such groups are not formed overnight and the complexity of their interaction develops and changes subtly over time. The development of the balance of power in this country has occurred gradually during the course of the last millennium. The power struggle between the monarch, the nobles and parliament has been proceeding for almost all that time. Its importance was defended by Charles I in 1642. He said,

> There being three kinds of government among men (absolute monarchy, aristocracy and democracy), and all these having their particular conveniences and inconveniences, the experience and wisdom of your ancestors has so moulded this out of a mixture of these as to give to this kingdom (as far as human prudence can provide) the conveniences of all three, without the inconveniences of any one, as long as the balance hangs even between the three states.[6]

He was facing a dramatic change in this balance as parliament made a challenge for outright power. Later there would be a partial reversal. In our own days we are witnessing the reform of the House of Lords. Charles was right about the balance of power. It is a good thing. Yet it can be expressed in far greater subtlety than these three orders of 'governmental being'. For example, it is clearly advantageous to develop a balance of function. Our own complex interplay of executive, legislature and judiciary has evolved over time and is precious. The Americans took tremendous trouble to copy this sort of principle into their constitution when they declared independence from us.[7] The extraordinary importance of a balance of power is that it can

---

[6] Harrison, *Democracy*, p. 67.
[7] Ibid.

result in a situation where everyone is accountable to someone else. So power becomes clothed with responsibility.

One sign of an emerging tyranny is when the leader acts to unravel such complex interrelationships. Hitler was a chief example of this. On the infamous 'Night of the Long Knives' in 1934, he commanded the SS to kill all his major rivals. He then proceeded to dissolve all other parties and declare himself both Chancellor and President. A balance of power is important and is something to be greatly valued. Anthony Sampson said this of Britain in 1962:

> The rulers are not at all close-knit or united. They are not so much in the centre of the solar system, as in a cluster of interlocking circles, each one largely preoccupied with its own professionalism, and touching others only at one edge … they are not a single Establishment but a ring of Establishments with slender connections. The frictions and balances between the different circles are the supreme safeguard of democracy.[8]

Jeremy Paxman, who uses this quotation, points out that all was not quite as rosy as it seemed, for access to this ruling elite was at that time still strictly controlled by a system of schooling and by tightly guarded relational networks, with the result that much of the power was exercised in a manner quite unaccountable to ordinary people. Nevertheless the presence of such balances of power is crucial to a good body politic. One view of the present difficulties of many governments in Africa is that radical disruption brought about by powerful western influence has destroyed the strength of their institutional life and so prevented the development of such stabilising balances of power.

---

[8] Paxman, *Friends in High Places*, p. 17.

Upholding the social order

At a psychological level, one vital stabilising influence in political development is love of the social order. We simply love the social world we know. It is the world we can negotiate with safety. We know its landmarks. We know where threats lie. The social order brings us safety. So we develop festivals and celebrations to act as a focus for the social order. It might be the last night of the Proms. It might be Remembrance Day, or a Harvest festival. Each will have their stated reason for being, but underneath each is the deep-rooted desire to celebrate and affirm the social order of which we are a part. One of the deep reasons for many of the biblical festivals was likewise to draw people together and acknowledge their common identity, so reinforcing the social order.

Perhaps the greatest exponent of this natural human tendency to love the social order was Edmund Burke. While Burke's views on situations such as that which prevailed in Ireland were liberal and reforming, the situation in immediate post-revolutionary France provoked an enormous reaction from him. His *Reflections on the Revolution in France* has since become a classic text for all who love and uphold the established order. For Burke the social affections begin in the family and his large and inclusive family life was home base for his life and thinking:

> To be attached to the subdivision, to love the little platoon we belong to in a society, is the first principle (the germ as it were) of public affections. It is the first link in the series by which we proceed towards a love to our country and to mankind. The interests of that portion of social arrangement is a trust in the hands of all those who compose it.[9]

Burke viewed the order of society as a precious inheritance to be treated with great respect and in large part not accessible to

---

[9]   Burke, *Reflections of the Revolution in France* (1790), p. 135.

rational enquiry. Britain had evolved in a continuous line from the days of the Magna Carta. Great energy had gone into maintaining a royal succession in order to secure the peace of the realm. Laws like habeas corpus or the petition of right were passed down through the generations. Our inheritance functioned as a constitution that could take on new ideas while retaining that which was good from the past. Burke looked for statesmen who had 'a disposition to preserve, and an ability to improve taken together'. And what he deplored was the sweeping away of everything in France. He sensed that there was an arrogance about the reasoning of Revolutionary France that had to lead to trouble. Much of what made a culture work was not known, and to sweep all away was to risk a breakdown in the instruments of trust that held it all together. 'I cannot conceive,' he said, 'how any man can have brought himself to that pitch of presumption, to consider his own country as nothing but *carte blanche*, upon which he may scribble whatever he pleases.'[10] Burke prophesied violence. As the reign of terror unfolded in France he was to see his prophecy fulfilled. There was something evidently right in his diagnosis. Love for a social order is not an idle love. The consequences of social chaos are tragic. In our own time people of African states like Sierra Leone, who have known years of social unrest, can testify to the destructive effects of disorder and to the violence, fear and despair that inevitably give rise to brutal new regimes.

Allowing challenge

Yet there is another side to all this. There is also a proper anger to be expressed by those who feel left out of a social system. The people who uphold the social order most strongly will include those who benefit most by that social order. That is why it feels

---

[10] Ibid., p. 266.

good to them. They are doing very nicely thank you and want to keep things as they are. They want to maintain their place in the hierarchy. But there are always others who feel excluded or unjustly treated. They will naturally be challengers of the system.

In Burke's day there was another prime mover. He was Tom Paine and he saw life differently. He was born the son of a corset maker and was poor and an outsider to the establishment of England. He embraced the thinking of the Enlightenment and found in its quest to test everything by reason a powerful tool with which to question the world of his day. 'Why uphold the aristocracy?' he railed at Burke. 'For what reason are they in power?' Why should we trouble ourselves about kings and their succession? It is a farce. The whole, English, so-called 'constitution' derives from 'a French bastard landing with an armed banditii and establishing himself king of England against the consent of the natives ... The plain truth is that the antiquity of the English monarchy will not bear looking into.'[11]

So the English king was no more than the 'royal brute of England'. Paine challenged the logic of Burke and on his own terms succeeded. These things could not be justified by reason alone. Yet the logic of the Enlightenment actually had no way of valuing what Burke valued. It could take no account of that vital tacit knowledge hidden in culture but inaccessible to rational enquiry. The French Revolution had produced a radical disruption of the social order and did not have the means to co-ordinate its life adequately without sliding down the snake to a brute power hierarchy, including Madame Guillotine, Robespierre and countless bloody coups. Paine himself was to discover the error of his ways, for within a few years, he fell out of favour in the increasingly violent France, was thrown in prison and in fear of death.

Yet in a sense Paine represents 'the challengers' well. They are people who stand on the edge and are brave enough to offer

---

[11]　Paine, *Rights of Man* (1791), p. 9.

criticism. He was angry and drew people with him. His book the *Rights of Man* sold two hundred and fifty thousand copies in two years and has been accounted the foundation-text of the English working class movement. Paine's own efforts continue to inspire. He was the first to advocate the sort of society that would include a welfare state. He insisted that the only legitimacy for government was the consent of the people. Paine was a challenger. He experienced and sympathised with the oppression felt by all who are unjustly treated by an established power. The establishment will always uphold the social order and suppress challenge. Walter Brueggemann's *Hope within History* says that establishment people naturally tend 'to manage the process, deny the hurt, eradicate the ambiguity. In a word they want to nullify and silence the voice from outside which keeps calling attention to that for which the system cannot account.'[12]

In the history of the UK we have a host of examples of this sort of behaviour. In 1807 the state was considering the possibility of sponsoring education. There was considerable opposition. One Mr Giddy, later to be President of the Royal Society, said that 'However specious in theory the project of giving education to the poor, it would be prejudicial to their morals and happiness; it would teach them to despise their lot in life instead of making them good servants in agriculture and other laborious employments; instead of teaching them subordination it would render them fractious and refractory.'

Subordination was the key motive, I suspect, behind Mr Giddy's ideas. Keep them in their place. Similarly the movement for electoral reform at that time met fearsome opposition, not least from the church. Reform agitators were brutally suppressed and accused of undermining the constitution. Magistrates and clergy were reported to go round pubs recruiting mobs to go and burn down the houses of known reformists. These mobs frequently marched under the banner of 'Church and King'. The

---

[12] Brueggemann, *Hope Within History*, p. 57.

chemist, Joseph Priestley, lost his books and laboratory to such a mob. Various laws were passed against sedition and leading reformers were tried and threatened with the death penalty. Fortunately few were killed, though many were transported.

The essential task

This leads to a conclusion. The essential task of any good politic is both to creatively uphold the social order and accept appropriate challenge. It is in effect to hold the tension between people like Burke who justify the system and people like Paine who properly challenge it. It is only in such a wrestling embrace that political progress can truly be made.

Martin Luther exemplified both sides of the dialectic in his own person. On the one side he was an extraordinarily brave challenger. The Catholic church at the time was trading on the fear of ordinary people by selling indulgences and thereby raising money for its own hierarchy. Beginning with this abuse, Luther launched a barrage of attacks against the Catholic hegemony using the Bible as a tool of liberation. Yet he also unwittingly inspired the rural folk of Germany who were suffering terrible hardship at the hands of their clerical landlords. When they gained access to Bible teaching, they were given new hope. 'It has until now been the custom of the Lords to own us as their property. This is deplorable,' they declared, 'because Christ redeemed and bought us with his precious blood, the lowliest shepherd as well as the greatest lord.'[13] How would Luther react to such sentiments? We might hope that he would rejoice that these people had also found liberating good news in the Bible. Yet Luther was by now beginning to feel responsible for the new social order that was in the making. There were seismic shifts in authority

---

[13] Hastings, *A World History of Christianity;* see essay by A. Pettegree, *Reformation and Counter Reformation*, p. 247.

taking place as secular authority grew to replace papal authority in many areas of governance. He was acutely aware that the social order was fragile. What is more he probably did not really understand these peasants. His own background was among the privileged intellectual fraternities. The result was that when these poor rural workers organised themselves to make a challenge in 1525, Luther advocated their brutal repression. His 'two kingdoms' theology put the power of governance firmly in the hands of the state, giving them an inalienable right and duty to suppress such challenges. He said in justification of state power that 'The hand that wields this sword and slays with it is then no more man's hand but God's, who hangs, tortures, beheads, slays and fights.'[14]

It was both a brutal theology and one that has convinced major parts of the Protestant church that governance is no part of their responsibility. As a result many Protestant Christians today ignore politics and are content to embrace a private pietism.

Yet Luther exemplifies this most basic struggle. The difficulty of the great snakes and ladders game of political progress is how to creatively uphold the social order while giving space for proper challenge and change. Certainly some cultures and belief systems will allow this tension to be held better then others. While Luther and many others have managed to develop oppressive theologies, there is a way of seeing the biblical story as truly pointing towards a much better process.

Political experiences of the Bible

The Bible is a particularly interesting story or set of stories, because it is rooted in the real life events of people and seeks to make sense of those events in terms of belief in a God who is the focus of all goodness, truth and beauty. This means first of all that

---

[14]   Forrester, *Theology and Politics*, p. 31.

it contains reflections on real political processes, but also that these reflections are cast into a tradition that is all the time pressing to know its God. To seek to know God was also to seek what was good in general, good for Israel and indeed good for all human people and communities. God is perceived as the focus of community life and yet is ever only partly known. The unity of the faith acted as a bond holding the community of Israel together, while the fact that God was only ever partly known kept the tradition open to new insight and potential challenge.

I will now try to demonstrate how this worked in practice and intend to use a section of the Bible that is one of humankind's earliest recorded reflections on political life. The story contains a number of really horrific aspects of realpolitik, including ethnic cleansing, which I shall consider further in a later chapter. For now I ask that we simply face the awful reality that was in their world and is still in ours. Human beings have not changed.

One key aspect of any politic is 'Who has knowledge of the good?' or 'Who knows what is good for us?' Is it the philosophers, as Plato taught? Is it the experts of Enlightenment social theory? One rather extreme biblical answer to these questions might be given through the story of Moses at Sinai. As Moses ascended the mountain to receive the commandments, we have one of the most awesome pictures of dominant authority. The authority of God merges with the human and political authority of Moses. He alone can approach God and therefore he alone has access to knowledge about what is good for the people. By contrast the people are cast as rebellious, fickle and unfit for power. The testimony of Moses was to become the fundamental source of appeal for the priests who would uphold the social order.[15] Its

---

[15] Consider, for example, the reforms under King Josiah (2 Kings 22–23), which originate with a book 'found' in the temple. Many scholars believe it to be Deuteronomy. Here the temple priests are using the authority of this book accredited to Moses to restore order in days of social unrest and theological confusion.

authority was vital in the face of competing social and religious forces, but political structures based on this story were to be challenged.

Samuel inherits such a model of priestly authority. The loose tribal confederacy of Samuel's time was a theocracy in which Samuel alone mediates between God and Israel. If the people suffer, it is Samuel who will cry to the Lord and God will raise up a deliverer. No one and nothing else is necessary. The problem for the people was that the priest before Samuel had corrupt sons and Samuel's own sons are poised to take over. They look poor bets for the future. What would happen when he died? The religious tradition and the social order were at stake. Furthermore the Philistines continued to be a threat and the people felt insecure.[16] Some of the elders approach Samuel and demand a king.[17] They encounter opposition, but finally obtain their request and set in train a series of events that will ultimately lead to David's succession to the throne. The political process between Samuel and David is fraught and might justly be described as a power battle. Commentators on these chapters no doubt rightly claim that several sources, both pro- and anti-monarchy, contribute to the whole.[18] Notwithstanding this, it is evident from the reported behaviour of the leaders in question that a real power battle did take place and this affected both Israel's subsequent politics and its theology.

Briefly, Samuel grudgingly accedes to their request for a king, but remains exceedingly wary about the new situation and looks to assert his power over Saul. Saul is entrapped by Samuel into

---

[16] Some have argued that there were also socio–political changes going on in Israel, with a move towards centralisation and new patterns of power. See Gottwald, Frick and Cheney quoted in Brueggemann, *1 and 2 Samuel.*

[17] 1 Samuel 8.

[18] See Brueggemann, *1 and 2 Samuel.* I am indebted to Brueggemann for much of the insight into the political intrigue that follows.

offering sacrifices and is roundly castigated for it.[19] Then Samuel
finds an ancient story of the misdeeds of the Amalekites and
decides without any provocation, that now is the time this score
should be settled.[20] Saul is ordered to engage in a round of ethnic
cleansing. Saul returns from the mission having failed to kill
everyone and everything. This is again interpreted as unfaithful-
ness. In both these situations Samuel is clearly asserting his
authority and the tide turns against Saul. Yet with David, new
hope dawns. The story makes clear God's involvement in the
process of election and the early successes of David. His future as
King is sure, but he too endures a protracted battle for power
with Saul. During the battle Saul exacts terrible retribution on
the priests by the hand of Doeg the Edomite,[21] and relations
between Saul and David degenerate as Saul senses David's threat
to his power.

This thumbnail sketch does no justice to the reality of power
and intrigue which the Bible records. Yet what is so interesting in
these accounts is that the political complexity is matched by a
theological one. Clearly a theological struggle about kingship is
also reflected in these writings. Brueggemann describes chapters
8–15 of 1 Samuel as 'an interpretive reflection on this difficult
and crucial relation between new forms of social relations and an
old, honoured, well-established theological tradition. The settlement between the two came only through an ongoing and
vigorous dispute and required a bold interpretive act.'[22] Overall
the editor of Samuel leaves us with the impression that the monarchy was allowed grudgingly by God.[23] The king was offered
kingship on the grounds that he had certain clear obligations to

---

[19] 1 Samuel 13.

[20] 1 Samuel 15.

[21] 1 Samuel 22:18, 19.

[22] Brueggemann, *1 and 2 Samuel*, p. 58.

[23] 1 Samuel 8:7–9.

God and the people.[24] It was a theology that would preserve a balance of power between priest and king and would be particularly important as the monarchy grew in status and was tempted to forget its obligations. The processes of political and theological change were linked together inextricably.

So we see in this story from the books of Samuel the creation of a balance of power in early Israel. Rule by priest alone becomes rule by king and priests. Later as the civil service developed, so other factors would further complicate and balance the developing power structure. For example, the wise men of the Royal court arose and produced their own theological challenge, from a multicultural and privileged perspective.[25] Such was the developing establishment of Israel. Overall the theology served to uphold the social order but was also able to adapt so as to develop more subtle balances of power.

Most importantly this theology allowed for a radical challenge to the establishment by outsiders, by those left outside the system and so most likely to suffer from it. This on the face of it was a surprising development. We would naturally expect that, despite balances of power in the ruling elite, they would, like other establishments, quite naturally deny the challenge of the poorest members of society. And yet in ancient Israel schools of prophets arose. Often led by people who felt themselves to be outside the system, they provided an acute challenge to the establishment on behalf of the marginalised.[26] In so doing they extended Israel's

---

[24] 1 Samuel 12:14, 15.

[25] The wisdom literature of the Old Testament comes from this source. It includes Proverbs, Ecclesiastes, Job and the Song of Solomon. It is distinctive in not recounting the founding stories of Israel but rather relating to an abstract general 'man' as it interacted with the new multicultural Royal court and so developed a wisdom from a privileged place in the society. See for example Scott, *The Anchor Bible. Proverbs and Ecclesiastes.*

[26] See, for example, Isaiah 5, 58, 59; Amos 8; Micah 2; Jeremiah 5 etc.

sympathies and enlarged their theology. Nevertheless there can
be no doubt that their work was a struggle. At one time
denouncing the wise,[27] at another decrying the temple ortho-
doxy,[28] they were bound to make enemies. The snippets of
biography in Jeremiah testify to their personal suffering.[29] Some
were killed.

Brueggemann notes three essential elements to their challenge. First, they offered a cogent critique of the dominant
ideology. They foresaw the coming exile not only because of
God's inevitable judgement but also because of the nation's
behaviour itself. In other words they were both prophets and
acute social analysts. In fact these two may have been inseparable.
Second, they worked by the 'public processing of pain'. They
brought the pain of suffering people into the public arena in a
formal challenge to the authorities. Third, they released a new
'social imagination'. The visions of such as Jeremiah, Micah or
Third Isaiah opened up the future of Israel to new possibilities,
transcending conventional dogma and reaching forward. God
was God of all. The essential vision of God was of a God over all
and for all. To that God every one was subject, even Israel's leadership, and it was that which allowed for such a challenge.[30]

Earlier we saw the need for a 'wrestling embrace' between the
likes of Edmund Burke who upheld the establishment and the
likes of Thomas Paine who challenged it. I believe in this
account of the prophets challenging the Royal–Temple establishment of early Israel, we see just that reality. It was
accomplished through a particular approach to faith. The beginning of the process was Moses going up the mountain alone. The
challenges of other power elites had broadened the political

---

[27]   Jeremiah 9:12, 23, 24.

[28]   Jeremiah 7:1–7.

[29]   For example, Jeremiah 19.

[30]   For another excellent introduction to this way of viewing the Bible
see Mason, *Propaganda and Subversion in the Old Testament*.

franchise. The visions of the prophets looked for greater possibilities. One of the greatest political and theological contrasts to the Moses paradigm would be uttered by Jeremiah. He said,

> The days are coming, says the Lord, when I will make a new covenant with the house of Israel and the house of Judah ... I will put my law within them, and I will write it upon their hearts; and I will be their God, and they shall be my people. And no longer shall each man teach his neighbour and each his brother saying, 'Know the Lord,' for they shall all know me, from the least of them to the greatest, says the Lord; for I will forgive their iniquity and I will remember their sin no more.[31]

Here was a vision of an inclusive and fully participatory society. Instead of one person having access to God and knowledge of the good, now all have access. The power-dominated society of the Moses paradigm was now contrasted with a vision of trust made possible through the knowledge of God.

I do not propose to examine the New Testament in any detail here. Briefly the social order on the big political level was now being upheld by the Roman authority. This allowed for a very radical reform of theology without disruption of the social order. Yet within the young church portrayed in Acts, the same fundamental processes of power, confrontation and negotiation are very evident as the church developed its theology. In particular the church struggled with the relationship of Jew and Gentile. Could the Gentiles be included in the new covenant and on what terms? It was a struggle that was to include serious confrontations between the leadership,[32] the development of factions within the church,[33] and even a special assembly of leaders in Acts 15 which has all the hallmarks of a political confrontation. These tensions were similarly reflected by the gospel writers as

---

[31] Jeremiah 31:31, 33, 34.
[32] Galatians 2:11.
[33] Galatians 2:12.

they carefully crafted their accounts of the story of Jesus so as to emphasise both the continuity with the Jewish inheritance and the dramatic changes provoked by Christ towards social inclusion. Here again we see politics bringing about theological progress. Ephesians 4 presents a summary of this church politic where the differences between people would be held in a bond of love based on the unity of God. A place where people should 'speak the truth' but in love, within the bond of peace. So the new church takes on the same essential political method of upholding the social order while allowing for proper challenge and embraces the same vision of working towards trust and inclusion.

Also the early Christians never abandoned the notion that what they had to say was relevant to the wider politic. It was implicit in their understanding of the sovereignty of God. As the early church grew in influence, so it would threaten the Roman Empire. Their belief in God automatically threatened the Roman gods and the social order that it justified. Christians died for refusing to acknowledge the deity of the emperor as the same age old political tensions manifested themselves.

So what am I really claiming for this theology? Firstly, one thing that I am not claiming is that the political structures of the faith community evolved towards perfection in the church. Every generation of people and society has to work out its own politics within its own situation. We have seen that the church has developed some ugly brutes of political institutions at times. What I do claim is the following:

1. The processes of Scripture formation illustrate the profound and intimate interaction between politics and theology. On a general level the process shows the vital relationship between political process and the belief system held by a society.
2. The deep structure of such a theology is extraordinarily in keeping with good politics, allowing a creative maintenance

of the social order and yet still being responsive to challenge by those who feel excluded.

3. The process of such theology continually presses toward a vision of an inclusive and participatory society.

4. Yet such theology is very realistic about the practical constraints on a human politic and the processes of power, negotiation and compromise that are necessary to the fulfilment of that vision.

Good politics

The word 'politics' is generally reserved for big government, but I think the above approach can make sense of all sorts of processes in society which are political in the sense of involving power and negotiation. While the main establishment of a society consists of a ruling elite, a well-balanced society actually contains a host of intermediate institutions, all of which might make representation of themselves to authority, but also all of which operate internally by the same processes of power. Thus a Trade Union makes representation to government, but within itself also has the need to uphold its order or tradition and yet allow challenge towards change. For any institution to lose order is to be dissolved; to fail to change, on the other hand, is to become ossified and irrelevant. Despite the fact that the unions in the UK have a deeply held identity, bolstered by stories of struggle, they recently came into internal conflict through their necessary alliance with a reforming Labour Party. Would they be able to cope with a change in the vital clause about public ownership and so sever their links with traditional socialism? It was a fight. The forces of change prevailed and, at least for some, it might be said that the tradition, or belief system, altered.

So society is upheld by, even consists of, a set of intermediate institutions, perpetuating their traditions, engaging in internal and external political struggle and facing challenges that cause them to reflect on their core beliefs. The church is one such institution. It is not above this process even if its members continually try to deny it. Sadly, institutions that ignore such power processes usually suffer for their naivety. Awareness of what constituted good politics might have saved the church much agony in the course of its history.

The political process begins at birth. A child faces the frustrations of maternal care. Food is not always there when required. There are discomforts. The child rages. It becomes aware of its mother as 'another' person, different from itself. The world no longer seems to revolve only round itself. There are 'others' and there needs to be compromise. Every group in society continues the process, bringing us face-to-face with 'other' people, forcing us to compromise in order to work together. It is a healthy, but painful process. Every group has its power structure. A family works out power, perhaps with great and intricate subtlety, perhaps with terrible tyranny or perhaps by never-ending negotiation, but every family has a structure of power. And the way it works out is important. At every level of our human society we need the wrestling embrace with the 'other' who sees the world differently from us, and tells a different story. We need others to enlarge our own grasp on the truth and we need them to see what is best for us all.

So how does all this relate to democracy? I have deliberately steered clear of the 'D' word, simply because everyone thinks they know what it is and I suspect do not. Democracy is seen as a necessarily 'good' word and tends to immediately associate in our minds with a method of decision making. In fact the concept of democracy is far more complex. Democratic decision making can actually be demonstrated in baboons.[34]

Hamdryas baboons forage as a group. Each day they have to decide which direction to set off in. First a senior male figure goes to the outside of the group and sits down facing the

---

[34] Dunbar, *Primate Social Systems,* chap. 11.

direction he thinks they should go. Then others come up to the male, presenting themselves to him, so as to signify their intention to 'vote'. They may go and sit facing an alternative direction. This process continues with other baboons gathering around the one who they think is right. Some shuffling occurs and when an appropriate consensus is achieved, they set out in the agreed direction.

Baboons may vote. What they lack is debate. And in our societies it is the processes of debate that tend to distinguish a good democracy from a charade. The logical justification for 'the people ruling the people', which is democracy,[35] depends on the assumption that, if people of divergent perspectives are somehow brought together and debate, telling their stories of life from their own perspective, then the resulting collective decision will be better than any that the individuals could have come to on their own. It is therefore a process worthy of committing oneself to.

Comparing this to the previous discussion, we can see that the process of facing a person or group up with the perspective of another is precisely what we have been referring to as good politics. What democracy adds to this is partially to build the structures of challenge into the social order itself. Sadly its common conception as a system of voting limits our thinking. Voting is a crude, non-relational process and is the end of a political process not its substance. It is a necessary procedure at a particular level of the body politic, but it can never replace the need for good public conversation with true negotiation and compromise.

If this is right and the groups we all belong to in society are the principle place where we learn that the 'other' is real and that we need to negotiate to work together, then the present disintegration of intermediate institutions in western society becomes a

---

[35] I am indebted to R. Harrison, *Democracy*, for highlighting the importance of debate in democracy.

source of great concern. At every level at the present time, associations between people are weakening. Families are falling apart; churches are losing members; so are Trade Unions. Many groups are bending over backwards to attract the 'consumer' and all are witness to the fact that bonds between people are much looser. The dangerous corollary of all this is that we may be failing to adequately engage with one another so as to force us to political compromises. If we do not like the group, marriage or whatever we get out and find one that we do. Such freedom to escape can be important, but if it means we lose the art of politics itself, then society is threatened.

10

The person in authority

Ernest Saunders was a man of considerable power and he had interesting ways of working. He rarely made records and kept few formal minutes. That gave him a certain freedom of action. He had turned Guinness around. It was now successful and looking for action. So Saunders set up a deal. He arranged for friends, banking colleagues and dealers to buy shares in Guinness so as to raise its share value and enable a take over of Distillers. These allies of Saunders bought £257 million pounds worth of shares, one quarter of the total shares in circulation. In return they received 'kickbacks' for their services of the order of millions of pounds each. Saunders himself once transferred £5.2 million through twenty banks in twenty-four hours. Part of the reason was to cover the fact that three million of this landed in his own account as his own personal pay-off for the deal. Of course he was acting illegally and was found out. The resulting scandal rocked the City of London, many of whose financial institutions were seriously implicated.[1]

The story illustrates some of the tensions about being a person in authority. It shows the perennial conflict between self-interest and public responsibility and illustrates the need for appropriate and enforceable regulation to constrain those who exercise

---

[1] MacLaurin, *Tiger by the Tail*, chap. 7.

power. But from where does all this derive? How can we make sense of it?

Making the powerful act fairly

Our first reference might be to the animal power hierarchy. The simplest hierarchy is an order of power, ruled by fear and threat. The animals at the top have maximum individual freedom, best access to all the necessities of life and need to be ready to fight to maintain their position. Such animals naturally have a concern to protect their status. Yet that is not the end of the matter, for animals in such positions may also be forced by their communities to accept constraints upon their action. This chapter will explore the development of such constraints around people in power such that power becomes linked inextricably with a certain social responsibility. We will show that such a blending of power with social responsibility establishes itself as a system of trust within a community and that the person in power thereby is acknowledged as being in 'authority'.

One of the first and most important stages in this development concerns the duty of fairness. All social animals have, as we have seen, a deeply felt need to uphold the social order. The most obvious one to do this, on behalf of the community, is the animal at the top of the power hierarchy. So it comes to be, for example, that the leader of a chimpanzee colony will often accept the responsibility of peacekeeping. If it looks like a damaging fight is likely to erupt, then such a 'control' male will intervene, asserting his 'authority', threatening both parties and keeping the peace. Frans de Waal has studied thousands of such interventions in primate colonies and makes the extraordinary observation that the control male tends to act fairly, that is, he will specifically not favour his own family or allies when they are involved in a fight. Furthermore when the disputants are unevenly matched, when we might say one was being 'bullied', then the control male intervenes especially to protect the weaker one.[2]

So it seems that chimpanzees at the head of the power hierarchy may naturally come to accept constraints towards fairness in their exercise of power. It could be that such fairness is part and parcel of any conception of a good person in authority. In the Judaeo–Christian Scriptures God is most fundamentally conceived of as the good person in authority, so how is God perceived to act? In precise accordance with this idea, we find a wealth of evidence to show that God is always perceived as acting impartially by those who acknowledge themselves to be under God's authority. It seems this idea of impartiality is linked inextricably to goodness and to the justice that must be displayed by a good person in power. Consider this extract from Deuteronomy: 'The Lord your God is God of gods and Lord of lords, the great, the mighty, and the terrible God, who is not partial and takes no bribe. He executes justice for the fatherless and the widow, and loves the sojourner, giving him food and clothing.'[3] God, as the person in authority, is understood to be fair and even to specifically intervene on behalf of the weak. This concept then becomes the model for human authority in the Bible. The ideal king of Psalm 72 is one who 'judges the people with righteousness and thy poor with justice'. Likewise the righteous magistrate is portrayed in Job as one who is scrupulously fair and has a particular concern for the powerless.[4] Bribery is condemned at many points as an attempt to pervert fair play.

So it seems that from every side of our enquiry, there is evidence of a deep sense that proper authority should carry a certain impartiality. This one principle, in fact, makes sense of a vast swathe of our experience. The battle is always to uphold this principle in recognition that people in authority will experience

---

[2] De Waal, *Good Natured*, pp. 128–32.
[3] Deuteronomy 10:17, 18
[4] Job 29.

real inner conflict between their own narrow self-interest and their public responsibility. They naturally want status, material wealth and recognition. A person at the top of their hierarchy has great power over the others below them. They also have the greater freedom of action. And they will be very keen not to lose this.

Consider the founding entrepreneur. Be it a supermarket chain, a religious congregation, or perhaps a new political movement, founding entrepreneurs enjoy being at the head of their organisations. The very existence of the organisation will affirm them. They will appreciate their status and the freedom of action it confers and being people of considerable creative imagination and executive courage they will prize these things and will defend their freedom to be creative. For all these reasons the founding entrepreneur will not want to share power with others and battles for power are almost certain to erupt.[5] They may ruthlessly defend their position and will do all in their power to avoid the constraints of accountability for fear of limiting their creative imagination or executive freedom. Similar considerations apply to every person in leadership. There will be reasons why they want to protect their executive freedom. Money and status will also be relevant considerations. And the whole package will add up to a natural resistance to any 'rules and regulations'. For some this will include a resistance to those rules designed to make sure they act in a properly impartial manner towards those they have power over.

Any society needs to develop systems of trust that are aware of this deep human conflict around leadership and which carry appropriate and effective disciplines against those who abuse their power. Many of our current issues in public life make sense on the basis of the struggle to maintain proper impartiality. Charges range from simple bribery to deep-level prejudices, but

---

[5] See, for example, the Branson story in chapter six

all are about the person in authority being properly impartial towards those over whom they have power.

For example, consider the ongoing struggles of the London Metropolitan police. Since the Lawrence enquiry, they have had to defend themselves against the charge of institutional racism. The police force is called upon to be impartial among the people they exercise power over, just like the 'control' chimpanzee in their colony. Similarly Northern Ireland is considering how to reshape its own police force in the light of the Patten report and the history of bias in its activities towards Protestants and Catholics. The aim is to recover public trust in the impartiality of policing in Northern Ireland.

Such issues are always at the forefront of our politics. Our newspapers have an important tradition of investigative journalism which aims to uncover corruption amongst those in power. Most of these cases can be understood by reference to this idea of impartiality. For example, Edith Cresson was put in the spotlight for appointing family and friends to top jobs in Europe. Why was this seen as wrong? Because she is a European Commissioner and has responsibilities to think and act towards all the people of Europe with a proper impartiality. The appointment of family and friends to key posts was thought to offer too great a temptation to arrange things in her or her friends' interest and not that of Europe as a whole.

Martin Bangemann was another case in point. He was European Commissioner for regulation in telecommunications. As such he had taken part in ongoing negotiations with Telefonica, a recently privatised Spanish Telecommunications giant. Suddenly he announced that he had taken a job with Telefonica at £700,000 p.a. and tendered his resignation from the Commission. He declared 'I have done nothing wrong', but the public were not convinced. The reason is that he was trusted as Commissioner to deal impartially with the telecommunication companies. The public were right to suspect that the possibility of a job offer by Telefonica may have tempted him to favour that company, making him biased in his dealings with them. In response to such situations our UK ministers have a strict code whereby they cannot accept jobs in industries related to their governmental roles until two years have elapsed since their vacating those roles. Such disciplines help to make for a working system of trust. They help the public to have a proper confidence in the impartiality of their leaders. The issue is always to constrain the person in authority against using their position to further their own, or their allies' interest and against the public interest.

One of the oldest and crudest methods of persuading the person in power to act unfairly is the bribe. In some countries like Nigeria, bribery has been so common that it has been very difficult to function without having recourse to bribes. In our own country, we have seen Neil Hamilton slug it out in court with Mohammed Al Fayed over allegations that Hamilton had received cash in return for asking questions in parliament. It was an unedifying spectacle, but public exposure of abuse by people in power is crucial to the development of public trust. Societies with high levels of corruption become deeply cynical about their leadership. If everyone is getting away with fraud, bribery and corruption, then despair sets in. One of the most important mechanisms for building public trust is an active, free, investigative press operating in a society with freedom of information and freedom of speech. Investigations into cases of corruption are crucial to a well-functioning political system. Public exposure is part of the discipline that prevents others from seeing it as worthwhile.

This process also has biblical resonances. The people of ancient Israel also needed to call their leaders to account for their actions. Their belief system allowed for their 'investigative-journalist-equivalents' to be called 'prophets', implying that their words came with God's authority and therefore must be heeded. It likewise allowed even the highest in the land to be questioned. So Nathan could go to David and accuse him of the conspiracy to murder poor Uriah in order to cover up his liaison with Bathsheeba. Or again, Elijah could confront King Ahab with his conspiracy to murder and defraud Naboth. These were real power struggles. Elijah's life was genuinely in danger, but the challenge was issued and was effective. Israel's kings learnt that they were not above public scrutiny. An effective system of trust arose.

Part of the wisdom of good government is in the design of these systems of trust. Badly designed systems make for almost inevitable corruption. In 1999 both the Labour and Conservative parties were subject to scandals regarding their own funding. The burgeoning requirement to fund political campaigns is an ongoing temptation to politicians. Michael Ashcroft has recently given several million pounds to the Conservative party. This is a substantial proportion of their total income and they have made him Treasurer. In 1999 *The Times* published articles alleging that his dealings in Belize fell short of proper standards for those in public life.[6] Yet the Conservative party are deeply dependent on him. He is their treasure as well as their treasurer: they are bound to treat him with kid gloves. Similarly the Labour party depend greatly on their Science minister Lord Sainsbury.[7] There is concern that his generous donations may influence government on the scientific issues close to Lord Sainsbury's heart and personal interest. Although we might be inclined to think so, the most important issue in both these cases may not be the corruption of the individuals, but that we need a wiser method of funding political parties.

In more general terms any society needs to establish boundaries around its people in authority. The Nolan report came up with seven principles applicable across the board. They were as follows:

---

[6] Letter by David Mackilligin in *The Times*, 16 July 1999.
[7] *The Times*, 9 September 1999.

Selflessness
Holders of public office should take decisions solely in terms of the public interest. They should not do so in order to gain financial or other material benefits for themselves, their family, or their friends.

Integrity
Holders of public office should not place themselves under any financial or other obligation to outside individuals or organisations that might influence them in the performance of their official duties.

Objectivity
In carrying out public business, including making public appointments, awarding contracts, or recommending individuals for rewards or benefits, holders of public office should make choices on merit.

Accountability
Holders of public office are accountable for their decisions or actions to the public and must submit themselves to whatever scrutiny is appropriate to their office.

Openness
Holders of public office should be as open as possible about all the decisions and actions that they take. They should give reasons for their decisions and restrict information only when the wider public interest clearly demands.

Honesty
Holders of public office have a duty to declare any private interests relating to their public duties and to take steps to resolve any conflicts arising in a way that protects the public interest.

Leadership

Holders of public office should promote and support these principles by leadership and example

These principles apply to all aspects of public life. The Committee has set them out here for the benefit of all who serve the public in any way.[8]

These principles can be understood collectively as an attempt to preserve the proper impartiality of those in authority and so build the public trust.

In terms of the global scene, the principle of impartiality has implications for the behaviour of western nations towards the rest of the world. Since the end of the Cold War, the western nations have risen to unchallenged dominance on the world scene. The most powerful international organisations currently include the United Nations, NATO, the World Bank, the International Monetary Fund and the G8 group of countries. There is some internal wrangling within these organisations, but generally it might be said that the western nations are dominant and the United States leads the team. This puts the west in the position of authority figure for the rest of the world. It means that, like the chimpanzees, we naturally begin to take the peacekeeping role. In 1999 we intervened in Kosovo. Then we rather belatedly accepted some partial responsibility for East Timor. As the year ended there was concern as to whether we should act to prevent the destruction in Chechnya. At the same time our economic situation gives us another opportunity to exert tremendous power over the poorer nations of the world. Such power rightly carries the demand for impartiality towards those we have power over. Indeed it requires even a specific favouring of the weak when they are in a serious power imbalance. Yet in

---

[8] From the 'First Report of the Committee on Standards in Public Life' (the Nolan Committee), p. 14.

fact the western nations are currently hopelessly biased in their own favour.

Our media give it away. As we saw in chapter five, western people simply count more than others in our press. At one level this is very understandable. We will of course be most interested in those who are closest to us. This is normal moral development. We start out aware only of ourselves and work outwards. But it will not do for those in authority. The call to them is impartiality. We have got to work to overcome our natural pro-western bias. There are signs that this will come to a head in the next decade or so.

In November 1999, the World Trade Organisation met in Seattle. This is where they set the global trade rules and in the past they have been notoriously biased against the interests of the poorer nations. Many suspect that multinational companies are now controlling the governments on these matters. Yet also present at Seattle were vast numbers of protestors. Their presence was partly co-ordinated on the Internet. The ensuing struggle was dubbed the 'Battle for Seattle' by the press. The conference had attracted people from all kinds of pressure groups, yet they were united in one theme, summed up by this flyer produced by Oxfam: 'At the World Trade Organisation there's no such thing as fair play … not when the major players make the rules to suit themselves.' The call is to impartiality. This issue will not go away, for we sense the injustice at the deepest level of our lives. If the person in power is impartial in the way that they behave, that is a good start. 'Firm but fair' is the old adage that would be applied to someone like a schoolteacher whom a class in fact respected. They kept order and did so without evident favouritism.

Other moral constraints

One further and related constraint on the person in authority is the call to be trustworthy. We have seen that a society is all the time seeking to build and maintain effective systems of trust around those in authority. These require discipline toward those who break trust, but are much easier to develop if people in general feel it is right to be trustworthy. If everyone thinks, for example, that it is really OK to lie and cheat, then it is hard to develop any effective system of trust. Any system of trust depends crucially on most of the people, most of the time not requiring the discipline. If everyone is breaking their word, taking backhanders, and free-riding on the system, then accountabilities are impossible to develop. So the general moral climate is a vital ingredient of a good society and this applies most particularly to those who have power over others. Their potential destructiveness is magnified by the extent of their power. Hence in a good society reputation is of prime importance. Great store is put on reputation and great effort made to protect it. This can, and arguably should, reach the point where the person in authority is willing even to work against their own short-term interest in order to maintain their reputation.

Another word for this would be integrity. Sometimes people in authority should suffer for what is right. Riyadh Ibrahim was Minister of Health in Iraq under Saddam Hussein. It is alleged that Saddam was using the ministry as a cover for the importation of chemicals for chemical weapons. Riyadh is said to have complained about this repeatedly. Finally in the middle of a cabinet meeting, in full view of his other colleagues, Saddam took out his gun and shot him.[9] Should Riyadh have stayed silent? He was between a rock and a hard place. Integrity demanded that he speak. A good society is built on people of integrity.

When British Airways was taken to court by Richard Branson over the alleged 'dirty tricks' campaign, BA settled with Virgin just before the leading BA executives had to give testimony. After the case Bernard Levin commented on the fact that these

---

[9] Ramadan, *In the Shadow of Saddam*.

executives remained in their places at BA. His view was that they should have resigned and thereby acknowledged responsibility for the behaviour of their company.[10] Taking such action would have been deemed a mark of integrity. There are moments when people in authority should suffer personally in order to maintain their reputation as trustworthy and so build a right confidence in the society at large. This principle was expressed by Jesus when he said, 'I am the good shepherd. The good shepherd lays down his life for the sheep. He who is a hireling and not a shepherd, whose own the sheep are not, sees the wolf coming and leaves the sheep and flees and the wolf snatches them and scatters them. He flees; because he is a hireling and cares nothing for the sheep.'[11]

The discussion so far should not be interpreted to imply that there is always a straightforward and self-evidently right path for persons in authority to take. Their role is never simply that of the peacemaker, nor are their issues confined to fairness. People in authority often act as a focus for the conflicts and debates within a society. Their role is therefore never comfortable.

One particularly important and difficult function for a person in authority is that of inter–group negotiation.

Difficulties of inter–group negotiations

People in authority have a vital role in the process of negotiation between collectives in a society. Inter–group negotiation is peculiarly hard. The difficulty derives at least in part from its structure. Typically, a group will appoint a person to represent it in a particular negotiation. Such persons from the different groups would meet together, not in their own capacity, but as representative persons, aware of their groups' own interests and aware

---

[10] Bernard Levin in *The Times,* 15 January 1993.
[11] John 10:11.

that their own power and reputation will hinge on the deal they can strike. They will also be acutely conscious of the fact that any decision that they reach, they will have to sell to their membership later. This awareness of the need to represent others introduces a cautiousness into inter-group behaviour that results in a limitation of moral imagination. While the person, as a human being, might sense the rightness of the settlement they agree to, they know that the whole process will fail if they cannot persuade their membership.

Those who have closely followed the Northern Ireland peace process may have sensed these difficulties. The negotiators seem so intransigent, yet in reality they walk a knife edge, for they must persuade the people they represent to put into action any deal they agree. The question of decommissioning of arms may turn, for example, not on whether Gerry Adams and co. are convinced of the rightness of such action, but rather on whether they still have the influence over the IRA to get them to do so, and whether they can sell it to them in terms that do not imply surrender. It is for this reason that a negotiator is almost always someone near the top of the hierarchy they represent. Most deals are compromises. That implies that ground must be shifted. It takes a person with some acknowledged authority to convince a group that any compromise is worth making.

So inter-group negotiation is fraught with difficulty. Groups of necessity tend to be formed as interest groups and so their interest is intimately associated with their identity. To offend the interest of the group may be to threaten its life. Very few groups will just pack up and die. Reinhold Niebuhr[12] suggested that, because of this, inter-group negotiation had to be seen as having a quite distinct moral base from that which pertained to individual morality. He saw that there would always remain a strong and ineradicable element of pure power in inter-group negotiations. The lack of moral imagination implicit in group dynamics makes

---

[12] Niebuhr, *Moral Man and Immoral Society.*

it so. Groups would never act except in their own interest. There is much truth in Niebuhr's critique, though I believe it inadequate in one respect. Groups can and do act against their own immediate interest in certain circumstances. To understand this we need to digress for a moment on the subject of group identity.

Stories and group identity

Every established group has a past. This constitutes the history of its purposes and actions. These purposes and actions coalesce into a tradition, or a story, that itself becomes a reference point for the future. The important thing is that these stories differ in character. Some are much more open to change than others. The tendency for all stories is to justify the predominant behaviour of the group. This arises quite naturally from the processes of their formation. As they draw together the purposes and actions of the group, they naturally offer an explanatory framework for that behaviour, justifying it. Such justifications can be held so tightly and so exclusively that the tradition is locked in and prevented from change by its story.

A particularly notorious example of this was the development of the Afrikaner tradition in South Africa under apartheid. The story has been told by Desmond Tutu in *No Future Without Forgiveness*. The Afrikaner identity was formed in battle. They saw themselves as re-enacting the biblical exodus as they escaped from British imperialism and occupied their land. On 16 December 1838, a Voortrekker band was attacked by *impis* (that is regiments of Zulus) and, so the story goes, made a solemn promise to God. They declared that if God would deliver them they would remember that day forever as a solemn day of covenant with God. They adopted a new strategy, forming a circle of wagons, or *laager*. The Afrikaners prevailed against enormous odds. Many thousands of Zulus died and 16 December became a sacred day in South Africa from that time on. Thereafter, on that day black people stayed indoors. It was the day of their humiliation, a day for racist bad mouthing and assault. It was around such stories that the myths reinforcing racism were constructed.

Another story helped to identify enemies. This was the threat of communism. For many years all people who raised a voice of complaint against apartheid were likely to be labelled communist. It is no coincidence that the undoing of communism preceded the liberation of South Africa. Additionally the law came to be upheld with a quasi-religious fervour. Tutu describes the judges of apartheid South Africa as 'god-like' in their stature. The law was beyond question. To disobey the law was therefore always and inexorably wrong.[13] These are the sort of stories that countries and cultures can use to justify their activities and affirm their own identities. Yet most of us would argue that such stories are inadequate. Such catalogues of self-justification can hardly allow for openness in dialogue with others. Yet there are other types of story that are able to encourage group identity more creatively.

Churches, for example, are embedded in a web of stories. These are not always as 'spiritual' as they seem. A major element of power in the Anglican church lies in the parishes of which it is made up. In Bristol, I remember a challenge that arose around a proposal that richer parishes should contribute more per head to the common church fund than poorer parishes. In the debate, representatives of the rich parishes were in a quandary. Many spoke for their particular parish's interest, tried to make a case for their peculiar difficulties and said things like 'The congregation simply will not do it.' Yet the church has a bigger story, that everyone was acutely aware of, about the weaker members being especially worthy of support, and this sat uneasily with the justifications of the rich churches. In the end, the proposal was carried, but it felt like a close thing.

---

[13] This perspective on the story of South Africa derives from Tutu, *No Future Without Forgiveness*.

This allows a guarded response to Niebuhr's pessimism which insisted that groups would never act against their own interest. Here we see an example of groups, namely rich churches, who did act against their own perceived interest. The important factor in allowing this sort of flexibility was the presence of a story that bound them in solidarity with others who were weaker. This openness to the 'other' is characteristic of a good story.

To summarise the argument of this chapter so far, we have seen that a person in power is naturally and deliberately constrained by the people they have power over. Such constraints can include a call to proper impartiality, to trustworthiness and to integrity. We have seen how important these factors are to the development of a functioning system of trust whereby people feel a proper confidence in their leadership. Yet people in power also have very real difficulties, as they become a focus for the conflicts within a society, as they mediate in inter-group negotiation and work with the very different types of stories that justify and give identity to these groups. One further factor that needs considering with regard to all people in authority is the way that they exercise their authority. How do they get things done?

How to get things done

With reference to the simple power hierarchy, the crudest method of sorting out issues as the person in authority is to do it by threat. For animals this means the threat of violence. In human cultures we also use the threat of violence. We threaten and smack children. We threaten and bomb other nations. Yet we have also developed other more subtle forms. A parent typically develops a range of threats for dealing with their children. These might include smacking or 'grounding' or the loss of the promised present. All are threats, but they are of different types.

Likewise a schoolteacher will develop a range of 'disciplines', the name on the board, the sending to the head etc., which their pupils learn and press the boundaries of.

Threats are also used against adults. A recent TUC campaign showed that five million people have experienced bullying at work.[14] Some might be bullied by a boss, others by colleagues, but it is all threatening behaviour. A person in work may also be threatened more subtly and indirectly by the withdrawal of public funding for what they are doing. Much of the workforce of the UK currently lives under the continual threat of unemployment. Such is life. But a society that lives solely under the coercive power of threats does not draw the best out of people. There is a better way, but its implementation is not easy.

I intend to argue that the principle alternative to threat as a means of coercion is to make an appeal to people on the basis of a story. A good society is always seeking to move from the use of threat through to appeal by means of story. In order to explain this, I would like us to return again to the Scriptures and to the fundamental understanding of God as the good person in authority. If people understood God in this way, how did they perceive God to act? For example, did *this* good person in authority use threat? The answer to this is clearly, 'Yes.' There are a host of examples of the experiences of the people being interpreted as the threatening action of God. Yet God is not only perceived to act in this way. There are other possibilities and the study of them becomes a reflection on the behaviour of people in authority in general. Let me explain.

Firstly, it is fascinating to note that threat stories about God are mostly concentrated at the beginning of the relationship between God and the people. That is, God is perceived as most threatening when God is least known or understood. For example, there are stories of people dying under strange circumstances. This absence of explanation is often made sense of in

---

[14] *The Times*, 1 December 1999.

terms of them contravening a 'holiness' command. They must have looked into the ark of the covenant.[15] They made the sacrifice wrong.[16] But these sort of events become less common as the story unfolds, the community comes to terms with unexplained suffering and grows in their understanding of God. With the knowledge of God come new possibilities for the way the relationship with God is perceived. One corollary of this in terms of human–human relationships would be the simple observation that threat is most likely to be used when the relationship between people is weakest and the understanding least. The history of international politics has been loaded with threat and has also been characterised by the weakest of relationships between peoples and minimal mutual understanding. Threat is most likely to be used when there is least understanding between people.

My second observation is that moments of perceived threat in the Scripture seem to particularly focus around times when the whole tradition is in danger of falling apart. The Pentateuch, for example, contains a number of stories of a highly threatening nature that would have been particularly used to uphold the religious tradition as it faced the secularising tendencies of the monarchy or of contact with other peoples. Most famous would be the Golden Calf episode. God invites Moses to go up the mountain alone. The rest of the people are told not to come near 'lest God break out upon them'.[17] While Moses is away, Aaron allows the people to make the Golden Calf, simulating worship of other gods. Moses comes down, sees what the people have done and God is understood to be furious. Moses commands the Levites to go through the camp killing with the sword. It is a terrible story, but one that would have been used by the priests to defend the tradition at moments when they sensed its life was

---

[15] 1 Samuel 6:19.
[16] Leviticus 10:1, 2.
[17] Exodus 19.

threatened. Frequently in the history of the people the whole tradition was in such danger of collapse that its very survival was in doubt. It was then, we can imagine, that the story of the Golden Calf episode would have been told. And it was a kind of threat.

This again suggests something general about relationships. We also tend to threaten when we sense the whole thing is about to fall apart. An unremitting squabble among children in a household might be halted by a loud parental shout. A teacher might reserve their most fearsome gesture for the moment when they are about to lose control. A team of directors might face up to the meeting that will decide the future of the company by drawing on every resource, including threat. So threat is used when a community sees itself to be in danger.

So, if that is an account of when threat is most likely to be used, we might suggest that alternatives to threat would arise most obviously as the people grew in their knowledge of God and when the tradition was relatively confident of its identity. Indeed it is so. From the earliest times there was a story developing about the loving purposes of God, but as the Scripture develops so this story is filled out and becomes a source of inspiration and appeal. For example, a prophet like Hosea will threaten in the name of God, but will also use the story of the release from Egypt as an appeal to people, based on the revealed character of God as one who loves. 'When Israel was a child, I loved him, and out of Egypt I called my son. The more I called them, the more they went from me.'[18] Here is a picture then of an appeal on the basis of relationship, on the basis of love and past evidence of concern. The possibilities for such appeal grow as the Scripture grows. By the time of the New Testament, we see appeal being used as the principle means of God influencing human behaviour. So in light of the life and ministry of Christ, the Gospel of John proclaims, 'God so loved the world that he

---

[18] Hosea 11:1.

gave his only son that whoever believes in him should not perish but have eternal life.'[19] This is the ultimate overarching appeal of God to humanity. Threat, in fact, is never quite removed from the story, as the words, 'should not perish' testify, but it certainly falls into the background. The main ground of God's perceived activity as the good person in authority is ultimately the story of God's loving purposes towards people.

The growing knowledge of God in the Scriptures therefore can also be read as something of a study in how any good person in authority should behave. In a positive sense it suggests that all good people in authority should give attention to the building up of relationships and to mutual knowledge and understanding. It further suggests the overriding importance of the stories that give any group their identity, for these can become a fruitful source of appeal in the management of people.

The story concerns the agreed common purposes of the group. In general, it is best generated by an inclusive process of high quality public conversation. A good company mission statement may function in this way. Many companies have worked hard at producing a mission statement that all can identify with. If it is truly owned by the people of the company, it can become a powerful source of appeal when change is in the air.

Deliberate strengthening of relationships in companies is in vogue at present and, I suspect, is of great importance. Many are opting for matrix management styles, which allow for working in teams around projects with little regard to status. The system has a downside in sometimes failing to provide adequate lines of accountability, but in certain situations it can provide for the building of mutual relationship and so reap the maximum benefit from co-operation and trust, with only minimal use of threat.

---

[19] John 3:16.

A less apparently good method of modern management is that of 'Carrot and stick'. This common phrase often denotes techniques that come close to appeal and threat respectively. Yet it is important to ask what particular things are being used as an appeal and what as threat. Often the carrot is not an appeal to story, but a manipulation by pay. The danger of such management is precisely that the term becomes an excuse for the manipulation of people. People are very sensitive to manipulation. The key immoral ingredient of manipulation is persuasion without due regard for the integrity of the people who are being persuaded. People are seen and treated as just 'workers', or 'consumers', or whatever, but not as people in their own right who have their own proper concerns and ability to judge. We rightly hate to be manipulated and sense that the people who do so have no real concern for us.

The fully developed story of the Scripture is special on two counts. One is that it is clear that the people count as individuals, not just as a collective. So there is no room for manipulation. Second, the story is about a God who is all good, so the appeal to divine authority is an appeal to their understanding of the sum of all that is good, to a big story which holds within itself all the tensions implicit in our humanity. Such an authority might be judged worthy of committing ourselves to.

Finally, an aside from America that illustrates that building strong relationships with people is easier for some than others. For a national politician, building good relationships with your people might be seen as an almost impossible task. How can it be done? Abraham Lincoln was at the top of his profession. He was the key player in America. Yet he also believed in keeping in touch with the people. Each week he set aside several hours to, as he called it, 'bathe himself in public opinion'. He invited all comers to tell him what they thought of the government. He was often shouted at, even spat at, as he entertained the public. But he thought it was important. His attitude was commendable. It reminds me of the one who spoke of being a servant and washed the disciples feet.[20] It is also a story that naturally leads on to a more general consideration of how we should be accountable.

---

[20] I refer of course to Jesus in John 13 who taught the disciples that they should follow his example as the undisputed leader and yet stooped to the servant's task.

11

How should we be accountable?

Bristol is famous for many things, not all of them admirable. Of late it has become the centre of a furious debate about account-ability. Two rather special groups of people have been involved. First of all there are the heart surgeons. They have traditionally been held in great honour. The public perception of their role could hardly have been higher. Secondly there were babies, the delight of their parents and always a strong focus of the general social concerns of a good society. Put these two together and we realise that heart surgeons who work with babies are in an excep-tionally highly charged environment. And it is an environment prone to tragedy.

The 'Wisheart Affair' as it has become known has dominated the medico-political agenda of this country for five years. The Bristol paediatric heart surgeons suffered a particularly bad set of results in one particular area of their work. Serious numbers of babies died. As this news broke, questions were asked as to why the surgeons continued to operate when it seemed that their failure rate was so high. The parents were naturally full of grief and looked for answers. The media focused in on the surgeons. They were demonised, but it made a good story. The public were enraged at the thought of babies dying unnecessarily. It became a test case for the General Medical Council. The GMC is part and parcel of the medical profession and there was much disquiet

expressed in the press to the effect that they were a body that
looked after their own and would not exercise discipline appropriately. There may have been discreet words from HM
government to the chair of the GMC saying 'you had better get
this right or we will reform your cosy little system'. All in all it
added up to a massive pressure on the GMC to return a guilty
verdict and they duly did so. But several of the leading consul-
tants in Bristol were deeply disturbed by this process. They
thought there had been a miscarriage of justice and looked to the
promised public inquiry to expose the truth.[1] At the time of
writing the inquiry has not yet set down its findings, but the difficulties are already clear.

Paediatric heart surgery at Bristol was done on a shoestring.
The limited resources of the health service and the inadequacies
of the internal market had led to a situation where the heart
operations on babies were done under extreme circumstances.
Babies would be shuffled between several different sites. They
were operated on by teams used to working on adults. Post-oper-
ative care was often in the hands of non-specialists. This resulted
in the surgeons working long hours, deep into the night in fact,
to ensure proper care was given to those recently operated on.
Surgery is team work. There are a host of factors involved in the
success of an operation. Yet there is a tragically real and determinative performance indicator. Babies die. And the question is,
'Why did the surgeons not respond to the signs?' Or did they?
Large teams agreed operations. Why are they not being called to
account? Whose fault is it anyway? These are questions the
inquiry will try to answer as it seeks to lay down best practice for
the future. But there is no doubt this is something of a seminal
case for accountability.

---

[1]   Dunn, 'The Wisheart Affair', pp. 1144–5.

Methods of calling to account

All establishments tend to protect themselves. In chapter nine we saw how the political establishment tends always to close ranks against challenge from outside. Similarly we can expect a medical establishment or a teaching establishment to do the same. For this reason there must always be accountability mechanisms greater than peer review. Likewise we must always expect some internal wrangling within establishments, with people seeking to make their name, establish their departments and put their results in the best possible light. This again is only natural and methods of accountability have to take this into account.

None of this is new to the commercial world of course. Business professionals have always been prone to doing deals among themselves that were not in the public interest. We have learnt to break up such informal coalitions of the powerful by competition. RMC, the suppliers of mixed concrete, were recently fined £34 million for agreeing with the other concrete suppliers in eastern Germany to carve up the market and so artificially inflate prices. It is their second offence in this area.[2] Aware of this tendency, anti-trust law has developed to break such cartels and to insist on true market competition as the means of making firms work for the wider public interest. Competition can be relied on to keep the prices as low as possible.

Governments too have attempted to use aspects of market competition as a means of disciplining our own public sector. They have scanned the structures of public institutions looking for places where market principles could be applied. Such 'marketisation' of public services has been of dubious value. Its purpose, of course, is not just to discipline the professional elite, but to call the whole organisation to account. Many aspects of a public service can fail to serve the public interest. An institution can fail to manage its life effectively. It can become a home for

---

[2] *The Times*, 2 November 1999.

free riders of all sorts who are no longer working well. Local councils have been suspected of this sort of incompetence for years. Alternatively the institution can develop its own ideology that ultimately works against the interests of those they are serving. Teaching in the sixties and seventies was full of whacky ideas. The aim of 'marketisation' was to call these institutions to account, to re-engage them with the wishes of their users and make sure they were acting efficiently. The problem is that these sectors of society do not work as markets.

The internal market of the health service is a case in point. A senior consultant recently said to me, 'The problem is that the government has treated the health service as if it were a can of baked beans.' Making and marketing a can of beans is a fairly well-defined process. There is immediate accountability to the public, who will actively choose the beans they like best at the best price. The system naturally utilises new technologies and every management advance that will provide a better output at a keener price. Not so an institution like the health service. Here there is no one product. Rather there is an array of 'products' all of which contain elements that are intrinsically beyond measurement. New technology may make for obvious efficiency, as in day surgery, but may equally result in the possibility of new and more expensive 'products', i.e. treatments that the public will want. Similarly there is frequently no real competition and the public does not know enough to make informed choices, even if they are available.

Marketisation of the health service can be analysed according to Oliver Williamson's approach to transaction cost economics. He shows that where there is a special relationship in a supply chain whereby each party is seriously dependent on the other, then the system is prey to exorbitant transaction costs.[3] In other words, doing the deals is notoriously inefficient. The purchaser/ provider set up of the NHS internal market is a classic example of

---

[3]   Burke and Goddard, *Internal Markets*, pp. 381–96.

such unhealthy dependencies. One would expect such systems to be hard to set up and to be particularly exposed to abuse at the point of re-negotiation of contracts. This would explain why between 1989 and 1991 the number of managers in the health service rose from 4,610 to 12,340.[4] This was part of the extra transaction cost necessary to establishing the internal market. Similarly the system caused serious imbalances of power as GP fundholders flexed their muscles in unhelpful ways, negotiating impossible deals with hospitals and forcing them to adopt practices deleterious to patients. All this was quite predictable.

The use and abuse of performance indicators

There was, of course, always an acknowledgement that the market could only do so much and other approaches would be needed to operate in tandem. Accepting that the products of the public sector were complex, the aim was to isolate performance indicators that could be used to judge whether the institutions were performing their task and doing so at the least cost. For example, we used examination results and SATS tests to compare schools. The aim of a performance indicator is to allow comparison of one school with another, one council with another or even one surgeon with another. Resources can then follow best practice, and discipline be imposed on poor performers. In short, performance indicators act to set up a competitive process much like biological evolution.

As we saw in chapter six, evolution works through the limited system of signals that co-ordinate much of animal behaviour. Such signals are employed by animals as a means of comparison of one animal with another. They decide the issue of who gets to mate and so propagate their genes. In traditional biological language, they are tests of 'fitness'. Take the Bower bird for example.

---

[4] Baggott, *Health and Health Care in Britain*, p. 195.

The courtship display of the Vogelkop gardener Bower bird includes the building of a hut out of twigs. This is a huge endeavour. The resulting construction is big enough for a man to climb into. The roof is thatched with the stems of orchids. The ground in front is moss. On top of the moss the bird neatly arranges piles of brightly coloured objects as a display. Birds may spend up to nine months of the year tending their bower. Some species of Bower bird even daub the walls with dye and carefully arrange the lighting by moving twigs in the roof. And it is all useless, apart from the fact that it is what the female birds measure as their sign of the male's fitness to mate. Females tour the bowers built by the males. Having selected their mate, the bower is finished with. It has served the competitive purpose.

Although this behaviour is extreme, the same sort of phenomenon is found throughout the animal world. The animal fixes on a sign, a performance indicator we might call it and that becomes the measure of their 'fitness'. So two great stags might clash in a ritual measurement of strength through the engagement of antlers. Fish may measure another's prowess by a sweep of the tail. The Argus pheasant has fixed on the length of the wing feathers as their measure. The result is that the male's wing feathers have grown to such a length that the bird can scarcely fly.[5] All this goes to prove the maxim, 'What you measure is what you get.' It is deeply embedded in our behaviour. As an animal fixes on a particular measure so this aspect of their lives is elaborated, comes to dominate their behaviour and purposes, even to the detriment of any bigger or different view of their overall purposes. And of course we do the same.

A succession of governments has recently betrayed an unhealthy fixation with waiting lists as the measure of health service performance. The results have been bizarre. Health authorities have fallen over backwards to change their systems according to the new measure. The waiting list was measured

---

[5] For a host of examples of this see Lorenz, *On Aggression*.

from the time of seeing the consultant. Keeping this down could be done by slowing down the stage between GP and consultant. The queues built up there instead. More than that, health service practitioners were distracted by the measure. Their eyes were necessarily on the length of the waiting lists and not on any of the other vast array of other possible measures of patient care. The present government appears to be backtracking somewhat on waiting lists and is going for heart disease and cancer therapy instead. That will introduce a new bias into the system. Poor use of performance indicators leads to Bower bird behaviour, that is, it leads to the elaboration of immensely inefficient systems of behaviour through the failure to take a proper overview of the overall purpose of the organisation.

Yet some sort of performance indicators are probably necessary. Everyone would agree that public accountability should be fair. One hospital or school should be compared fairly with another. The need for such comparisons demands measures. Otherwise it is like trying to play a competitive game without rules. Such games would not last long. Everyone would soon go home in disgust. So we need performance indicators, but on what basis should they be designed? A government might fix on waiting lists because their focus groups tell them this will be popular with the voters. Such crude populism is not a sign of good government. There is a better way.

Any complex, co-operative venture like a health or education service is actually based around big and overarching perceptions of purpose. Questions like 'What good does this business do?' or 'What does it mean to be doing this business well?'; these engage with the big purposeful stories. It is around these questions that good performance indicators are built. Of course there are many different answers to these questions, but this is the real debate that a society needs to have with itself. What do we really want for our children's education? What should local authorities be doing? What would a good health service look like? How does that go together with what we are willing to pay taxes to provide it? Out of these questions come relevant performance indicators. The importance of good performance indicators is that they relate strongly to the overall purpose, bearing on all facets of the big story that sustains the community's views about the subject. This is precisely what other animals cannot do. They cannot take an overview of what they are about. Hence they get trapped in useless spirals of fruitless activity. Not so the human being. We can imagine; we can debate; and so we can do better.

The important feature of good performance indicators is that they are so designed that they together exert pressure on the institution to be faithful to the big story that gives them purpose. The recent government proposals about 'best value' may begin to approach this. The performance indicators for local authorities are drawn from the various different stakeholders in society. The government and audit commission set down certain limited objectives that it feels must be required of any competent council. In addition local people are to participate in drawing up their own measures for the delivery of council services and these will also feed into the process. How it works remains to be seen, but the provision of a rounded set of indicators bearing on the overall purpose is commendable.

The importance of things that cannot be measured

Performance indicators are, however, not enough. The concept of a local authority or health service setting indicators and then working to enhance their performance year on year sounds good, but is inadequate: we are not rational automatons. A world built around external measures of life would be a cold, sterile place, more the stuff of computers or machines than the vibrancy of human life. In fact any complex, co-operative venture is a function of much more than what is measurable. To concentrate only on the measurable aspects is to value only that which is measurable. This means that that which cannot be measured is left aside and is prone to wither.

For example, all the systems we have spoken of above are actually not products of an assembly line process, but are products of a system of human relationship. As we saw in chapters two and seven, much of human culture needs to be understood as a system of trust. Accountabilities are an integral part of such systems. Effective discipline is necessary for the whole community to trust the system. If free riders are perceived to dominate any public institution then all are tempted to cheat and co-operation becomes the sucker's game. It is everyone for themselves and society breaks down. So effective disciplines are vital in any system of trust. Yet trust is the basis of the arrangement and trust is not susceptible of measurement and therefore is in danger of being ignored. Overplaying performance indicators can diminish trust.

Consider the parent who submits their baby to the heart surgeon. There is a huge amount of trust in this process. The child's life is literally in the hands of the surgeon. There is real risk involved. Some will inevitably die. What allows that system to work? In the past the surgeon's role was veiled in mystery. The 'top man' was doing the operation. The child was in good hands. The parents could relax. This veil also protected the surgeon. After all who would accept this risk? Who would allow themselves to be put in this position of such vulnerability? – that one slip of their fingers and they would be considered responsible for the child's death. A person doing that would need some protection, the implicit support of the community, a willingness to forgive when things went wrong. Something of the awe in which the surgeon used to be held gave them such protection.

Instead imagine what would happen if the parent was told this. 'Your child will be operated on by Mr/Mrs_____. He/She is currently ranking twenty-seven in the country for this particular operation. Here is the list showing their current place in the league table.' How would that feel? Of course everyone would scream for access to the person who was number one on the list. That is natural. For the surgeons the pressures would be intolerable also. No one would want to do life-threatening operations at all. Such openness cannot inspire adequate trust. If we are committed to undoing the old professional mystique of the surgeon, we need to think very carefully about what to replace it with. *Glasnost* destroyed Gorbachev's Russia. Openness, on its own, destroyed trust. Facing the ugliness of their social institutions was okay but there was nothing to simultaneously give pride. *Perestroika,* the industrial rebuilding, was going to take far longer to have a positive effect on morale. Such is the case with our own institutions. We need to take care to maintain public trust.

Many of our institutions in the UK have been subject to radical restructuring over the last two decades. The positive purposes of such reformation include the rooting out of poor practice and free riders, but some have been through several cycles of change. If they were actually just rational organisations this would be no problem, but they are not. They are systems of trust. A school, a hospital or a council work as a system of relationships. Much about their lives is learnt and absorbed but never expressed propositionally. People learn the ropes and as they get to know the system they develop efficiencies along the way. All this knowledge is lost in a radical restructuring. A process of continual radical change leaves people psychologically at sea. We are built to work in relationships. Relationships give us our sense of place in the world. If they are always changing we feel lost.

Related to this is the issue of vocation. Many people in our public sector would currently describe themselves as demoralised. They have been through such a mill of radical restructuring that their own professional identity has been eroded. The story of their life is bound up with their work. They see their work as good in some wholesome sense and therefore they receive a considerable sense of their own worth from the practice of it. I remember talking to a social worker. She recounted sadly that she had entered the profession with a vision for counselling and helping others. Yet she now felt reduced to a care manager who visited people, assessed their care needs, designed a 'package' to suit them and then left. The new structure was efficient in one sense, but it had also drained her of vital motivation. She had lost her vision. A similar story is told by doctors, teachers, university lecturers and people from a host of other professions. The new systems of accountability have resulted in a loss of the holistic vision that sustained their purpose. They are demoralised. Part of this is due to over-concentration on performance indicators which give only part of the picture and so tend toward such loss of vision. Such demoralisation is another symptom of the breakdown of the trust that sustains a society.

Systems of relationship in all workplaces depend on a whole set of virtues that are ignored by performance indicators since they cannot be properly measured. In the health service for example, it matters how people feel they are being treated. They can sense compassion, but it is hard to measure and so easily ignored. Then there is the wisdom that arises from knowing people, how they behave and the best way to treat them. Who can measure wisdom? Wisdom is traditionally associated with older people. Is it surprising that a large proportion of older workers feel undervalued? They are not up with the latest techniques. Change comes harder to them. But in a sticky moment, they may know what to do when no one else does. Because they understand people. They have seen this sort of thing before. We need to honour wisdom.

Trustworthiness is another essential characteristic of a good worker in a system of relationship. Any system of trust is dependent on trustworthy people. With trustworthy people you can have the best work environment. If they are all layabouts and wasters then only harsh discipline can make the place function. Yet we have no measure of trustworthiness today. Interviews tend to be skills-based. They look solely for qualifications and relevant experience. Previously, issues like trustworthiness and integrity were covered by references. Today, references have themselves fallen into disrepute, because the referees were not trustworthy. Too many people were writing good references to get rid of bad employees. There was also the fear of litigation if you said anything bad about someone. So the system broke down. Trust, compassion, wisdom, integrity and trustworthiness all play a vital part in what it means for any complex, co-operative venture to be done well. Their presence has a dramatic impact both on the cost efficiency of the project, and also on the general feel of the working environment as experienced by the workers and users of the service. To ignore these things because they cannot be measured is disastrous.

A better way

There are various ways round these problems, but they generally demand a more holistic, and therefore inaccurate and subjective, measure of the life of the organisation. The aim must be to encompass these deeper and relational aspects of corporate life within the overall appraisal. It may be that a process like Ofsted can, at its best, perform this sort of task. Ofsted has certain stated criteria for judgement, most particularly the delivery of the National Curriculum, but it does its assessment in a process of relationship that can implicitly take in many other aspects of good teaching. It has the downside that this relational aspect can cause serious problems when it is done badly by a heavy-handed or prejudiced band of assessors.

One interesting approach is to build interpersonal as well as task objectives into performance appraisal. (If you achieve your set tasks only by walking all over everyone else in your department, it will count against you.) This creates an environment where relational abilities become valued and people have more of a sense of working as one of a team.

Another holistic approach is to define tasks in more general terms. This encourages the creative imagination. Even very general questions can be used like, 'Tell me six things you have done in the last year that have been to the good of the business.' Such questions look for real initiative rather than the useless hurdle jumping common to set-indicator systems. Also it allows for the possibility that people can be assessed as teams as well as individuals. This in turn encourages mutual responsibility rather than the individualism that is fostered by individualist appraisal.

All these more imaginative systems of appraisal have another necessary ingredient. Since they are more subjective, then great care needs to be taken with the actual appraisal process. In one innovative system that I am aware of, several reports are gathered for each individual appraisal, both from those above and below the person in the hierarchy. People are encouraged to say directly to the person what they write about them in the report. Also the appraiser is themself appraised in their appraisal of another. If you imagine such a process, it is easy to see how this system of everyone reporting on each other could descend into mutual recrimination with everyone feeling suspicious and resentful. Its success requires a certain sort of culture. It might be called a 'low blame' culture or a culture of mutual understanding and support. I suspect it also has other possible expressions, but to see that we need to review where we have got to on the subject of accountability.

The root of good accountability is in the debate about the story that gives purpose to the organisation. As people offer their perspectives on the organisation, they implicitly reflect their own values, their own sense of what is good about what they are doing. The debate is therefore ultimately a debate about the good and its root form is the story. A person may relate the story of how they were treated when they were told they had cancer. A doctor might tell the story of how funding restraints were putting pressure on the whole service. All sorts of points of view might coalesce through a healthy process of consultation into versions of the big story of what the health service is really for and how it should work. Out of this story are derived healthy performance indicators that reflect a rounded view of the aims of the institution.

It is not hard to see how this relates to the biblical quest described in previous chapters. The community of faith struggled together towards a view of the good which was held in their understanding of God. They had different perspectives and these were in tension. They also saw themselves as accountable before God for what they did. God was the good, and therefore just, person in authority who must therefore judge their behaviour. So there was this reference to a big story about what was good and a real expectation of accountability whereby they would be judged on the basis of that goodness. Yet God was only known in part. They knew their understanding of what was good was partial. There was much hidden, we might say immeasurable, about the good. And the question was how they should be accountable to each other.

The story of accountability develops through the Scriptures. Initially they try to interpret every calamity as a sign of the judgement of God. Although this provides a great moral spur to their debate about the good, it is an understanding that ultimately cannot hold. Clearly innocent people suffer. In this light the focus shifts to the *future* judgement of God and comes to a particular watershed in Jesus' ministry. Jesus is understood to proclaim the imminent coming of God as judge. This God knows all the secrets of our hearts. God understands our real motivations, the struggles that go on within us that no one else has access to. Only such a God is able to judge justly. In this awareness Jesus teaches that we need to be *careful* how we judge one another, for we do not know it all. 'Judge not, that you be not judged', he says. 'And the measure you give will be the measure you get.'[6] If you judge others harshly, then you will be judged harshly. There is need for mercy, kindness and a readiness to forgive.

---

[6] Matthew 7:1, 2

This is of vital importance to our discussion because we too must recognise our limitations. We simply do not know all that we need to know in order to make just judgements. We need systems of accountability. People must be called to account in this world. But at the same time we need to recognise the limitations of our own understanding in that process. Who really knows the true motivations of the heart surgeons who operated on the babies who died? We can guess that they had within them all the same tensions that we have. No doubt they had some concern for their status, their reputation, their department. They also wanted to work well for the children, whom they deeply cared about. How were these tensions resolved? And how were they mediated by that most terrible performance indicator, the death of a child? All our inquiries will never get to the bottom of that, for it is not given to us to know the secrets of the heart. Yet we need to act. We need to try for justice. We need to call to account. But I believe the Judaeo–Christian story would suggest that we need to do so with a certain kindness, a mercy and a willingness to forgive. There is an anguish at the heart of the human condition. There are issues that will remain unresolved and there will be those who bear unjust suffering. That is a necessary feature of our human situation. And there is a certain mercy that is essential if we are to get along with one another in the best way possible.

Of course this also applies to the more mundane matters like conventional performance appraisal. We have seen that there is much about our human relationships that cannot be accurately measured. Many of these things are yet vital to our ability to co-operate well. Some sense of them can partially be had from more holistic measures that take in our relationships with one another. Yet because we cannot accurately measure these things, then neither can we be absolutely fair about them. Any human group that tries to work on them is going to need to develop systems of trust that are implicitly forgiving. It will need to accept that people will get things wrong. It will need to try to prevent personal vendettas. But most of all it will need to foster an environment of mutual vulnerability, where there is an understanding that we all fail at times, where there is mercy and kindness. This is the sort of culture that was encouraged by Jesus and commended to his followers.

Stephen Egan is Director of Finance and Corporate Resources at the Higher Education Funding Council for England. He is also a Christian. He wrote the following short piece about the process of appraisal specifically in the light of the Christian culture anticipated by the Sermon on the Mount. I believe it clearly expresses the connection between good accountability and the Christian faith.

> Every year I review the activity of my staff for the year and allocate a mark which translates into pay. I have six managers who report to me. Some are very good at their job. Some perform at lower levels. Performance appraisal is always a stressful time. At stake is far more than money. An individual's sense of self worth and value can be affected by the review. So how can the Sermon on the Mount help?
>
> *Blessed are the poor in spirit.* As an appraiser it is possible to assign to others our own faults. Psychologists call it projection. What we say about others often says more about ourselves. If we recognise our own faults and are open with these to God we have taken the plank out of our own eye and are more likely to see clearly the speck in our brother's. It also means we can recognise where our own behaviour at least partially is part of the problem. Our judgement is more likely to be sound. So before I appraise anyone else I should first appraise myself.
>
> *Blessed are those who mourn for they will be comforted.* It is right to be concerned about the impact of the plank in one's own eye on the behaviour of others. It is right to say sorry and mean it. When staff are equally open about their own faults the right response is comfort and support not blame and recrimination. From such an attitude everyone can learn and come out stronger.

Blessed are the meek. An appraiser should consider first the needs of the appraisee. The question is, 'How can I support them?' How can I deliver a message sensitively? How can I affirm rather than destroy? Humility enables honesty which helps issues to be recognised and tackled.

Blessed are those who hunger and thirst for righteousness. If a member of my staff is unfairly treated by say my boss, it is my responsibility to try and sort it out. For instance, not to put up with abusive language, bullying or discrimination. I should be more concerned with any injustice or hurt to my staff than to my own interests.

Blessed are the merciful. I must always consider the circumstances of the individual. Bereavement or illness can cause poor performance. I must also be prepared to accept an apology and desire to improve. That's the start of something very positive.

Blessed are the pure in heart. It is important I go to the appraisal free of all prejudice, envy or other unworthy attitudes. This is not a time to settle scores or to remember a grievance. It is time for a rational evaluation and an attitude that is not based on self.

Blessed are the peacemakers. Forever look for reconciliation. Look for ways to change a negative attitude into a positive one. Do not give up on people.

Blessed are those who are persecuted. It is possible to be deceived. It is possible to be ridiculed. It is possible to shy away from just decisions for a quiet life. It is possible to be accused of being too soft or too hard. I am not sure this is real persecution but it is certainly true if one is open about one's own faults this can be abused, although I have to say abuse rarely occurs.

By conducting performance appraisals in this way it does say a lot about my personal values. People know I am Christian. It is mostly by my actions that I can demonstrate a sense of what this

means. I am far from perfect. Even as I write I can see where I
need to improve. But I do try to pray about the appraisals and
thank God when they go well.

12

At the bottom of the pile

I was sitting in a bedroom of a seedy Paris hotel reflecting on my situation. For the last nine years I had been vicar of an inner city parish in Bristol. It was a place high on every indicator of social deprivation and many people struggled. Day after day I had listened to the stories of people in great need. Often the process had left me reeling from shock and for days life would seem out of focus and bizarre. As vicar I had been a sort of grief dustbin, a repository, a safe place for the anguish of others. As I stared at the window in the hotel, I came to focus on drops of water through the mouldy net curtains. Were these drops of water on the inside or the outside of the window? It was not clear. The net curtain prevented a clear view. As I reflected on that scene, the drops became tears, the tears of anguish and tragedy that I had experienced through this time in the inner city. I could no longer tell whether these tears were on the outside or the inside, whether they were my own tears or the tears of others. My life had become filled with the tragic. Tears were always close by, under the eyelids, pressing for their release. It was time to leave. And I did.

It was easy for me to leave. I was the vicar. I was expected to leave. But for most of the residents of the area leaving was not even a possibility. Most were council tenants with little hope of moving. Few people in other parts of town wanted to swap to go there. They had to live on and life could be very tough. Many of those I came to know and be concerned for had lives marked by multiple difficulties. There was no one nice circumscribed issue that could be dealt with; their lives were a story of interlocking anguish. There may have been abuse when they were children. This may have led to eating disorders or alcoholism. Their children might likewise have been abused. The children may have grown up to be difficult, fomenting trouble in schools, then in the neighbourhood. Drugs might have come into the picture. That would lead to theft and the whole scene would become violent. People would live from day to day. Life would happen to them. For many people with such a complex web of struggles, simply managing to live was a triumph. Sadly, I buried a continuous stream of those who succumbed to the pressures and killed themselves directly by suicide or indirectly with alcohol or drugs. There were also many good things to say. There were many fine examples of humanity. There were many people who were able to carry immense burdens and still live and live well. I knew some of these people and they remain an inspiration. Yet the grief needs talking about.

The perceived importance of rank

Perhaps we can get a perspective on these problems from studies of animal behaviour. In his *Primate Social Systems*, Robin Dunbar considers the plight of primates who are at the bottom of the dominance hierarchy. From a socio-biological point of view, the animals can be understood to be embroiled in a continual search for the highest possible rank. High rank confers priority of access to all those resources on which successful reproduction depends, such as food, safety and sex. The tragic corollary of this is that those who are left at the bottom of the heap get the worst deal. They have the most stressful and violent life. The stress can even be so severe as to result in reproductive suppression. They have least access to food. When the food supply is limited, it is they who go without. The result is that they weigh less. More seriously, when primate colonies suffer heavy mortality, it does not fall evenly. The young die first, particularly young females. This again can be related to rank.

Dunbar's study leads to the following conclusions about animals at the bottom of a dominance hierarchy. In general they:

1. Suffer most violence
2. Have least access to the necessities of life
3. Have least freedom of action
4. Are the first to suffer in crisis

If this is true of animals, it is also still true of human beings. These phrases typify the experience of those I have spoken of. Areas of deprivation are always areas of multiple deprivation and their people are often people with multiple difficulties to overcome. For example, successive British crime surveys show that the heaviest concentration of crime is amongst the urban poor. The perpetrators of violent crime are often people who have been victims of violence themselves. More than nine out of ten violent offenders aged ten to seventeen have suffered abuse or loss in early life.[1]

The incidence of crime is in turn linked to unemployment and poor education. Poor education limits opportunity, or freedom of action. Such freedom is also curtailed by low income. Many will not have access to a car and will be unable to move house. When things go wrong, they are the first to suffer. They will be located at the poorest end of the city. They will suffer the most pollution. They will experience worse health than the rest of the population and will even die more quickly than other people. The clustering of these factors in specific areas and

---

[1] Bristol Audit of Crime and Disorder.

people may then be related most fundamentally to rank. It is the experience of those at the bottom of the pile.

Part of the reason for the separation of people into areas of deprivation is that the rest of us avoid them like the plague. An animal always seeks to rise in the hierarchy. The higher places are safer. In social terms, gravity moves upwards. Everyone strives for the highest place they can get. It offers more freedom and potential. Those left at the bottom are there because they cannot get out. We so fear being consigned to the lowest places in society that we are even very careful how we relate to the poor. Charity is okay. Charity maintains the distinctions of status. Even voluntary work programmes that work with projects from offices can be okay. What we dread is being associated with the poor in any way that we might be mistaken for one of them. That would be a disaster.

A recent report by the Rowntree Foundation made a study of suburban areas. They were particularly interested in neighbourhoods that at one time were fashionable places to live and which are now avoided. Michael Gwilliam, one of the authors of the report, came to the conclusion that suburbs are in a form of continuous social competition with one another. Their fortunes wax and wane according to how they are perceived by people. It seems that we are very sensitive to signals that an area is going, as we would say, 'downhill'. If the shops close, bars are fitted to their windows, and more houses are put out to rent; if there is vandalism, a spate of burglaries or noisy neighbours, then people move, if they can, to a 'better' area.[2]

One interpretation of such behaviour is that it is a response, not only to the simple sign of, say, the closure of shops or vandalism, but to its deeper meaning which is that this area is becoming a place where people of lower rank live. This is a threat. Those who can, therefore, move out and seek a place that maintains

---

[2] Joseph Rowntree Foundation, *Sustainable Suburbs* (Feb. 1999), commented on by John Harlow in the *Sunday Times*, 21 March 1999.

their perceived social position. It is happening all around us. I currently live in a new estate. It is fashionable. Many are selling up and moving here. There is massive investment in new shops and roads. Yet in a few years another area will be the place to be. Many will go there and any that stay will risk losing status.

Many of us are urbanites. Reflect for a moment on your town or city. It will have its poor area. Now let me ask you this, what do people say about the people who live in the poorest area of town? If you went into a pub, or were at some sort of gathering of people in your area, what would they say about the people who live in the poorest places of the city? I strongly suspect such conversations would rapidly point to the failures of the poorer people. 'They are lazy.' 'They drink it all.' 'They are all single parents (and therefore immoral)' – or words to that effect. Many such conversations would unearth massive prejudices in people. How are we to understand these pronouncements? Basically they are an attempt to show the difference between us and them. They prove that 'we' are different and they serve to justify that difference, showing why 'I' deserve to be higher in the hierarchy.

The importance of our place in the hierarchy is one of many reasons why unemployment hits us so hard. A friend of mine is a safety engineer. He was called into his manager's office immediately after Christmas one year and told, 'Your work is totally unacceptable, clear your desk and leave.' He was dumbfounded. Only weeks before he had been representing the company at official meetings. Anyway, suitably chastised, he left with his tail between his legs. Only later did he discover that several others had also been laid off that day and that the cause was almost certainly simple cost saving not poor performance. The experience led to several months on the dole during which he had thirty interviews. At last he secured a job. The only snag was that it was two hundred miles from home and his family was not in a position to move. The result was that he left his wife and children at six on Monday morning, lived in a lonely bed-sit all week and returned on the Friday night often past midnight. His new firm recently announced that they would be laying off around thirty per cent of the workforce. Such an announcement would strike dread into the most courageous soul.

The harshness of this sort of treatment is evident. Parents need to feed and care for their families. That is one of our strongest impulses and we will move heaven and earth to try to do it. But we also need a sense of place in the world and in the west that is increasingly focused on our work. The corollary is that those without work find it increasingly difficult to maintain their own sense of self-esteem. We are the first society to expect all its mature and fit individuals to undertake paid work. Now we all have to take our place in the market. If we do not, or cannot, we easily feel worthless. I have personally taken a few years out of formal employment to study and write, this book, among other things. It has meant that I do not have a formal role. The interesting thing is that people do not know how to relate to me. Other vicars describe me as having a 'sabbatical', a term they understand but which bears no relation to the amount of work I am doing. I myself take a deep breath when someone asks me what I do. It is hard to explain and yet is important to how they will see me. We need a sense of place in the world. Part of that is inevitably to do with where we rank in the hierarchy.

We can get a larger perspective on this issue by considering the relationship between western nations and the peoples of the Niger Delta. Poverty is a complex issue and not all poverty is relative. Simply surviving is less hard in the UK than it is in many other areas of the world. Yet people at the bottom of the pile experience the same sort of things wherever they are in the world. The phrases we have alluded to namely, 'suffer most violence', 'have least access to the necessities of life', 'have least freedom of action' and are 'the first to suffer in crisis', are common features of the human animal at the bottom of the pile.

The west has reaped several harvests from the Niger Delta. First there was the slave trade. Many African American people of today derive from this region. Then it was colonised by Britain and its indigenous farming activity was subverted to cash crops for export. Since then the whole area has been utilised by the oil industry, drilling around a thousand wells with its associated pipelines. Despite all this economic activity, the peoples of the region remain poor. They have around thirty per cent unemployment, while per capita income and educational achievement are both below Nigeria's national average. They have suffered from a poorly controlled oil industry which has failed to observe standards of practice that are normal in western countries. A series of attempts by local people to gain some control over the oil industry and protect the lives of the indigenous people have been ruthlessly put down by the Nigerian government, who are of course themselves seriously dependent on the oil moguls. We have heard of Ken Saro Wiwa. We have not heard of countless others who have been put to death for working, usually quite non-violently, to get their story heard and for a place in the political arena. There are those who have got rich in the Delta. There are those who are greedily aspiring to the oil revenues, but the mass of the people are neither of these. Ike Okonta, a Nigerian academic and writer, tells of

> … the millions of poor peasant fisherfolk who stumble from one day to the next wondering what has gone wrong with the land and creeks on which their fathers and grandfathers before them had relied on to feed and clothe their children and what they could do to bring back the good old days again. When they cry out, when they wave a puny clenched fist of rage at booted Shell workers that rampage through their farms and fishing creeks leaving death and destruction in their wake; when their hungry sons and daughters haul their wiry, emaciated bodies against the machine guns of the Nigerian soldiery only to be mowed down like fleas, they do so not in the name of oil and American dollars. No.

> They rage and dare the deadly guns in the name of the land on which they depend for survival.[3]

Survival is the name of the game for those at the bottom of the pile. The peoples of this region are trapped in a web of exploitation. It is hard to see the way out. The whole Nigerian society is destabilised by the presence of the immensely powerful oil industry. A supervisor in the oil industry will be paid $800 US a month compared to $60 US for a university lecturer. A society cannot stand this sort of power imbalance. Systems of trust are inevitably undermined as corrupt practices become the only game in town. In Nigeria the government officials are themselves terribly liable to corruption. They give licences to drill. They can charge immense licit and illicit 'fees' for this service. The temptation to corruption is enormous. It is alleged that General Babangida salted away billions of dollars into his own personal coffers during his time as President.[4] Meanwhile life continued as usual for those who actually live in the Niger Delta. They are at the bottom of the pile. Ironically, if global warming really produces the predicted rise in sea level, the Niger Delta will suffer again. A one-metre rise in sea level will flood 18,000 sq. km. forcing 80 per cent of the population from their homes.[5] Once more they will be the first to suffer in crisis.

The most prevalent western response to this sort of analysis is to emphasise the corruption of the Nigerian government. The effect of this critique is to deflect attention from the western destabilisation and exploitation of the region. It is often accompanied by veiled or not so veiled racist judgements about Nigerian people. Overall it functions to justify our position in the hierarchy vis à vis the peoples of the Niger Delta, implying

---

[3] Okonta, *Litmus Test*.

[4] Ibid..

[5] This and other details of the Niger Delta are drawn from Ashton Jones et al., *The Human Ecosystem of the Niger Delta*.

that we deserve our higher rank among the nations. Judgements like this have been common fare in the response to the Jubilee 2000 campaign for debt relief for the world's poorest nations. In fact the situation in the Niger Delta illustrates many of the most fundamental issues regarding imbalance of power in the world today.

This is a bleak picture. What it suggests is that the issues of poverty and deprivation that the world faces have certain common characteristics that can be related to people's position in the social hierarchy. Furthermore it gives reason for the deep-level motivations and behavioural characteristics of both the powerful and the powerless. Fortunately it is not the end of the story.

If this condition is fundamental to the human animal, then it would have been experienced similarly by the biblical community and their reflection on it may have light to shed. In earlier chapters we have already seen how the prophets arose and confronted those in power with the stories of the downtrodden. This is one vital means by which the tragedy implicit in the power hierarchy is mitigated. Today it is possible to see people like Ken Saro Wiwa, or Nelson Mandela or Martin Luther King, as of the same type as the biblical prophet, bringing the stories of the powerless into the public arena. This is part of the story. The other part belongs to another in the line of the prophets, Jesus of Nazareth. He too spoke up for the powerless like the prophets, but he also employed another, and most interesting, method.

Challenging justifications of the heirarchy

In Jesus' day the people of Israel were stratified according to racial purity. The top jobs were only available to those who could demonstrate their pedigree. So only the racially pure could be priests, the top echelon of society. Only pure Jews could sit on local councils or be almoners. To be pure was to uphold the tradition and to be considered as trustworthy. Those men who worked in jobs associated with women were suspicious. Their work brought sexual temptations and they were therefore a threat to the nation. Women were totally excluded from public life. How else could one ensure the purity of the next generation?

This ranking by means of racial purity was upheld by an elaborate and detailed legal system. Proving your ancestry, upholding the traditions and keeping the law were all mixed together in a system that was designed to maintain Jewish identity in days when it was under threat, not least by the Roman occupation.[6]

It was in the context of this obsession with racial purity that the 'forerunner' John the Baptist came onto the scene proclaiming the revolutionary words, 'Do not presume to say to yourselves we have Abraham as our father,' he said, 'for I tell you, God is able from these stones to raise children to Abraham.'[7]

The gospel story that followed continued to challenge the social hierarchy to its roots. The law decreed the impurity of those with certain skin diseases. They were excluded from society. As Jesus touched and healed these people, he was performing more than a miracle of healing, he was giving a sign that he was concerned to re-integrate the alienated. 'Go and show yourself to the priest,' he said. Only then would they rise from the bottom of the pile. In daring to speak with women in public Jesus deliberately confronted the social order. It was the same with people in the despised trades, the prostitutes and tax collectors. The moral system kept them in their place. People recoiled from them, but Jesus encouraged understanding, openness and mercy and so questioned the dogmas of a rigid society, opening up people's moral imagination.

---

[6] This background study is drawn from Jeremias, *Jerusalem in the Time of Jesus.*
[7] Luke 3:8.

One corollary of this for our day is to see that what Jesus was doing was calling into question the means by which the society of his day justified its hierarchy. We have seen that we also justify our hierarchies. We will have set commitments in our attitudes towards those in the poorest parts of our community, just as we have set attitudes to the poor in foreign countries. Some of these will be simple prejudices that help us avoid the issues of injustice. Others of them will be structural. They will be expressed in law, in moral attitudes, and in the theory behind oppressive economic systems. Followers of Jesus today would therefore seek to bring a new understanding and mercy to these judgements. They would expose moral hypocrisy, subvert oppressive law and generally work to increase our moral imagination such that we cannot avoid facing injustice.

An example of this type of behaviour might be found in today's India. Orissa is one of the poorest areas of the country and has been the focus of a particularly vicious outburst of persecution of Christians by fundamentalist Hindus. The charge made against the Christians is that they are subverting the social order. It is said that they are proselytising and so undermining the traditions. The real reason, according to a recent report, is that the Christians are educating the poor and, no doubt, radically questioning the caste system, telling the untouchables that they are okay in God's eyes. It is suggested that the Hindu fundamentalist groups are probably a cover for the powerful of the land whose interest is to keep people in their place.[8]

One key positive element of this sort of challenge to the social order is to provide a healthy engagement with our social sympathies. To act compassionately we need to engage with deep level motivations that enable us to imagine the condition of others. In this Jesus also led the way. We saw in chapter one that there is a variety of evidence linking the development of social sympathies with the care of children. In caring for the child we appreciate

---

[8] D. Orr in *The Times*, 8 October 1999.

the position of the weak. The very shape and sounds of the child are signs to us that draw out our deep-level motivations toward caring for others. How apt then for Jesus, in instructing the disciples, to take a child and put it in their midst and say, 'Truly, I say to you, unless you turn and become like children, you will never enter the kingdom of heaven. Whoever humbles himself like this child, he is the greatest in the kingdom of heaven. Whoever receives one such child in my name receives me ...'[9] In terms of our explanatory frame this sort of action deliberately brought into conflict two of our most basic human motivations. On one side there was the prevalent desire for status, to achieve the best rank in the hierarchy that it was possible to achieve. That was the background to the saying. But the child is then used to draw out another strand of our being, our capacity to care for others. Jesus is aware that there is a tension between these two and forces this question with the demand to humble oneself like a child. He was asking people to do the unimaginable, to identify with the weak, to allow our own identity to merge with the weak, risking our own status on the way.

This was a teaching that Jesus was himself to act out as he was crucified. The early church was to understand his death precisely in these terms, as a humbling, an identification with the weak. The first Christians were to see this as a central part of their calling. Paul quotes what was probably one of the earliest Christian hymns as he says,

> Have this mind among yourselves, which is yours in Christ Jesus, who, though he was in the form of God, did not count equality with God a thing to be grasped, but emptied himself, taking the form of a servant, being born in the likeness of men. And being found in human form he humbled himself and became obedient unto death, even death on a cross.[10]

---

[9]   Matthew 18:3–5.
[10]   Philippians 2:5–8.

Death on a cross was the ultimate humiliation. It was the death of a criminal. The story that God incarnate had undergone such an identification with the weak and vulnerable of the world so as to die in this way was the ultimate challenge to those seeking to justify their place in the social hierarchy. It remains so today.

13

Who is to blame?

They were only going to a football match. It was to be an afternoon out, a fun time. Yet ninety-six of them were never to return home. Such was the Hillsborough tragedy. Their life was crushed out of them as fans flocked into the stands. And, of course, there was a massive public outcry. 'Who was to blame?' Many lessons were learnt about crowd control, police methods and proper lines of authority and communication. Football grounds up and down the country were re-examined in light of the tragedy.

Another time, some children were at school. It was a normal day. The quiet babble of little voices could be heard up and down the corridors. Teachers were here and there attending to all the usual class business. Then in came Thomas Hamilton and the nightmare of Dunblane began. Sixteen children and a teacher were shot dead. When the shock subsided, again there were serious questions asked about blame. The perpetrator was dead, but the anger, grief and tragedy had to provoke questions. How could this happen? What could have been done? How can we make sure this never happens again? They are good and important questions. School security has been increased. A new handgun law has been passed. There is an ongoing debate about the best treatment of the mentally ill.

The importance of blame

In both these situations, a normal, quite unthreatening, situation turned horrific. Any society that experienced such things would naturally ask hard questions about the incidents. The sheer fact that such things can happen is offensive. While they are unexplained, then we all feel threatened. If it can happen there, it can happen anywhere. The possibility of such horror undermines our basic trust in the society of which we are a part. So we strive with all our energy to make sense of it and put right the defects that are highlighted. There may be a public inquiry. New procedures, moral understandings and laws will often be established. There will also be some allocation of blame. But though the cry to locate blame is often particularly insistent, it is also rather problematic.

We have recently had a number of young people develop 'New Variant CJD' and die. Any person's death through illness is a tragedy, but this was a new disease. It was therefore particularly threatening. How many will eventually succumb, we all wondered? What is it? Is it linked to the 'mad cow' disease BSE? These were vital questions. Here science was able to address the issue in part and came up with evidence strongly supportive of a link between the animal and human diseases. Many such problems have an element that can be investigated profitably by science. But science cannot solve it all, because issues involving society ultimately interact with human purposes and actions. Where people act, then moral explanations have to be given; people have to be held responsible for their actions. In this case, it was not enough to know that BSE and new Variant CJD were linked, but questions needed to be asked about when the government could be said to have had evidence of a potential problem and how it acted on that evidence. People wanted to know whether they had covered up BSE in order to protect the interests of the farming lobby. Again we are talking the language of blame.

The social order is important to us all. Social animals have a deep-level motivation toward upholding the social order. Occasionally signs of chaos impinge on our society. Violence erupts in an unforeseen place and we act with massive energy to bring that place of chaos back into order. Our response to signs of chaos is rather like that of sailors responding to their ship springing a leak. We concentrate all our energies on plugging the hole, restoring the order, making it good. If we do not manage it, the whole company is in grave danger. One important weapon in our arsenal at these times is blame. Blame acts as the spur, encouraging moral improvement, defining new lines of acceptable behaviour, and new and more appropriate law. But blame can also become a problem in itself.

When blame goes wrong

The United Kingdom has recently been called a blame culture. It seems that we are increasingly caught up in spirals of mutual recrimination. John Humphrys[1] points out that in the event of major tragedy today, claims for injury will come not only from the directly injured or their relatives, but also from the professional people who were responsible for treating those injured. So there were claims made by the police at Hillsborough that they had been exposed to trauma through negligence. A paramedic recently sued his Health Authority over psychiatric distress caused by attending road traffic accidents. Similarly a doctor sued after being pricked by a needle, claiming that she should have been counselled more thoroughly for her fears about the potential (presumably AIDS) contamination. Humphrys is right to point out the strange nature of these claims. It seems that we are in danger of becoming a society where everyone is blaming everyone else and we become hooked into a cycle of blame that

---

[1] Humphrys, *Devils Advocate*.

we cannot get out of. The health service now has 20,000 claims for compensation a year, costing the tax-payer £250 million. Doctors are increasingly concerned about their own insurance protection. Likewise every public organisation is most careful to give public warnings of every conceivable danger for fear that they might be sued. Health and Safety officials in workplaces can bring the whole show to a halt on some petty regulation that contributes more to their need for power than the public safety. It is not without good cause that we have been called the 'nanny state' and we have ourselves to blame. Caught up in an endless cycle of blame, we sue everyone for everything. This means that we all have to cover our backs, developing a plethora of new regulations. The result is that we no longer perform many good and proper practices because of some slight risk that under previous circumstances we would be happy to bear.

The causes of such a blaming society are complex. The legal environment is important and there can be little doubt that the transition to no win/no fee charging will contribute to the growth of litigation and the attempts to blame. But there are deeper things going on.

Risk is a scientific concept. Safety engineers will calculate quite dispassionately that these points on a railway line will fail once in three million hours of use. They will tell us that this figure can be extended to one failure in ten million hours by the expenditure of x million pounds and someone will judge whether we will be willing to pay the resulting fare increase. Such calculation seems all too cold and calculating for those whose relative is on the train that crashes. Yet governments and railway managers do have to make this sort of decision and they need to make some equation for what the public is willing to pay. The difficulty is that risk and blame are linked inextricably. Risk is a scientific concept and blame is not, but both are important.

However well we manage life, it will contain risks. However much we fuss over our food, at the end of it all, some will be dangerous. Our transport systems will fail. People will do mad and bad things. When things do go wrong, we will try to allocate blame and so learn all that we can about doing it better. Yet the only way for human society to be risk free would be for it to conform to a perfect machine, and that would not be thought desirable by any of us. We are stuck with risk. And one important function of any society must be to learn how to bear the necessary risk associated with life.

One of the lessons illustrated by the BSE crisis is that the quality of public conversation is important to the bearing of risk. If the public are fully informed, and are able to hear the stories and fully debate the issues that are associated with any risky situation, then they are more likely to be able to bear any tragedy that ensues. Sadly the quality of public conversation in the UK has diminished dramatically over the twentieth century. The media now inform us of great risks with their 'shock horror', soundbite reporting, but most of the public have been reduced to passive recipients of this news. The disintegration of civil institutions, clubs, societies and the like has meant the loss of social space in which people formerly had quality conversations about things that were of concern to them. Now we just flop in front of the TV. Loss of good conversation leaves us fearful in the face of potential threats and more likely to lash out in inappropriate blaming behaviour.[2] People can bear risk, when they feel fully involved and consulted. Conversation generates common stories and values, which bind the community together and allow it to function even through tragedy. Without mutual bonds or moral consensus, we are prone to a competitive individualism where everyone tries simply to get the best deal for themselves and minimise their own risk. This is the blame culture.

Blame is clearly difficult to manage. It is a form of massive energy probing social chaos. It is like lightning seeking an earth. Just like lightning it can also be highly dangerous. A community can turn on people. After a horrific bombing campaign by the

---

[2] Bauman, *In Search of Politics.*

IRA, the police were under great pressure to locate the blame and nail the culprits, and they arrested and charged the 'Guildford Four'. It took many years to establish the miscarriage of justice. The public wanted to blame someone.

Similarly during the Cold War, the United States grew particularly adept at blaming the problems of the world on communism. Their own leaders were continually examined for their anti-communist credentials. If the spotlight turned on you, it would be hard to prove your innocence. Arthur Miller's play *The Crucible* highlighted a parallel between the McCarthy era and the days of witchcraft trials. When America needed someone to blame, the communists were a ready target. The lightning of blame found its earth.

The persistence of cultural and racial antipathy

The most dreadful examples of blaming in human societies are due to cultural or racial antipathy. This subject is so important that I must now digress upon it. Having done so, I shall return to the more general subject of blame towards the end of the chapter.

I guess we hoped that the Holocaust would be the end of it. Six million Jews died that we might change our ways. A massive effort has been made to understand racism and eliminate it, but this is a problem that refuses to go away. In Rwanda, the Hutu leadership incited its fellow tribespeople to rise and liquidate the Tutsis. It is estimated that one machete-wielding gang could mutilate and kill one thousand Tutsis in twenty minutes. Such estimates of efficiency remind us of the gas chambers of Auschwitz. Much closer to home the conflicts in the Balkans have claimed thousands of lives as Serb turned on Croat, Muslim turned on Christian and vice versa. John Simpson, surveying the tragedy of Sarajevo, declared his inability to sort out one side from another, or right from wrong, in the mess that had ensued. He said that all that remained in that shell-shocked town was the distinction between those who had power and those that did not.[3]

We might comment that the Balkan conflict is not strictly racial, or not entirely racial. This actually becomes a clue to its unravelling, for none of these conflicts are strictly racial in any properly defined sense of the term. Race is simply part of the justification for the conflicts, not the root of the behaviour. The behaviour that we call racism is part of cultural antipathy in general. To make sense of it we must return to some of the most basic characteristics of our society and to ourselves as social animals.

Any animal seeks to make sense of its environment, to learn where threats lie and where safety and nourishment can be found. An animal on their home territory is more confident and rightly so. A wandering animal will frequently follow the same path at the same time of year. So a swallow might return from right across the other side of the world to the same barn. It worked last time. It is likely to work again. We might say that animals are highly traditional creatures.

Social animals are distinctive in that they have a relational landscape to negotiate as well as a physical one. Here again they are likely to develop patterns of working together, methods that work tolerably well, and stick to them. In human societies we call these cultures. They are the gradually evolving means by which we co-ordinate our social lives. The social order is vital to our existence, so we come to value those traditions we follow and always seek new justifications of them. Much of our learning of culture is something we absorb. We do not teach it propositionally in school. A child grows to understand itself as a person of this particular 'way'. It becomes part of their identity and is bolstered by the stories that confirm that culture.[4] It is their home territory in a social sense.

---

[3] Simpson, *Strange Places, Questionable People*, p. 445.

[4] See, for example, Bloom, *The Social Psychology of Race Relations*.

Part of this process of enculturation is the learning of who is within and without this culture. To see something is to be able to distinguish it from its background. In just the same way, the formation of culture implicitly involves the identification of those who are outside that culture. We spot outsiders. We spot those who are different. They may represent a threat to us or our social order. They are to be watched. Being animals that are particularly sensitive to visual clues, we are prone to differentiating people on the basis of skin colour or other visual signals. This gives rise to what we call racism. The whole process of enculturation means that we have an inbuilt tendency to view people of other cultures almost as if they were people of another species. Erikson has called this 'pseudo-speciation'. The history of racist thought is full of the sort of comment that says, effectively, that these others are not really humans, they are savages and of no account. Theodore Roosevelt, for example, said in the early twentieth century, that the most righteous of all wars 'is a war with savages, though it is apt to be also the most terrible and inhuman. The rude, fierce settler who drives the savage from the land lays all civilised mankind under a debt to him.'[5] Such sentiments underlie all racist thought and easily develop into a structure of justification. Simplistic Darwinian logic was a powerful tool in the hands of such people. Houston Chamberlain wrote his famous book justifying racism on 'scientific grounds' and Kaiser Willhelm II described Chamberlain's theories as a 'magic wand' that created 'order where there was chaos and light where there was darkness'. This is the great urge of racist thought, to provide order, a social order, to make sense of the world and remove threat. For many years the Japanese were known as the 'yellow peril'. They fought a long struggle for racial equality in the League of Nations but, just when they had gained a majority in favour of their proposals for equal treatment, Woodrow Wilson, the chair, steam-rollered their motion out of existence. At one point

---

[5] Quoted in Lauren, *Power and Prejudice*, p. 62.

Roosevelt sent the US fleet to the Pacific as part of his tactic to prevent Japanese immigration into America. He saw it as absolutely essential to protect our 'white civilisation' justifying it with the phrase 'self-preservation is the first law of nature'. [6]

Such fears about the social order and the perception of threat have an unfortunate tendency in the human psyche. We tend to blame the perceived outsider for our own defects. Blame, as we have seen is a problem for any society to deal with. Very often, as a society goes through a period of weakness or struggle it looks to bolster its own identity. Germany between the wars provides a classic example. They were suffering, as was all Europe, from the Great Depression, but they had the added burden and humiliation of reparations from the First World War to contend with. In the face of such weakness, it is a typical strategy to put the blame for the present situation on a perceived 'outsider'. In Germany's case the Jews were a useful target and Chamberlain's theories of racial supremacy a convenient peg of justification. So Hitler accused the Jews of destroying civilisation itself by spreading decadence, supporting bolshevism and 'crawling like a maggot in a rotting body'. [7] Mary Midgely relates this to the psychological tendency to project these deepest and most disliked parts of ourselves onto the outsider, so disowning them. She sees the process in society as like a glass lying round 'our' society, with everyone 'else' outside in the darkness. Against the background of such darkness we see the reflection of ourselves in the glass. [8]

The necessary corollary of all this is that there will be no end to racism and the cultural antipathy from which it takes its root. We will never 'deal with' the problem. It is in us. It is part of our make-up as animals and as people. We will be able to lessen its effects by considering the factors in society that promote or

---

[6] Ibid.

[7] Ibid., p. 122.

[8] Midgley, *Wickedness. A Philosophical Essay.*

diminish these attitudes. We will be able to expose its spurious justifications, but we will never eradicate it.

If racism is indeed endemic and part and parcel of the human condition, then we should expect such attitudes to be present in the stories of many traditional societies, even the Bible. As the Hebrew people established their identity and sought to maintain it so they developed all sorts of traditions, doctrines and rituals that both upheld their social order and implicitly alienated the outsider. They were the 'chosen people'. That meant there were others that were not chosen. They went into the 'Promised Land'. They justified their wholesale destruction of the other peoples of the land under the description that such treatment was 'devoting them to the Lord'. Similarly their elaborate sacrificial and dietary laws had a secondary social function which was to keep them distinct from other peoples. The strictures about food preparation made it hard to sit round a table with others. In fact all the factors that built the special identity of the community implicitly sought to differentiate Israel from the outsiders and therefore increased the likelihood that others would not be perceived as truly real, that blame would be inappropriately foisted on them and that their destruction would be deemed authorised.

Such is one strand of the tradition. Yet on the other hand, the experiences of the Hebrew people gradually encouraged them to feel for the outsider.

The story of the captivity in Egypt, with its slavery and oppression, translated into an understanding of God who showed some concern for the outsider. In response to this, they elaborated laws that commanded special provision for the widow, the orphan and the alien and set conditions around slavery. Typically these would be introduced by the phrase 'Remember that you were once slaves in Egypt.'[9] So the experience of being the outsider provoked sympathy for outsiders in general. Similarly many of the prophets were themselves on the edge of the tradition.

---

[9] See for example Deuteronomy 14:28ff.; Deuteronomy 15:15.

They thought and felt like outsiders and were so clear in their sympathies towards those unjustly treated, even the foreigners, that they were occasionally moved even to deny the great justifying stories of God's election.[10]

As the people go into exile and then return, the same tension holds. On the one hand there is the concern to maintain the tradition. Intimate contact with a foreign culture truly threatens to undermine the tradition. As the people return, Ezra seeks to re-establish their identity, embarking on an austere programme of purification designed to re-establish their racial and cultural purity. Yet at the same time the people in exile have grown to appreciate some of the foreign people. The book of Genesis is written, describing God's creation of all people. The book of Ruth is written, celebrating the mercy and love implicit in intercultural loyalty and mixed marriage, something that would be anathema to Ezra's ears.[11] So there is a debate, a tension within the community. There are those who sense the need to maintain the tradition. There were others who were developing social sympathies towards those outside the tradition. Both were of vital importance to the future of the community.

It was a tension that remained into the New Testament period. Jesus is understood by the gospel writers as both upholding the inherited tradition and being extraordinarily radical in his inclusion of those who were perceived as outsiders. It was a narrow road to walk, but it led to a transformation of the faith, first preached and acted upon by the convert Saul of Tarsus. Saul, or Paul as he became known, was brought up as a Pharisee, a Hebrew of Hebrews. He was converted to the Christian faith and had to struggle with his own identity as a Christian. Jews had defined themselves over against everyone else. The world consisted of Jews and Gentiles. The Gentiles were simply non-Jews.

---

[10] See chapter three.

[11] Williams, 'The literal sense of scripture', pp. 121–34 explores this idea of Scripture being formed in a process of tension.

When Paul realised this new faith was for all people, Jew and Gentile, he had a problem on his hands. In some way he had to show his loyalty to his Jewish inheritance. Yet how could he do this and also include the Gentiles? The letter to the Romans is a continual struggle with this issue. Yet through it all, Paul does attain to a vision and it is a vision for a new sort of community, a community that is able to hold its order and identity whilst always reaching out to be inclusive of all. In Galatians he announces that 'There is neither Jew nor Greek, there is neither slave nor free, there is neither male nor female, for you are all one in Christ Jesus.'[12] Similarly he declaimed to the Greeks at Ephesus, 'you who once were far off have been brought near in the blood of Christ. For he is our peace, who has made us [Jew and Gentile] both one, and has broken down the dividing wall of hostility …'[13]

His vision of Christ, melded into this vision of a new community which could resolve this essential conundrum of our humanity, providing a means of upholding a social order whilst always looking to embrace the outsider. In a sense the vision transcended the specifics of culture, bringing all cultures into question before God and the knowledge of goodness, beauty and truth that God had inspired. It implicitly provided for a certain interrogation of cultural dogmatism, those aspects of a society's life that might be rigidly but unnecessarily upheld by the strictures of culture. So Paul found himself arguing passionately that circumcision and much else of the Jewish law did not need to be practised by the Gentile converts. Christ was setting people free. It was therefore an argument for a peculiarly liberal and tolerant society, yet one that should always be pressing forward toward that which is good and beautiful and true. It is a vision the church has never realised in practice, but one which continues to inspire.

---

[12] Galatians 3:28.
[13] Ephesians 2:13–14.

So we have seen that the scriptural story develops from positions of outright racism and cultural antipathy. The source for this tendency can be readily traced to the simple need to uphold the community tradition. The tradition of monotheism may well have been lost if they had not held firmly to that path. Yet at the same time, sympathetic social feelings naturally arise as they experience being outsiders and come into contact with other peoples. These two tendencies produce a fruitful conflict within the believing community that comes to a focus in Christ, the Christian community thereafter setting out with an inspiring new vision of an inclusive community. At the very least this is an instructive history.

Many of the factors important to an understanding of racism, can be illustrated from the biblical story. Upholding the social order is still the ardent cry of the racist. Nationalism so easily turns into direct enmity of other cultures and inappropriate blaming behaviour of one sort or another. Yet contact with people of other cultures does indeed soften our hearts, making us more understanding and less threatened. In the seventies, the Cold War was still very much a reality. I remember asking a youth group what we could do to work for international peace. One of them replied astutely, 'Get to know some Russians.' How right she was. It is as true today as it was in biblical days that real relationship with people of other cultures is the best antidote to our besetting tendency to feel threatened by such people and to blame them for our ills.

Sadly the vision of the church as a new and inclusive community has never been truly and fully lived out. Indeed the church has behaved atrociously at times, but the whole story of the Bible does give us something of a vision for the process of development that is required as we work for the best society. Some evaluation of moral progress in this area can be gained by measuring contemporary societies against the biblical development.

The Boers of apartheid South Africa, for example, were stuck right at the beginning. Their doctrines about South Africa being the Promised Land and God helping them subdue the *impis* were taken from the earliest and crudest biblical understandings. In these developmental terms the rest of the Bible need not have existed for them.

Or to draw a different parallel, during the last few centuries many societies have been going through an engagement process, rather like the exile, where they have come into considerable and intimate contact with other cultures. In some this has produced a retrenchment, an Ezra-like response, which protects their own society. At other times a new understanding and sympathy has been forged. We press on toward the vision.

Dealing with the excess of blame

Yet we still have to deal with blame. Blame stalks our lives and our societies. Capable of good use in the development of more appropriate morality and law, blame may also be displaced. If blame is not placed inappropriately on the outsider, as in racial and cultural antipathy, then it might home in on the hurt person themselves. The children of separated parents are well known for blaming themselves for the split. Even more seriously, an abused child may turn their own anguish in on themselves. Blame may then turn to anorexia or bulimia, as the fight to regain control becomes the fight to somehow purify a body that is blamed for its abuse. Illogical perhaps, but these things are devastatingly powerful in the lives that are affected by them. Blame is an important issue for us all.

In the aftermath of violence or pernicious injustice, a society can be faced with such a terrible backlog of blaming to do that the system is overwhelmed and might never recover. Thousands of Hutus languish in Rwandan gaols today. It is difficult to know what to do with them. Many are guilty of outrageous acts of brutality, but there is precious little evidence that can withstand scrutiny and the justice system is overwhelmed by sheer numbers. How is the society to recover? The people of newly liberated South Africa tried an interesting experiment. Instead of opting for a Nuremberg type of process that would last for decades and still probably not be satisfactory, they tried their 'Truth and Reconciliation Committee'. It was a bold step. They offered amnesty in exchange for confession. The government gave small tokens of reparation to those wronged. Much was revealed that would never otherwise have seen the light of day.

For example, the headquarters of the South African Council of Churches was bombed. At the time Mr Adrian Volk, the then minister of law and order, announced that the African National Congress were to blame. They were 'terrorists' and 'communist-inspired'. He went on to accuse a certain Ms Shirley Gunn of the bombing and detained her and her infant son for six months without trial. Most of the white community believed this. Yet later, the offer of amnesty by the Truth and Reconciliation Committee induced Mr Volk to make a full confession, admitting that his own police officers had planted the bomb. At last the cover was off. Now everyone knew that many of the other stories were also likely to be the work of the police force. The police were not keeping law and order, but actually fomenting trouble, systematically and viciously. It was worth hearing. Other more heart-rending episodes were expounded in the Committee. In Archbishop Tutu's words it allowed some to reach a point of 'closure', at last they could hear the story of how their loved one was killed. No longer was their son just another unexplained disappearance, they now had an account of the tragedy or murder. Without assuaging the grief, they could now live with it. Nevertheless, some left the proceedings feeling robbed of justice. Too many had walked away scot-free. [14]

In the end, every human system of blame allocation will be inadequate. There are always a large number of tragedies, accidents and misfortunes. There will always be a massive weight of

---

[14]   Tutu, *No Future Without Forgiveness.*

grief following these. This grief will search for someone to blame, but it will never be satisfied. There is much we do not know or understand about people's motives. There is even less that we can prove. This means that any society must have a way of dealing with its blame, of earthing it, safely. One aspect of religion that can be considered here is sacrifice.

Meyers Fortes, an anthropologist, describes sacrifice as a ritual of defence against affliction or misfortune.[15] We are inescapably vulnerable in this life. Sacrifice in religion generally provides a way of dealing with the dangers of life. In the Judaeo–Christian religion the system of sacrifice took its place within the overall structure of life in relationship with God. Things going wrong were generally perceived as being due to some failure in their relationship with God.

Mary Douglas, anthropologist and theologian, has shown how the sacrificial system in Leviticus works with concepts of wholeness and order. God is perceived as one who has ordered the world, both morally and physically, such that any offence against this order requires sacrifice if danger is to be averted. Leviticus offers a very long list of potential offences including using mixtures of cloth, menstruation, men dressing in women's clothes as well as ethical matters such as lying and cheating. All these were offences against a natural order as it was perceived. What God intended was whole, pure and ordered.[16]

Of course it was impossible to live a life in keeping with these extraordinary standards, so people made sacrifice regularly. It was as if failure to keep God's requirements was expected. Indeed many sacrifices were offered for unintentional sins, things that one might not even have been aware of, but yet might put a person or the community in danger. It was as if people were saying, I know I will have done wrong somewhere so, here, I make my peace. In a sense it was the acceptance of blame and its

---

[15] Fortes's preface to Bourdillon and Fortes, *Sacrifice.*
[16] Douglas, *Purity and Danger.*

earthing in the poor, hapless animal. As the worshipper drew near to the priest to offer his animal, he would lay a hand on the animal as a sign and say words that clearly located his 'sin' on the animal in some way.[17]

The sacrifice was a ritual that assuaged blame. Of course the sacrificial system did not stand alone. Included within it were proper ethical concerns. Some sacrifices demanded concurrent reparation to injured parties. All the same, like all rituals of forgiveness, the sacrificial system could be misused. It could easily become a cop out for not taking the moral issues raised by the situation seriously enough. The prophets dared to question the legitimacy of the whole sacrificial system on account of this failing and forced the development of the people's moral understanding.[18] Yet I suspect the system of sacrifice did serve a communal purpose. Consider the Day of Atonement for example.[19]

Once a year the High Priest would make special offerings for the whole people. The idea was that the society had gradually become 'polluted' through the year. There was much unintentional and undealt with sin. So on this one occasion, this great day, the High Priest would solemnly prepare himself, enter into the holiest place of all, and offer sacrifice for the sins of the people. In a sense we could say he was discharging blame. Part of the ritual was the scapegoat ceremony in which the priest took the goat, laid hands on it confessing the sins of the community, and then sent it away into the wilderness. It was a sign that their sins had been carried away. And so had all the blame that might linger in the society.

For all its faults, and there were as many in that society as there are in ours, they did know something about dealing with blame. Subsequently, as the biblical story unfolded, so the story of

---

[17]   Wenham, *The Book of Leviticus.*

[18]   Jeremiah 7:21–28; Amos 5:21–24; Micah 6:6–8; Isaiah 1:10–17.

[19]   Leviticus 16.

sacrifice came to an extraordinary finale. The gospel accounts of Easter week are all different and complicated by several factors, most particularly by an apparent bias that sought to place the blame for the events on the Jewish people.[20] Nevertheless it seems that the crowd turns from the frank worship of Jesus on Palm Sunday to a situation on Good Friday when they are nasty, vicious and willing to kill. This needs an explanation. At the same time the authorities are reported to have calmly considered whether it was expedient for one man to die for the people. What was going on here? Perhaps the people were behaving like so many others do when their culture feels under threat. They were looking for someone to blame. In that fragile time, when the whole society feels weak and struggles under the oppression of the Romans, we can imagine the terrible urge to locate blame rattling around in the society, and then quickly, and finally, that blame is located on Jesus. The lightning bolt strikes. 'Crucify him' is the cry and the innocent one goes to his death. He was the ultimate scapegoat. In the eyes of the early church, he fulfilled the prophecy of Isaiah. 'He bore our griefs and carried our sorrows … The Lord has laid on him the iniquity of us all.' [21]

As the early church grew to understand Jesus as God incarnate, so this killing assumed even more gigantic proportions. It was firstly the killing of an innocent one, but to kill the one who was God, could there ever be a more monstrous crime? 'This Jesus whom you crucified,' said Peter, 'God raised from the dead.' There could be no greater wrong. So Jesus' death presents us

---

[20] There are those who see this anti-Jewish undercurrent in the New Testament as part of the evidence that Christianity has always been the true source of anti-Jewish feeling in the world, e.g. Ruether, *Faith and Fratricide: the Theological Roots of Anti-Semitism*. I think this view does not do justice to the basic human disposition toward racism and that Christianity is more truly accounted for as the development of a truly liberal society in the way I have described.

[21] Isaiah 53.

with a powerful example of the barbarity that so easily erupts in human populations. It makes God the victim of such barbarity and so judges that behaviour. There could be no more powerful story to encourage us against such inappropriate blaming.

In subsequent Christian thought the cross was to be the central means by which people came to terms with blame. In a sense the cross was understood to bring a certain interim 'closure' to the pain and injustice of the world. It is both an appreciation of pain and a signpost to judgement. The horror of the cross tells us that justice matters. There must always be an attempt by us to secure justice, even if we know that it will be flawed and inadequate and that some final judgement must await. Yet at the same time, the cross points to the inevitable fact that there will be pain to bear in this world. So it becomes the call of God to endure that suffering and an appeal for a spirit of forgiveness.

This religious understanding of the world therefore offers an approach to the difficult subject of blame. The relationship with God, which is embraced by the sacrificial system, opened people up to the possibility that there was much that is 'wrong' in the world. There was much continuing anguish, much unlocated blame. And it provided a means in ritual for this to be publicly acknowledged and dealt with. As we reflect on the blame culture of the present UK, there is something positive here that resonates with our deepest psychological needs. As the religion developed, so animals ceased to be used for the location of blame. The cross of Christ interposed as the ultimate sacrifice and became the focus for the faithful. Yet perhaps ritual is a particularly helpful means of dealing with pernicious problems like blame, and sacrifice was soon to be replaced by alternative religious expressions with a similar purpose.

The confession rituals of the church bear considerable resemblance in function to the old sacrificial system. Both personally and corporately there is an acknowledgement of all sorts of ways in which we may have failed to live up to God's standards, both intentional and unintentional. An atmosphere is deliberately generated where none can boast of righteousness. And so blame is earthed. Similarly the Holy Communion becomes a memorial, or even a re-enactment of Christ's sacrifice. However it is precisely understood, the service points to the death of Christ for the sins of the world. There is an earth for our blame. This is of profound importance.

Part three

Seeking vision

14

In search of goodness, truth and beauty

I was once asked to take the funeral of a man who had died after a fire. In preparing for the funeral, I discovered that he had led a tough, wild and tragic life. He had taken comfort in the bottle and, after decades of alcoholic bingeing, had accidentally set fire to his flat while under the influence. It was a sad, but all too common, story. What was not common was the music the relatives requested at the service. Playing tapes and CDs has become a common feature of the modern funeral and relatives usually choose music of a sentimental character. Whitney Houston, Frank Sinatra or *You'll Never Walk Alone* are favourites. This time the relatives said, 'We want *Bohemian Rhapsody* by Queen.' I gulped. I had not faced this one before. How would the congregation cope with words like, 'Beelzebub has a devil put aside for me', 'anyway the wind blows' or 'nothing really matters to me'? Apart from that how could I square it with myself as a Christian minister? Strangely, I felt a sense that it might be appropriate and decided to go for it. The day of the funeral came and as the searing anguish of Freddie Mercury throbbed through the building, I became calm. This music was bringing home the agony of the tortured and tragic life that we were remembering that day. It helped us to grieve.

There is something about that sort of occasion that still speaks
to me. There are many whose lives are caught up in tragedy and
who feel that there is no purpose in life. Freddie Mercury
himself, knowing that he was dying of AIDS, was to cry out 'Can
anybody tell us what we are living for?' It was not just his cry. It is
the cry of humanity at the turn of the millennium. For centuries
philosophers like Nietszche, Sartre, Camus and Voltaire have
railed at us about the stupidity of our lives. Fundamentalist scientists have gravely decreed that life has no purpose. And we have
been left without vision and without hope.

So where can vision be found? This book has tried to lay out a
new approach to understanding our human society. It is built
upon an analysis at three levels. First of all, there are the deep-
level motivations that we inherit as animals. Second, there is the
expression and transformation of these within human culture.
Finally, there is the possibility of an appropriate theological
expression and reflection, which in turn allows integration of
conflicting tensions and the generation of vision for public life.
At every level there will typically be tension. For example, the
discussion on racism in the last chapter might be understood in
these terms:

Animal motivation

Fear, aggression,   sympathetic social
perception of threat .... *tension* .... feelings

Human experience

Culture formation,   experience of being
alienation of outsider............ *tension* .... outsider

Theology

God mandates purity,
ritual, separation,   God as concerned for
ethnic cleansing   .... *tension* .... 'other'

These tensions become focused in the concept of God and are
held together by the community of faith such that the biblical

story becomes the story of a society which is seeking all that is good and true and beautiful as held together within their understanding of God. As the biblical story develops, so the vision of the good society develops with it. The previous chapters have shown how this process was able to integrate simplistic visions of success into a bigger worldview, call dominant leaders to account and engage the society in the quest for justice and inclusiveness. We have seen how it specifically encourages trustworthiness, forgiveness and mercy, how it allows for the generation of balances of power and for the story of the powerless to be brought into the public arena. There is scarcely any area of public life that it does not bear upon. Yet it all begs a question that now we must face. It may be an inspiring idea that there is a God. It may even be a very fruitful idea, but ultimately we have to ask the question, Is it true?

Testing truth claims about God

In the earlier chapters, I argued that truth about human purposes could only be sought by means of story. As people experienced life so they continually sought to make sense of experience in terms of stories. Stories are an attempt to draw together our lives into a coherent whole. Without them we should be lost in a blur of disconnected experiences. In forming stories we are implicitly testing our overarching commitments about life. Every story has its commitments. As we share stories we are essentially appealing to others to see the world as we do. They will probably demur, at least in part. The process of conversation then becomes the pursuit of truth, in which we negotiate not only the superficial experiences of life, but also the deep commitments that underlie our interpretation of them. It is an intrinsically uncertain process, much less determinative than the methods of science. Yet it is still a proper quest for truth and, in fact, the only means by which truth can be sought where human purposes are concerned. My claim is simply that the process of the formation of the Scripture is precisely such a pursuit of truth by means of story and as such it is testing a particular, overarching theory of life, or paradigm. This theory understands there to be a God who is personal, in authority and the source and focus of all goodness, beauty and truth. The scriptural record is the story of the testing of this theory and its further elaboration towards a vision for a good society. On what grounds then can it have any claims to be true?

One important aspect of biblical reflection was that it was an attempt to make sense of real human experience. In this it bears a clear relationship to scientific method, which likewise takes the data of experience as real and seeks to make sense of it. Other religions and philosophies have taken very different views of the external world and how it impinges upon us. Descartes, for example, found his certainties in the ideas of his mind and much about human experience could for him be illusory. Hume had a pronounced scepticism about whether the world would make sense in terms of regularities. If this stuff is bread today, there is no reason to think it will be bread tomorrow.[1]

Both these attitudes also have their religious corollaries. Some eastern religions have strong threads of 'illusion' about the world. God can even be a god who deceives. True spirituality can be found by inward retreat. This is the religious analogue of Descartes' philosophy. Likewise polytheistic religions are akin to the scepticism of Hume. There is no overall sense to be made of the world, the only thing that can be done is to recruit the favour of this god now for that purpose. Obviously the moral possibilities of such religious approaches are slight. They cannot force a resolution of the competing interests that are around in every society. Furthermore neither of these philosophical or religious positions is consistent with a scientific view of the world. Science is actually committed to a view that the world will make sense and is

---

[1] Hume, *Enquiries concerning human understanding and concerning the principles of morals* (1748), section 4.

real. It is our primary experience. Judaeo–Christian theism is precisely in accord with such a scientific view of the world. It takes experience seriously. Nowhere in the Scriptures are we told about a tragic experience, 'Do not worry about it, it is not real.' Everyone has to face the real experiences of their life, even death on a cross. Also, there is the continual search in the Scripture to make sense of the world in terms of a relationship with the one God, and therefore in terms of that God being all goodness, beauty and truth. This is to trust in some regularity, albeit relational and not mechanical, at the heart of the world. The commitment is that at some deep level the world makes sense because there is a God. Therefore there is goodness; there is justice; and these are to be searched for. Judaeo–Christian theology is then actually asking the hard question. It is trying to make sense of the world as a whole and it is taking the data of human experience as real. The next question is whether it can make any claim to have done so successfully.

Science has its own methodology. In chapter five we explored some of the parallels between scientific method and the pursuit of truth in the realm of purpose. Scientific method was seen to be a particular subset of the whole human search to make sense of the world. Such making sense of the world always involves the testing of big, overarching views or paradigms. So science originally tested the corpuscular theory. Historians of science have paid particular attention to the great paradigms that science works with and to moments when those paradigms shift. In particular it seems there often comes a moment when the available experimental evidence is interpretable on both paradigms, when there is no decisive judgement between the two. At this moment of uncertainty, scientists still seem able to make quite accurate judgements about which view will turn out to be right. Take Einstein, for example. He knew that relativity was right long before the Michelson–Morley experiment set out to test it. How did he make such a judgement? Michael Polanyi has analysed this sort of moment in science and come up with four criteria that work to make a new theory carry conviction. A new theory carries conviction when:

1. It gives an accurate account of experience up to that point
2. It fits with all the other systems of knowledge
3. It is relevant, having practical, predictive power
4. It is persuasive, for example, through sheer elegance[2]

These criteria are interesting in themselves. The link between beauty and truth has been noticed and commented on by many scientists and can been used alone as an argument for the existence of God. A new mathematical theory is often compelling by virtue of its elegance and the coincidence of truth with such elegance can suggest a greater creative mind behind the world.[3]

Yet if these things are pointers to truth in the narrow confines of science, the question needs to be asked whether they might be of value, in a reformed sort of a way, in the realm of purpose and the testing of paradigms by storytelling. These criteria are after all about making judgements about paradigms at moments of uncertainty. Knowledge of human purpose is intrinsically uncertain and so, of necessity, will be any paradigms that purport to make sense of it. Let us consider the paradigm about God on this basis.

A theory is likely to be true if firstly it offers an accurate account of experience. A scientific theory may be tested by experiment. A paradigm about purpose will be tested by negotiation through story and conversation over time. Does this story make sense of our experience? That was the question. There is no doubt that some of the biblical paradigms did fail that test.

---

[2] Polanyi in *Personal Knowledge* uses terms such as certainty, systematic relevance and intrinsic interest. He also speaks of our fundamental heuristic quest, trying to make sense of life.

[3] J. Polkinghorne in conversation with Roger Penrose, *Third Way*, Jan. 2000.

The story that you would be successful if you obeyed God was tried and found wanting. There was a paradigm shift. Innocent suffering was on the agenda. This coupled with a change in the theory of judgement. Originally judgement was understood to be accomplished in this world. Later the emphasis shifted to a final reckoning. Similarly the detail of the 'theory' of God filled out in the process of history. More was understood of God. More was understood of the good society. Yet overall the essential, overarching paradigm remained. The commitment that there was a God, who was the source of all goodness, beauty and truth, prevailed. It proved an adequate reflection of the experience of the biblical community through time. It made sense of their life.

Second, a theory is likely to be true if it fits in with all the other systems of knowledge. This has been a major headache for religious people since the Enlightenment. How can religious faith be stated in such a way as to be consistent with other forms of knowledge? Fortunately the arrogance of science as a totalising 'theory of everything' has diminished in recent years and we are beginning to see our way through the fog. This book has tried to plot a new path, based around the story as the most basic means of pursuing truth in the realm of purpose. This method, I would argue, is the essential method whereby truth is pursued in all the humanities. Wherever history, sociology, anthropology or any other of the humanities has to embrace the purposes of human beings, they need to use what is essentially a story methodology. This is not to suggest that they always employ a formal story structure with a beginning, middle and end. Rather it is to say that wherever these disciplines try to make sense of human purposes, their proper method is to try to imaginatively enter the world of the people they are describing and create an holistic account of their activities, making sense of their behaviour in terms of their understandings of life and deepest motivations. Their descriptions have to work, by necessity, with the deep-level commitments, both of the storyteller and the people under consideration by the storyteller. Likewise the biblical writer has theological commitments and constructs stories to make sense of the world from within this paradigm. But this process is not entirely different from that of the other humanities. They are all story formed. Moreover the theological commitment is to a God who is all goodness, truth and beauty and this theological pursuit therefore implicitly understands itself to embrace all the other disciplines. All becomes contained within the theological vision. In this way it may be claimed that theology truly fits in with other systems of knowledge.

Third, a theory must be relevant and make practical predictions. I hope the relevance of this approach to theology has been proven in the preceding chapters. In almost every substantial area of public life, this biblical approach offers insight and understanding. As a scientific theory might make practical predictions for experimental investigation, so this God paradigm offers vision to live by. We have seen how the overarching view of the good society develops through the Scripture so as to provide us with guidance as to what we are aiming for in commerce, in politics, in leadership and in justice. Such a vision can constrain us, forcing an integration of our lives and so delivering us from destructive addictions, but it can also liberate us to pursue all that is good and true and lovely.

Finally there is, I believe, something elegant and intrinsically beautiful about such a faith. The vision of God is one of all beauty, all goodness, all truth. That for me is something of beauty in itself. I cannot explain that to you if you cannot see it.

Evidence for a real relationship

So it seems that scientific criteria for truth concerning paradigms can be applied, with appropriate modification, to the belief in God that gave rise to the Scriptures. My reason for laying this out like this is to emphasise the continuity between science and faith. Yet there is at least one sense in which this parallel is quite inadequate. The biblical paradigm was essentially about a relationship not an idea. The people's commitment was that they were in a relationship with this God. They did not just have a good idea that there might be a God and work with that. The vision was to live in harmony with this God who was all beauty and goodness and truth. Scriptures that look forward to the possibility of a full relational harmony with God might typically use a refrain like 'and you shall be my people and I will be your God'. There was a hope for intimacy, safety and rest in God. Such relationships are hard to examine in any adequate propositional manner, but there may still be some useful indications as to its reality.

The evidence about the relationship with God is really contained in the preceding chapters. In each chapter we have seen a development of understanding, often from very crude beginnings, towards a fuller vision for the good society. This development has proceeded by mutual engagement of people with very diverse perspectives, each of which believed they knew God and spoke for God. This diversity produced enormous tensions. It was held together within a community who shared the overarching paradigm and by its belief in a relationship with God, but at times, little else.

One thing is immediately evident about any relationship this people had with God. It was not an easy or transparent relationship. At the very summit of the whole biblical narrative, Paul owns up to the difficulty. He says 'for now we see in a mirror dimly'.[4] Mirrors in his day were of polished metal. Their reflections were dim and imperfect. Paul was saying that, even after all the light that Christ had brought, his relationship with God was no better than the vague and difficult to discern images of such a poor mirror. Or in more archaic language, he saw 'in a glass darkly'. This is important in a positive as well as a negative sense.

---

[4] 1 Corinthians 13:12.

The people of faith have always struggled to know God. Yet it is this very struggle that allows the diversity of expression that we find in the biblical account and the subsequent development of the vision for a good society. If all had been clear about God from the start, there would be no development and no need for a story at all. The poverty of the relationship with God is actually the key to the openness of the quest and so its ability to be inclusive, to listen to the perspective of the minority, to challenge the leadership and all the other very good features of the biblical process. It is because the priests accepted that they may not know it all, that they had to listen to the prophets, that they had to allow the appointment of a king and all the other developments towards a more subtle and benign society. The lack of knowledge of God made them open to the perspective of the 'other', who might yet bring revelation. I shall explore the importance of this more fully in the next chapter as we consider the proper role of such faith in today's diverse society.

Despite the struggle to know God, I believe the accounts still have certain features that suggest that the relationship with God was real. First of all, the diverse stories of the Scriptures add up to a remarkably self-critical account of the tradition. The Scriptures are the 'product' of a religion in a marketing sense. The Gideons place Bibles in hotels and schools in the belief that the Bible will lead people to faith. Occasionally it does, but when it does, I suspect this is by special grace, because the Bible is found by most people to be an extraordinarily confusing book. This confusion arises both from its diversity and its implicit self-criticism. What company would market a product by giving details about problems in production and difficulties with its workforce? No, they would present you with a glossy flyer, designed to emphasise everything good about the product. Is it not rather odd that the Judaeo–Christian Scriptures then present us with this most tortuous story replete with all its failures and problems? Talk about washing your dirty linen in public! Yet perhaps the nature of this account is a perverse indication of its truth. The people certainly

did not know God well, but *together* they may have grown to
know God. As they heard the diverse perspectives of 'others', as
they battled with the incipient conflicts within and without their
society, so maybe they did truly grow to know more of this God
they were committed to. I personally find such a process believ-
able and in keeping with a God whose goodness would allow us
the freedom to explore life, to struggle for the good and own it
for ourselves.

At the same time as being extraordinarily self-critical, the
Scriptures portray a great capacity to keep hoping. This too may
be evidence of relationship. At the time of the exile, the people
had apparently lost everything. Transported to a strange land,
amidst a strange people with strange gods, there was every temptation to pack it in. Terminal despair would have been a huge
temptation. Yet always in this situation, there came the prophetic
voice of hope. 'Comfort, comfort my people,' says your God.
'Speak tenderly to Jerusalem and cry to her that her warfare is
ended, that her iniquity is pardoned ... '[5] And such things were
not only said, but heard, and the tradition survived. Time after
time in the Bible it seemed that the light was about to go out and
the tradition would be extinguished, but it persists. And new
hope dawns. Whence came this continuing possibility of hope?
Is it further evidence that the relationship with God was real?

Such exclamations of hope were drawn from the imagination
of the prophets. This imagination may also be a sign of relationship. Imagination is the key to all storytelling. We imagine the
situation of another. As the prophets felt for the poor and
oppressed in their land, they did so through their imagination. As
they considered what God might be saying about this, they used
their imagination. So too, all the people of faith were people of
imagination. It was this quality that sustained their hope in the
darkest days. And this imagination was, most importantly, both
the imagination of the plight of other human beings and the

---

[5]   Isaiah 40:1.

imagination of the God of all goodness whom they served. You could say that imagination mediated the relationship between God and the realities of life. It was the vitality and breadth of this imagination that drove the development of the biblical story. That too might be seen as evidence of the reality of the relationship with God.

There is one further factor concerning this relationship with God. It is simply this. Each chapter of the middle section of this book puts different parts of public life under the spotlight. In each case there were aspects of the biblical account that were found to relate to the public life issue in hand. These biblical stories were developmental. They were directed towards increasing knowledge of the good. In each case the life of Christ naturally forms a focus for this development. I have not always made this explicit, but I think readers may see for themselves that this is so.

For example, take the development of the awareness of the reality and worth of people of other nations. At first, this is scarcely on the agenda. Other peoples are ruthlessly exterminated and the tradition made secure in that way. Gradually the people become open to others. The prophets cry out a message with sympathies for all. The exile forces a new openness. Yet only with Christ does the tradition find the ability to formally recast itself as for *all* people, breaking down the division between Jew and Gentile.

Similarly the religious story naturally embraces the success paradigm at first. Obey God and all shall be well. This expresses itself in attitudes to commercial activity that justifies a materialist, success-driven account of life. Gradually stories of obviously unjust suffering impinge on the tradition. The prophets cry out for the poor and alienated. Finally in Christ there is the watershed and a new extraordinary possibility is brought into focus. God may actually call people to suffer for the sake of what is right. This becomes real in the very suffering of Christ. So again, the story develops and comes to a new resolution in Christ.

Similarly we saw how blame came to a focus on the cross. Christ died as the scapegoat and as a terrible sign of our besetting tendency to blame people unjustly. Or again we followed the struggles of people in authority as they battle with their individual concerns for status and creative freedom against the proper constraints of public office. We noted briefly how these came to a focus in one who washed the feet of others and who was the shepherd that gave his life for the sheep.

Time after time the Bible develops within a certain tension. These tensions are found to be implicit in our very human nature. They derive from our animal inheritance. The Bible presents us with a people struggling with inner conflicts and reflecting those struggles in the formation of their society. Each of these tensions comes to a new and inspiring resolution in the life of Christ. That is my claim, and for me it points to why it is so appropriate for the Christian church to make the commitment that Christ was in some way a special person. He was one who made the character of God clear to us, who even, as Christians say, *was* God in human form.

It is not the task of this book to develop these thoughts into an orthodox Christian theology, though I hope that I have said enough to indicate that I think this can be done. What I have tried to do is to relate the stories of the Judaeo–Christian Scriptures to public life in a way that might invite the interest and even commitment of others. I hope that the above might go some way towards making it clear that Christian belief has every reason to make the claim for its own truth. It also has every reason to be considered as part of the main-line quest for the good society, even by those who do not share its particular faith commitment. It is to the role of such a religion in a diverse society and the particular needs of the west, that we must now turn.

15

Our common future

The human animal has been extraordinarily successful. The planet now lies wounded at our feet. Yet as we set out on a new millennium, there is a need to recognise where danger lurks. The human species will enter a crucial period in the next fifty years. Our future will depend on how we handle it. It is my hope that this book may give us a better understanding of our condition and help us to see our way towards a good future. Let me try to explain how.

The need for a global culture

The human animal has proved to be remarkably innovative and adaptive. From the small, bounded communities of traditional societies, we have now extended our reach right across the world by the use of technology. New powers of communication and mobility are revolutionising our lives. The range of our potential relationships and knowledge is now immense. The latest generation of phones will make the whole of cyberspace available to the free-floating person with a mobile phone. We can video-conference across the world in real time. A snapshot of human activity would now show vast numbers of people travelling, shuttling around the world, co-ordinating activity across the globe.

Global interaction must lead to global interests and concerns. What happened in the small traditional community was largely its own affair. It was of little concern to the rest of the world if they lived or died. How could it be, if we scarcely knew of one another's existence? Today we are aware. Moreover we interact. The market is now global. The whole world is dependent on the activities of a few oil companies. Power blocks dictate the rules of the international market. Film companies, news agencies and other parts of the mass media tell the stories to the world and so shape our understanding. The scale of this worldwide interaction is quite new for the human being. New technologies are changing the way we relate, yet we remain animals and it is sobering to recognise the constraints that makes upon us. Our greatest challenge in the next fifty years will be to develop a human culture that can embrace the extent of our technological power.

At present worldwide interaction is co-ordinated principally by market mechanisms. It is the market that harnesses and employs the new technologies. Market mechanisms have proved able to transcend and override the particulars of culture. Arising as a means of co-ordinating interaction between strangers, the market is ideally placed as the first means of interaction between hitherto estranged peoples. Yet the market is inadequate on its own. It is locked into a competitive evolutionary system that has a ready capacity to destroy us, either by abusing the planet or by failing to take account of our inner psychological needs.

Anthony Giddens has coined the term 'disembedding'[1] for the process by which technological change has lifted us away from both our settled geographical locations and from the cultures which had grown up around these locations. There is a new dynamism and radical openness implicit in the structure of modern society. Giddens remarks that 'The modern world is a "runaway world": not only is the pace of social change much faster than in any prior system, so also is its scope, and the

---

[1] Giddens, *The Consequences of Modernity.*

profoundness with which it affects pre-existing social practices and modes of behaviour.'[2] The tendency for such a technological, market-driven society is therefore to sweep away previous cultural norms and practices and to fail to provide an adequate environment for their re-formation. I would argue that the very future of humanity is dependent on growing other complementary systems of trust to take their place alongside the market and so constrain it towards a larger view. All human cultures have recognised the need for a law, a political establishment, a moral base and most have recognised some role for religion. These things now need appropriate expression on the world stage as well as their renewal within cultures presently dominated by the market. The material in this book may help us reflect on this task.

For example, several embryonic global institutions are already feeling their way toward their future task. We have the World Trade Organisation, United Nations, the World Bank and the International Monetary Fund. We have some semi-formal groups like the G8 group of countries that powerfully influence economic structuring. We have held various summits on the environment. Of course all these organisations are currently inadequate. They are not yet working as systems of trust. Many are still dominated by simple power play. All reflect the perspective of the powerful northern hemisphere in matters of consequence. It is often hard to see how resolutions on, say, the environment will be enforced, that is, how free riders will be disciplined. Yet this is all just what we would expect of such embryonic institutions. Like all politics, they will begin in confrontation between power players. If they work well the various power alliances will give rise to a balance of power and result in a situation where each can be called to account by another. A balance of power will develop into a truly inclusive and just institution only when the voice of the marginalised is brought powerfully into the public arena. The Jubilee 2000 coalition has

---

[2] Giddens, *In Defence of Sociology*, p. 16.

offered an important example of this process as it has brought the reality of life in the poorest, indebted countries to world notice. This type of development was described in chapter nine. It is common to many cultures through history. It will not be surprising if the development of a new global culture follows roughly the lines of other human cultural development. Unfortunately our situation presents particular problems.

Stories and the importance of public conversation

The key method in all human cultural development concerns storytelling in the pursuit of truth and right. I hope I have made it clear that this is to be conceived as a radical engagement of people of different perspectives. Traditional cultures were formed as different individuals, bound together in a common future, negotiated their understandings of life. Debate was at the heart of life and the quality of that debate determined the adequacy of the systems of trust that resulted. We have a problem with such storytelling.

In the past our society was shot through with an array of associations of people. We had families, clubs, unions, churches, a whole host of institutions. The relative stability of society meant that these groups developed a life of their own to which people were committed. The group's members accepted that they shared a common future and therefore they had to work out their differences. Powerful negotiation was commonplace. Moreover these groups themselves formed power blocs within the wider society, providing an opportunity for proper representation of the group interest. A more flexible society finds it much harder to maintain such a diverse corporate life, and the strength of all the voluntary associations of the UK has declined during the last half of the twentieth century. Flexibility and mobility mean that if you do not like the group you can get out. It has the downside of making for inadequate engagement with one another. We do not need or want to go through a painful debate in the hope of a resolution. It is easier to leave. Marriage is a case in point. The current wave of house building is not due to a rise in the UK population. A major factor is family breakdown. Yet this is simply a part of the wider malaise affecting all our voluntary associations and characterised by the breakdown of previously strong systems of relationships.

The market has worked together with new communications technology to produce a heady cocktail. The power of the media means that now it tells the stories of us all. Everyone must use the media to communicate their concern to others. Other forms of relationship are thereby rendered useless. If someone wants to get something on the news, they dress up, climb a tree or do something as outlandish as possible to attract the cameras. The 'Battle for Seattle' took place outside the World Trade Organisation conference in 1999. It provides us with a useful picture. Vast numbers of organisations took to the streets. People were dressed as animals, they danced, they charged, they screamed, they shouted. And all to get the attention of the cameras, because only through the cameras can you enter the public world. People complained that the quality of the debate engendered by the protest was poor. Of course it was. Soundbites are an impossible means of debate.

The new scenario maroons the individual. In traditional society the frequent presence of others acted to affirm us. Face to face conversations gave credence to our stories and so under-girded our own sense of identity as well as giving community solidarity. Today we are left free-floating. The only project left to us is the self-project which links our basic desire to succeed with that awesome need to find ourselves, express ourselves, or in fact do anything that helps us feel real. A host of commentators describe how anxious and insecure the people of the west have become.[3]

---

[3] See for example, Bauman, *In Search of Politics*; Gould, *The Unfinished Revolution*.

This insecurity is expressed in an all-pervasive cynicism towards public life and most particularly towards politicians. Confidence in politicians ebbed away during the last decades of the twentieth century. In 1958, seventy five per cent of Americans believed they could trust the government to do what was right. That number fell over time until, two years after Clinton took office, only eighteen per cent of the population trusted the government to do the right thing.[4] A similar pattern might be noted in the UK. Philip Gould, one of the architects of New Labour, wrote a document called 'Fighting the Fear Factor'. He said it was his campaigning 'bible'. 'It argued,' he said, 'that modern electorates are insecure, uncertain and anxious. They are "more afraid of things getting worse than they are hopeful of things getting better." The mood of anxiety about the future allowed the right to use the tactics of fear, enabling the Conservatives to dominate politics for the 1980s and 1990s.'[5] New Labour addressed this by bending over backwards to reassure people of their trustworthiness, but in our media-dominated world, this led to some strange behaviour. While having many seriously thought-out policies, New Labour had to strive to condense these into marketable, media-friendly soundbites like 'Enough is enough'; 'Britain deserves better'; 'People not privilege'; 'Future not the past'; 'Leadership not drift'. Immense energy was poured into the development of these phrases, because they were, in effect, the debate. Focus groups of marginal voters became vital sounding boards for each new phrase or public event as it unravelled. To deploy the new strategy, Labour found a new headquarters at Millbank and employed a considerable team to manage the image of the party. Rebuttal units were set up so that as each new Tory offensive was launched, they could reply within hours, catch the media tide and not suffer any

---

[4] Renshon, *High Hopes*, p. xvii.
[5] Gould, *The Unfinished Revolution*, p. 181.

damage. It was a very effective operation in terms of gaining power, but what does it say about the future of democracy?

John Humphrys calls the new methodology 'consumer populism'. It is politics according to the ebb and flow of gut public response. Its danger is obvious from a remark once made to Mrs Thatcher. She was advised that one way of increasing her popularity at a stroke would be to casually link unemployment and immigration.[6] It was to her credit that she did not go down this route. But others have and others will. Consumer populism does not serve the good society. Of course, one might argue, as Gould does, that the public are actually very discerning about these things, but even so this soundbite-oriented process cannot properly be termed debate; it is simply marketing. Nevertheless these are the realities of political life with the media. This is what you must do to get elected and stay in power. It also has a tragic downside.

Most people are left out in the cold. They are really not part of the process. In fact they are subject to continual manipulation. People do not like being manipulated. At some point they will react. Just now we are still content to sit in front of the TV. The programmes supply us with hype, more and more excitement to fuel our frenetic lifestyles. Our attention spans grow shorter year on year. But one day, perhaps quite soon, I suspect that people will grow to realise that they are being controlled. That will be a new day.

The difference between manipulation and a healthy public life is the quality of public conversation. John Humphrys offers the telling phrase, 'Real citizenship is about being participants in an argument.'[7] That, I believe is the heart of the matter. The chief task facing us at the turn of the millennium is the renewal of public conversation. There are two basic ingredients of good public conversation. One is the sense that our lives are bound

---

[6] This story from Humphrys, *Devil's Advocate*.

[7] Ibid., p. 254.

together in a common future and therefore we have to work this problem out. The other is to include the broadest possible perspectives in the process. To listen to one's enemy, to hear the story we refuse to hear, this is good public conversation. And good public conversation leads to good culture. I have likened the process to a 'wrestling embrace'. We wrestle with each other as we struggle with our different perspectives and yet we are bound together in the embrace that comes from sensing that we share a common future. Furthermore, to renew public conversation we need the social space in which to do it, a situation where this conversation can take place.

This brings us to the role of religion in society. In what sense can a religious approach to life help in this process? What is the proper role of religion in the society of the future?

The place of Christianity in public life

We live in an age that is wary of all truth claims. It might be said that many, particularly of the postmodern school, glory in our confusion and seek to perpetuate it at all costs. They have a point. Fundamentalism comes in many guises, but it is united by claims to inappropriate certainty. Very often such claims have done damage. There were Christians who thought they should go and fight the infidel. There were scientists who thought they could prove the superiority of the Aryan race. Communists thought they could plan society. They were all wrong and the reason they were wrong is because it is only given to the human to see in the glass darkly. Our knowledge of truth and good and right is partial. That very inadequacy makes for an open society in which we need to seek the perspective of others, where we need to be always striving to understand better and so form our common life more appropriately. But it does not mean that we should be lulled into a hopeless despair. We need some guidance to live by. We need to form stories and act upon them. The question is what role religion should play in this.

In this book I have tried to offer an understanding of the Christian faith that relates in a positive way to the public life issues that every society needs to address. I cannot pretend that this has been the understanding of the church for the last two millennia. It has worked with many different theologies, some far more adequate than others. I have deliberately kept away from all the established theological categories like sin, redemption, justification etc. and simply tried to recover something about the process through which the Scriptures were formed and what that means. It is, I think you could say, a sort of 'ground level' theology.

Central to this theology is the idea that the people who formed the Scriptures were essentially testing a paradigm about God. This God was one with whom they were in relationship, who was in authority and was the source and focus of all goodness, beauty and truth. They rarely stated this paradigm, but I believe the writings give enough traces of these commitments to justify such a claim.

This led, as we have seen in this book, to a situation where the development in understanding about God was also a development in understanding about what a good society would look like. The process of Scripture development admitted the most basic inner, conflicting dispositions of the human animal, but continually sought to draw these together into new resolutions that would give a comprehensive vision both to the individual and the society. In the process, the Scripture commented on many of the besetting problems of our human society, such as market dominance, our addictive lifestyles, the continuing abuses of political power, the ingrained tendency to racism, the need for good accountability and adequate means to deal with blame. Each of these is embraced by the scriptural process in such a way as to offer potential vision for the future.

I believe that the importance of this approach to the wider society is in the substantial overlap between the biblical process and the striving for the good that is common to every human community. Each culture shares the same deepest motivations. Each needs to negotiate about human purposes and their meaning by means of story. All share the common search for truth and goodness and beauty and all see 'in a glass darkly'.

This leads to several conclusions about the relationship between the church and the diverse societies of which it may be a part. Firstly, as the Christian faith seeks to know God and so understand all that is good and right and true, then it must accept that which is good, right or true whatever source it comes from. This will include truth as presented by others who do not share the particular faith commitment. The uncertainty in our knowledge of God demands a radical openness in our faith and insists on both internal debate within the church and engagement with those who do not explicitly share the faith.

On the other hand, it would also be proper for the society to acknowledge that a faith stated in this way can truly take its place in public life. The church and the society are both seeking the same things. The conclusions of the church are then relevant to the whole. The stories of faith in the Scripture then become, at very least, exemplars of the process of culture formation, and the quest to know all that is good. In this way the Christian faith might properly stand at the heart of human society.

In fact there are several reasons why such an understanding of the Christian faith may be particularly important to cultural development at this time. We need to develop new systems of trust that have global reach. We need to reinvigorate a culture that is in danger of losing its coherence in the face of market dominance. At the heart of the growth of all culture is the trustworthy person. Personal honesty, integrity and trustworthiness are the key virtues required for building any effective system of trust. The Christian faith is set up as a system of trust between people and God. As such it specifically encourages the development of these virtues in people. The church has many failings, and I have not hesitated to mention them, but it does have this general reality. People are encouraged, by their faith, towards being trustworthy. Where this works well the church can potentially become a centre for cultural formation and a force against all corruption and cheating in a society. This is of major importance.

The church likewise remains a major social grouping in a country such as the UK, when many other institutions have been almost destroyed. As such the church has the potential to playing a major role in the renewing of relational life in our society. The renewal of public conversation must be the goal. Churches might be seen as nuclei of corporate life, able to spawn new communities, new groups, new associations of people in a world where all group life is falling away. For it to play such a part, the church will have to wake up to its responsibilities in this area.

I set out on this book because I felt there was a crying need to restate what we believe in terms that make sense and which apply to the whole of life. I am all too aware of its inadequacy. While each chapter has tried to set out some of the most basic issues of public life, I have been only able to give a mere taste of their potential resolution. I believe the Scripture can give vision, but I am clear that I do not have the detail of that vision, or even a small part of it. The detail needs to be filled in by public conversation. The prize we seek is that of an integrated life, release from addictive behaviour, a proper balance of challenge and trust, accountability and mercy, justice and forgiveness. We can only work for this together, in conversation, and I believe that the church could be an important focus for this necessary coming together, if it can rise to the challenge.

The Christian church may still represent a serious body of people, but many of its members languish in the pews without any encouragement in their work or in political understanding or engagement. If we are to rekindle vision and hope, we are going to need to work for that vision. We are going to need to join together in conversation about public life. We are going to need to re-engage with the resources of our faith and also join together with, and honour the insights of, many who do not share our faith commitment. Large numbers of church people get to the age of forty or fifty and really wonder why they attend church at all. The easy formulae of their initial church experience no longer satisfy. The complexities of responsible jobs press in on them and the church offers little or nothing. It is time for a change and that change could be that the church should lead the way in the renewal of public conversation.

Our need is for a global vision. The church believes in a God over all creation, a God who is not partial among the nations, before whom every tribe, language and nation lives and one day will be judged. Sadly, it has frequently identified God with a national culture, a racial identity or some other partial view. This was understandable when we were all locked into the limited perspectives of our traditional cultures. Globalisation must be the spur that forces the church to shake off these partial outlooks. If it can do so, the vision of God that it offers the world could help to bind us together and give vision for our human society as we face what is inevitably our common future.

Appendix

Chance, God and evolution

Ever since evolution was first mooted, it has been controversial in all sorts of respects, not least with the religious. In recent years there has been a whole succession of scientific writers that have polarised the discussion about evolution and God and left many people feeling that a Christian has to choose between belief in God and belief in evolution. As this book has progressed, building as it does from evolutionary perspectives through to faith in God, I am aware that there may be some that have nagging worries about this issue.

Recent contending scientists have not always intended to undermine religion itself. Most often their aim has been to expose spurious arguments for faith. For example, in *The Blind Watchmaker,* Richard Dawkins seeks to demolish the Argument from Design as used by William Paley in the eighteenth century. [1] He agrees that the complexity of the natural world does indeed naturally provoke a wonder that says 'This could never have happened by chance', yet first impressions can deceive. Dawkins argues persuasively that the organic complexity we now experience can be derived from chance events, but not one single, highly improbable act of chance. Rather evolution occurs in a succession of steps, each of which has a plausible chance of

---

[1] Dawkins, *The Blind Watchmaker.*

occurring and the whole process is organised around a clear logic, namely that of gene propagation. Of course, he does not, and cannot, describe all the innumerable steps in the pathways of evolution and detractors will always try to point to 'gaps' in the argument, saying, 'but how could this particular thing evolve or that come to be'. With a historical process of such complexity there is no hope of ever completing the theory in the sense of filling in all the details and so the argument will always rest on its overall explanatory power and plausibility. 'Does this *make sense* of the world as we experience it?' That is the key question. The vast majority of biologists today affirm the basic evolutionary process. They may argue over details, but the overall understanding is perceived as unassailable.

This is important for Christians to appreciate. Believing that there is an irreconcilable gulf between faith and belief in evolution, Christians have taken up an array of defensive positions, some quite subtle, others frankly dull and reactionary. These defences can become a hindrance to our understanding if, as I contend in this book, there are important things that humans need to learn about their place in the evolutionary process. For me the theory of evolution does indeed offer vital insights into the animal world. It has unique explanatory power. I hope the reader may have appreciated from this book that such insights can be of real help to us as human beings in our search to understand ourselves, our societies and the origin of some of our deepest motivations. Yet we have also seen that faith has a vital role to play in society. We have considered the possibility that human beings can indeed have a real and personal relationship with a God who is the source of all goodness, beauty and truth. We have examined the basis on which such a faith can be properly claimed as true and seen how important it can be in shaping a human society for good. So how can this faith in God be put together with belief in evolution? Chance is commonly perceived as the nub of the problem. Einstein famously decreed, 'God does not play dice' and many people of faith today would

agree with him. A world that came into being by chance cannot
have place for a creator God. The two appear to be logically
incompatible. But I wonder?

First of all we must make the argument harder. Issues of
chance and God cannot be limited to evolution. The biology of
human procreation is fairly clear and uncontentious. It describes
the process through which every one of us was formed. Yet it is a
process permeated at every level by chance occurrences. Within
our parents' bodies sperm or ova were formed by a process
known as meiosis. This repackaging of DNA includes a recom-
bination of genes rather like the shuffling of a pack of cards and
equally the subject of random chance. Meiosis has been investigated thoroughly. It is at the heart of genetics and its very
randomness underlies a great deal of the proven predictive power
of that branch of science. As far as I know no Christian has ever
disputed this on scientific or other grounds. Yet it shows that
there is something very random right at the heart of the formation of our beings. The rest of the process is equally troubling.
On one particular day, father ejects around forty million sperm,
all of which are different. One of these, largely by chance, meets
with the particular ovum that the mother has produced that
month, this ovum being one at random out of the huge number
produced in her lifetime. Out of this extraordinarily random
series of events we all arise. And yet the Christian contends by
faith that somehow God was involved in this process. Somehow
they were intended to exist and are known personally by the
Creator. Psalm 139 claims,

> For thou didst form my inward parts, thou didst knit me together
> in my mother's womb. I praise thee, for thou art fearful and won-
> derful. Wonderful are thy works! ... My frame was not hidden
> from thee when I was being made in secret, intricately wrought
> in the depths of the earth. Thy eyes beheld my unformed sub-
> stance; in thy book were written, everyone of them, the days that
> were formed for me, when as yet there was none of them.

This shows us the real problem and it is not limited to the theory of evolution. There are parts of our life that are quite incontrovertibly based upon chance, and yet the Christian readily interprets these as somehow under the hand of Almighty God.

In our daily lives things happen to us that at one level have to be seen as the result of chance. Yet the person of faith will often interpret these in some sense as within God's concern. In general we have shown through this book how the events of life can be interpreted fruitfully in terms of a relationship with God and actually constitute such a relationship. We search for purpose and meaning through the events of life. Of course, many of the great catalogue of events in a human life are not by chance. They have an evident human or other causes and reflection on them helps to develop our moral capabilities. Yet some are almost pure chance. We might think of a car accident, serious illness, chance meetings with people or even chance associations of ideas. Very often the Christian, after reflection, will settle on the idea that even these events were somehow part of God's intention. There are some rather unbalanced people who try to interpret every chance detail of their lives as guidance and get themselves in a hopeless mess, but a more subtle sense of guidance by event, even chance event, is common to many people of faith.

It is not often appreciated that believing in God's guidance and inspiration through chance is a position adopted by the people of faith in the Scripture. It is not the advent of modern science that has raised this essentially philosophical conundrum. The people of the Old Testament appeared to regularly use systems of lottery to divine God's will. Of course, as the faith developed so the resources for discerning the will of God grew and so choice by lot became a relatively minor part of religious observance. Yet it was always there as an option. For example, in the story of the failure of the attempt to conquer Jericho, the people presume that one of them has sinned. How do they discover who has offended God? The rather terrible consequence of this theology was described as follows: 'In the morning you shall be brought near by your tribes; and the tribe which the Lord takes shall come near by families … and the household which the Lord takes shall come near man by man. And he who is taken with the devoted things shall be burned by fire …'[2] Many commentators would see a form of lottery behind the words, 'the Lord takes'. Casting the lot is specifically mentioned in a similar incident in 1 Samuel 14:42 where Saul tragically identifies his own son Jonathan as guilty of breaking his command. In this case the people stand by Jonathan and cry out for his life. It seems that in pre-exilic times, priests were regularly called upon to use the lot as an aid in decisions of major national consequence. When they needed to decide whether to go out to meet an enemy, the priest would be brought to deliver a verdict 'by Urim and Thumim' and, although the details of this process are lost to us, it is very likely that it involved some form of choosing by lot.[3] Likewise in the New Testament the disciples had to choose another disciple to replace Judas. How did they do it? They drew lots.[4] It was clearly therefore a self-conscious and deliberate part of faith throughout the Bible that God somehow used processes that were based upon chance. Not that all decisions were made in this way, far from it. But where there was nothing else to guide them as to God's will, they felt free to use chance.

This leads us to the conclusion that it has *always* been a part of faith to embrace the paradox that God could somehow still be sovereign over events that were known to be pure chance. This paradox turns out not to be the peculiar defining problem of evolution and faith, nor even of science and faith, but rather it turns out to be implicit in the whole concept of there being a God who interacts with a world such as our own.

---

[2] Joshua 7:14, 15a.

[3] See 1 Samuel 14:36–42; Numbers 27:21; 1 Samuel 23:9–12; Exodus 28:30.

[4] Acts 1:26.

This should take the heat out of the evolution debate. If the paradox about faith and chance is as old as the hills, then there is absolutely no reason to focus it on evolution or for Christians to take defensive positions against the rest of the biological fraternity. The paradox has been part of biblical faith from the beginning. Those who now seek to continue it by declaring that evolution did occur by processes of chance *and* God was somehow sovereign over the whole process, actually hold a position in accord with the historical faith, not against it.

It is interesting that in times past the people of faith did not seem to have a problem with upholding God's sovereignty over events that were clearly chance ridden. They were content to affirm mystery at the heart of the way God interacts with the world. The modern difference is the construction of the scientific mind-set that has prevailed over western civilisation since the Enlightenment. Typically scientists would argue that the methods of science are adequate to reveal all that counts as truth. P.W. Atkins in his book *The Creation* affirms at the outset, 'I take the view that there is nothing that cannot be understood.'[5] He is going for a world of total rational explanation. For some reason that I cannot fathom, he thinks the human mind capable of all things. I wonder why we should consider the human mind able to resolve all the ideas implicit in its own existence?

Atkins's method, common to many post-Enlightenment theorists, is actually to limit human knowledge to that which can be plotted on the grid of theory built up through scientific method. Such a method proves to be inadequate for almost everything that has been discussed in this book. Science has its place. It has proved remarkably fruitful and accurate in its analysis of the material world. Yet in the early chapters of this book, it became clear that once organisms have arisen bearing minds of spontaneity and creativity, then knowledge concerning their purposes had to be pursued in an holistic, integrating manner and different

---

[5] Atkins, *The Creation*, p. vii.

from that of traditional scientific reduction to clear and distinct ideas. The use of story was expounded as a proper means of the pursuit of truth in the humanities. Such a method resulted in knowledge that had a necessarily open and incomplete character, such that it can never be fully defined. Against this background the scientists' demand for a world of total rational explanation becomes a fiercely limiting commitment. This may be the reason why so many scientific texts attempting to deal with the humanities feel so arid to the reader. At least they do to me! Most of what a human being counts as real is not included in the system of rationality employed.

Another way of saying this would be to note that science simply cannot describe how human beings act purposefully. Its grid of knowledge only admits ideas about probabilities, necessities, chaos and suchlike. Its method denies such necessarily holistic realities as purpose. Yet every one of us believes truly that we act purposefully each day. Purposeful action lies at the base of all our understanding of society. It is assumed by our system of justice, by our calling people to account, by our moral capability and much else besides. Nevertheless science simply does not have the language or concepts to describe purposeful action. If science cannot adequately describe how human beings act with purpose, it is no wonder that the purposeful acts of God are likewise beyond its scheme of knowing.

In light of all this the fact that such a limited system of rationality as traditional science comes up with paradox when considering evolution, human beings and their relation to God, should not be surprising, but rather *expected*. Even in its own world of definition, science has had to thoroughly revise its worldview at times: witness the transition from the Newtonian/ mechanical worldview to that of the New Physics. How much more should such struggles and revolutions of perspective be expected when human beings, relationship, societies and God are in view!

In conclusion I would argue that the apparent paradox between belief in God and belief in evolution is actually an artificial construct of scientific methodology and the western mind-set that now dogs so many in our modern society. Scientific method has its own sphere of proper application. It is remarkably fruitful and accurate within that sphere, but it cannot adequately encompass all that human beings count as true. In particular it cannot adequately relate to the humanities and to their open pursuit of truth, nor to the relation of the human being with God. The subject matter of chance, evolution and God necessarily crosses all these boundaries. The nearest human beings can come to truth in such a study might be to express it as paradox.

Bibliography

Ardrey, R., *The Territorial Imperative – A Personal Inquiry into the Animal Origins of Property and Nations* (London: Collins, 1967)

Ashton Jones, N., S. Arnot, and O. Douglas, *The Human Ecosystem of the Niger Delta – An ERA Handbook* (Nigeria: Environmental Rights Action, 1998)

Atkins, P.W., *The Creation* (Oxford: Freeman, 1981)

Baggott, R., *Health and Health Care in Britain* (London: Macmillan, 1994)

Barnett, A. 'Hey, big spender – the extravagant lifestyle of the Irish Elk led to its doom', *New Scientist*, 165: 2231 (25 March 2000)

Bauman, Z., *Intimations of Postmodernity* (London: Routledge, 1992)

—, *In Search of Politics* (Cambridge: Polity Press, 1999)

Best, S. and D. Kellner, *Postmodern Theory. Critical Interrogations* (London: Macmillan, 1991)

Bloom, L., *The Social Psychology of Race Relations* (London: Allen and Unwin, 1971)

Bourdillon, M. and M. Fortes (eds.), *Sacrifice* (London: Academic Press, 1980)

Branson, R., *Losing my Virginity* (London: Virgin, 1998)

Bristol Audit of Crime and Disorder (Nov. 1998). Prepared on behalf of Bristol Community Safety Partnership by Bristol City Council Community Safety Team and Avon Somerset Constabulary

Brueggemann, W., *Hope Within History* (Atlanta: John Knox Press, 1987)

—, *1 and 2 Samuel*, Interpretation (Louisville: John Knox Press, 1990)

Burke, E., *Reflections of the Revolution in France* (London: Penguin Classics, 1986)

Burke, C. and A. Goddard, 'Internal markets: the road to inefficiency?' *Public Adminstration*, 68 (1990), 381–396

Cassirer, E., *The Philosophy of the Enlightenment* (Princeton: Princeton University Press, 1951)

Coleman, J., *The Foundations of Social Theory* (Cambridge, Massachusetts: Harvard University Press, 1990)

Committee on Standards in Public Life 'First Report of ...' (London: HMSO, 1996)

Crowley, B., The limitations of Liberalism: The self, the individual and the community in modern British political thought with special reference to F.A. Hayek and Sidney and Beatrice Webb' (PhD Thesis, London School of Economics, London University, 1985)

Daly, H.E. and J.B. Cobb, *For the Common Good. Redirecting the Economy Towards Community, the Environment and a Just and Sustainable Future* (London: Merlin, 1989

Davidson, J.D. and W. Rees-Mogg, *The Sovereign Individual. The Coming Economic Revolution. How to Survive and prosper in it* (London: Macmillan, 1997)

Davies, N., *Europe – A History* (London: Pimlico, 1997)

Davis, S. and C. Meyer, *Blur. The Speed of Change in the Connected Economy* (London: Capstone, 1998)

Dawkins, R., *The Selfish Gene* (Oxford: Oxford University Press, 1976)

—, *The Blind Watchmaker* (Harlow, Essex: Longman, 1986)

Descartes, R., *A Discourse on Method. Meditations and Principles* (London: Dent, 1994)

De Waal, F., *Good Natured – The Origins of Right and Wrong in Humans and Other Animals* (Cambridge, Massachusetts: Harvard University Press, 1996)

Douglas, M., *Purity and Danger – An Analysis of Concepts of Pollution and Taboo* (London: Routledge and Kegan Paul, 1966)

Dunbar, R., *Primate Social Systems – Studies in Behavioural Adaptation* (London: Croom Helm, 1988)

Dunn, P., 'The Wisheart Affair. Paediatric Cardiological Services in Bristol 1990–1995', *British Medical Journal* 317 (1998) 1144–1145

Economic and Social Research Council, *The Politics of GM food – risk, science and public trust*, Special Briefing no. 5 (Oct. 1999)

Eibl-Eibesfelt, I., *Love and Hate: On the Natural History of Behavioural Patterns* (London: Methuen, 1971)

Faringdon, B., *The Philosophy of Francis Bacon* (Liverpool: Liverpool University Press, 1964)

Forrester, D., *Theology and Politics* (Oxford: Blackwell, 1988)

Fortes, M. and C. Evans-Pritchard (eds.), *African Political Systems* (Oxford: Oxford University Press, 1940)

Freedman, N. and D. Graf (eds.), *Palestine in Transition* (Sheffield, England: Almond Press, 1983)

Fukuyama, F., *Trust – The Social Virtues and the Creation of Prosperity* (London: Penguin, 1995)

Giddens, A., *The Consequences of Modernity* (Cambridge: Polity Press, 1990)

—, *The Transformation of Intimacy: Sex, love and eroticism in modern societies* (Cambridge: Polity Press, 1992)

—, *In Defence of Sociology, Essays, Interpretations and Rejoinders* (Cambridge: Polity Press, 1996)

Gottwald, N., 'Early Israel and the Canaanite Socioeconomic System', in N. Freedman and D. Graf (eds.), *Palestine in Transition* (Sheffield, England: Almond Press, 1983), 25–37

Gould, P., *The Unfinished Revolution* (London: Abacus, 1999)

Harrison, R., *Democracy – Problems of Philosophy* (London: Routledge and Kegan Paul, 1993)

Hastings, A., *A World History of Christianity* (London: Cassell, 1998)

Herman, E.S. and N. Chomsky, *Manufacturing Consent – The Political economy of the mass media* (London: Vintage, 1994)

Hume, D., *Enquiries concerning human understanding and concerning the principles of morals.* Reprinted from the 1771 edition with introduction by L. Selby-Bigge (Oxford: Clarendon, 1975)

Humphrys, J., *Devils Advocate* (London: Hutchinson, 1999)

Jennings, H., *Societies in the making. a study of development and redevelopment within a county borough* (London: Routledge and Kegan Paul, 1962)

Jeremias, J., *Jerusalem in the Time of Jesus – an investigation into economic and social conditions during the New Testament period* (London: SCM Press, 1969)

Kermode, F., *The Genesis of Secrecy – on the interpretation of narrative* (cambridge, Massachusetts: Harvard University Press, 1979)

Konner, M., *The Tangled Wing: Biological constraints on the human spirit* (London: Penguin, 1982)

Kottak, K., *Assault on Paradise. Social change in a Brazilian village* (New York: McGraw-Hill, 1992)

Kuhn, T., *The Structure of Scientific Revolutions* (Chicago: University of Chicago Press, 1962)

Lauren, P., *Power and Prejudice: The Politics And Diplomacy Of Racial Discrimination* (Boulder: Westview Press, 1988)

Lorenz, K., *On Aggression*, tr. M. Latzke (London: Methuen, 1966)

Lyotard, J.-F., 'ThePpost modern condition: A report on knowledge', in *The Theory and History of Literature*, vol 10 (Manchester: Manchester University Press, 1979)

Macintyre, A., *After Virtue, a study in moral theory* (London: Duckworth, 1985²)

MacLaurin, I., *Tiger by the tail – A life in business from Tesco to cricket* (London: Macmillan, 1999)

Mair, L., *An Introduction to Social Anthropology* (Oxford: Clarendon, 1972)

Marks, H., *Mr Nice – an autobiography* (London: Vintage, 1998)

Mason, R., *Propaganda and Subversion in the Old Testament* (London: SPCK, 1997)

McIntosh, M., D. Leipziger, K. Jones and G. Coleman, *Corporate citizenship – Successful strategies for responsible companies* (London: Pitman, 1998)

Middleton, J. and B. Walsh, *Truth is Stranger than it used to be* (London: SPCK, 1995)

Midgley, M., *Beast and Man: The roots of human nature* (London and New York: Routledge, 1979)

—, *Wickedness. A philosophical essay* (London and New York: Routledge, 1984)

Mill, J.S., 'On the definition of Political Economy and on the method of investigation proper to it', essay V in *Essays on some unsettled questions of Political Economy*, from the Collected works, vol. 4 (London: Routledge and Kegan Paul: University of Toronto Press, 1967)

Niebuhr, R., *Moral Man and Immoral Society* (London: Scrivener, 1932)

Nisbet, R., *The Sociology of Emile Durkheim* (Oxford: Oxford University Press, 1974)

O'Hear, A., *An Introduction to the Philosophy of Science* (Oxford: Clarendon Press, 1989)

Okonta, I., 'Litmus Test', *ERAction*, the quarterly magazine of Environmental Rights Action/Friends of the Earth, Nigeria (Jan.–Mar. 1999)

Paine, T., *Rights of Man* (London: Penguin Classics, 1969)

Patten, C., *East and West* (London: Pan, 1998)

Paxman, J., *Friends in High Places* (London: Penguin, 1990)

Polanyi, M., *Personal Knowledge* (London: Routledge, 1958)

—, *The Study of Man. Lindsay Memorial Lectures* (London: Routledge and Kegan Paul, 1959)

—, *The Tacit Dimension* (London: Routledge, 1967)

Popper, K., *The Logic of Scientific Discovery* (London: Routledge, 1959)

—, *The Poverty of Historicism* (London: Routledge, 1960)

Ramadan, M., *In the Shadow of Saddam* (London: GreeNZone, 1999)

Renshon, S., *High Hopes – The Clinton presidency and the politics of ambition* (London: Routledge, 1998)

Richardson, D., *Eternity in their hearts* (California: Regal Books, 1981)

Ricoeur, P., *Time and Narrative* (London and Chicago: Chicago University Press, 1984)

Ridley, Mark, *Animal Behaviour – a concise introduction* (Oxford: Blackwell Scientific, 1986)

Ridley, Matt, *The Origins of Virtue* (London: Viking, 1996)

Rorty, R., *Philosophy and the Mirror of Nature* (Oxford: Blackwell, 1980)

Ruether, R., *Faith and Fratricide: The Theological Roots of Anti-Semitism* (New York: Seabury Press, 1974)

Schmidt, W., *Primitive Revelation* (St Louis: R. Herder, 1939)

Scott, R., *The Anchor Bible. Proverbs and Ecclesiastes* (New York: Doubleday, 1965)

Sheed, F. (tr.), *The Confessions of St Augustine* (London: Sheed and Ward, 1944)

Schluter, M. and D. Lee, *The R Factor* (London: Hodder and Stoughton, 1993)

Sennett, R., *The Fall of Public Man* (London: Faber and Faber, 1974)

Simpson, J., *Strange Places, Questionable People* (London: Pan, 1998)

Smith, A., *An inquiry into the nature and cause of the wealth of nations* (London: Penguin, 1982)

Thompson, E.P., *The Making of the English Working Class* (London: Penguin, 1963)

Tinbergen, N., *The Study of Instinct* (Oxford: Clarendon, 1951)

Trivers, R., 'The Evolution of Reciprocal Altruism', *Quarterly Review of Biology* 46 (1971), 35–57

Tutu, D., *No Future without Forgiveness* (London: Rider, 1999)

Urbach, P., *Francis Bacon's Philosophy of Science* (London: Open Court, 1987)

Wenham, G., *The Book of Leviticus, NICOT;* (Grand Rapids, Michigan: Eerdmans, 1979)

Williams, R., 'The literal sense of scripture', *Modern Theology*, vol. 7 (Oxford: Clarendon, 1991), 121–134

Williamson, O., *Economic Organisation – Firms, markets and policy control* (New York: New York University Press, 1986)